MW01014268

The Strange Case of
Ermine de Reims

THE MIDDLE AGES SERIES

Ruth Mazo Karras, Series Editor
Edward Peters, Founding Editor

A complete list of books in the series
is available from the publisher.

The Strange Case of
Ermine de Reims

A Medieval Woman
Between Demons
and Saints

Renate Blumenfeld-Kosinski

PENN

UNIVERSITY OF PENNSYLVANIA PRESS

PHILADELPHIA

Copyright © 2015 University of Pennsylvania Press

All rights reserved. Except for brief quotations used for
purposes of review or scholarly citation, none of this book
may be reproduced in any form by any means without
written permission from the publisher.

Published by
University of Pennsylvania Press
Philadelphia, Pennsylvania 19104-4112
www.upenn.edu/pennpress

Printed in the United States of America on acid-free paper
1 3 5 7 9 10 8 6 4 2

Library of Congress Cataloging-in-Publication Data

Blumenfeld-Kosinski, Renate, author.
The strange case of Ermine de Reims : a medieval woman
between demons and saints / Renate Blumenfeld-Kosinski.
pages cm — (The Middle Ages series)
Includes bibliographical references and index.
ISBN 978-0-8122-4715-2 (alk. paper)
1. Ermine, de Reims, approximately 1347–1396.
2. Visionaries—France. 3. Women mystics—France.
4. Visions—France—Early works to 1800.
5. Mysticism—France—History—To 1500.
I. Title. II. Series: Middle Ages series.
BX4705.E66994B55 2015
282.092—dc23
2014040343

CONTENTS

When I first read *The Visions of Ermine de Reims* in June 2000, I was stunned and very moved. Reading about her tribulations brought tears to my eyes, not a very scholarly reaction to be sure but one that motivated me to pursue her story for many years. She interested me because she seemed to fit into two broad categories that characterize my research: issues of sanctity and mysticism and the politics of late medieval France. André Vauchez, with whom I had many conversations about Ermine, wrote about her in the preface to Claude Arnaud-Gillet's excellent 1997 edition;[1] he saw that worries about the Great Schism of the Western Church seemed to be a central part of the *Visions*. It certainly seemed strange to me that such a simple peasant woman should be concerned—or even know—about this decades-long division of the Catholic Church. This puzzlement about the attitudes of laypeople in the face of this grave crisis was at the origin of my 2006 book *Poets, Saints, and Visionaries of the Great Schism (1378–1417)*, where I devoted a few pages to Ermine. But she continued to haunt me, and I wanted to know more about her. In 2010 I published a long article about her in *Speculum*, but I still felt there was more to know and to say.[2]

Although the modern editor chose to entitle the text that Ermine's confessor Jean le Graveur composed *The Visions of Ermine de Reims*, Jean himself refers to Ermine's experiences mostly as adventures (*aventures*). *Adventure* means literally "things that happen to us," and this term truly captures the happenings in this peculiar text. The word *adventure* also evokes medieval romances, of course, texts in which realistic and supernatural elements had coexisted for centuries. One only has to think of the Arthurian romances and those dealing with the Holy Grail to understand how a medieval audience may have reacted to the term *aventures*. But in truth, Ermine's experiences were so unusual that both the editor of the *Visions* and the German scholar Paul Gerhard Schmidt agree that she and what her confessor wrote about her were "unique" in the fourteenth century. No other holy woman, Schmidt states, was frightened at such length and to such an extent as poor Ermine.[3] Indeed, Ermine being battered and mocked by demons ceaselessly for the last ten months of her life (interspersed with a few divinely sent revelations and consolations) is the gist of the *Visions.* A reader cannot help but ask what the matter was with Ermine. Was she mad? Was she ill? Did she suffer from hallucinations?

Throughout the years I worked on this book, I conversed with my friend and colleague Paula M. Kane, who was studying an equally strange case but a much more modern one: that of Margaret Reilly, known as Sister Thorn, a New York stigmatic living in the community of the Good Shepherds in Peekskill, whose experiences made her famous in the 1930s.[4] Many of her tribulations were exact copies of Ermine's: demonic assaults on her body and also on her belongings, like furniture or dishes, of the kind Kane calls *Poltergeist* vexations. We were aware of course that over the centuries certain models and patterns for both divine and demonic visions had been established; nonetheless, these similarities led to long discussions about possible ways of understanding our peculiar women. For an analysis of a holy woman in the 1930s numerous conceptual frameworks are available: medicine, psychoanalysis, interwar American Church politics, and more; these are brilliantly explored by Kane in her book. But what about a holy woman in the fourteenth century?

Frameworks

In his fascinating 2012 study of hallucinations Oliver Sacks observes that the supernatural and the pathological were often separated in the medieval and early modern periods, although the symptoms may have been identical. He states that "until the eighteenth century, voices—like visions—were ascribed to supernatural agencies: gods or demons, angels or djinns. No doubt there was sometimes overlap between such voices and those of psychosis or hysteria, but for the most part, voices were not regarded as pathological."[5] Sacks highlights that the term *supernatural* can refer to divine or demonic actions. Indeed, it was always difficult to distinguish between the two. Was a visionary woman granted divine grace or possessed by the devil?[6] Did she suffer from hallucinations, perhaps caused by some mental illness? Certainly, medieval scholars did not exclude medical causes for seemingly supernatural experiences. Bartolomeus Anglicus, the famous thirteenth-century encyclopedist, for example, "spoke of natural causes of mental illness in the region of the brain around the lateral ventricles." In the tradition of the ancient medical writer Galen, "medieval medical psychology was biological, not demonological. But not experimental either."[7] What was crucial was how supernatural phenomena were interpreted.

Of course, it is hard to resist the desire to diagnose a case like Ermine's. If I wanted to practice retrospective medicine, I would consult Dr. Sacks and ask him to examine Ermine in the framework of hallucinatory states. Since many of Ermine's experiences involved apparitions and voices just when she was about to or had just gone to sleep, one might be tempted to describe them as "hypnagogic hallucinations," that is, those that occur on the threshold of sleep. Sacks quotes Andreas Mavromatis's 1991 study that tells of a man in 1886 who reported seeing "animals that have no fellows in creation, diabolical looking," thus repeating centuries of visions that fill hagiographical accounts from antiquity to modern times.[8] Mavromatis defines hypnagogia as "the unique state between consciousness and sleep," which has some similarities with "dreams, meditations, trance." Anyone who has studied medieval visions knows how difficult it is to distinguish between these different states.[9]

Mavromatis's "hypnopompic" or waking hallucinations are also similar to some of Ermine's. He describes one person's visions of hideous animals, black angels, an ugly man lying on the floor, and even of "a little devil riding a bicycle at the foot of his bed." Sacks summarizes:

> Given the outlandish quality of some hypnopompic images, their often terrifying emotional resonance, and perhaps the heightened susceptibility that may go with such states, it is very understandable that hypnopompic visions of angels and devils may engender not only wonder and horror but belief in their physical reality. Indeed, one must wonder to what degree the very idea of monsters, ghostly spirits, or phantoms originated with such hallucinations. One can easily imagine that, coupled with a personal or cultural disposition to believe in a disembodied spiritual realm, these hallucinations, though they have a real physiological basis, might reinforce a belief in the supernatural.[10]

Sacks makes two crucial points here: that these kinds of hallucinations can be accepted as physical reality and that they reinforce belief in the supernatural. Sacks' argument seems to me the key for an understanding of Ermine's visions. What she sees and hears is represented unambiguously as real; her confessor reports in a matter-of-fact way things that are so outlandish that we want to cry out: but they can't be real, she must be hallucinating, she might be crazy!

Ariel Glucklich rightly notes that over the centuries "the Church had struggled to distinguish between mystical experience and various forms of 'insanity,' such as epilepsy, possession, humoral imbalance, and others."[11] For quite a long time scholars had accepted the idea, popularized by Gregory Zilboorg in his 1941 *History of Medical Psychology*, that all medieval people considered mental illness a form of diabolic possession and that the only "treatment" was exorcism or even death. Thirty years later Jerome Kroll debunked this idea in a by-now classic article. He showed that most often mentally ill people were seen as such and treated more or less compassionately by the society of their time. He also argued that what we might consider extreme "pathological behavior" today was often accepted as "normal, if possibly peculiar" in the fourteenth century and that what really mattered was the "the determination of whether the behavior was in the service of Christ or in the service of Satan."[12]

Another twenty years later the French historian Muriel Laharie explored medieval ideas about and attitudes toward madness in an excellent study that analyzed medical explanations of mental illness and the many remedies medieval scholars proposed to cure it. Both natural (herbal potions as well as psychological help) and supernatural means (in the shape of healing saints) were enlisted in this curative process. She also showed that in addition to being part of medieval medicine—and even what one could call psychotherapy *avant la lettre*—mental illness, often divided into different manifestations such as mania or melancholia, was integrated into a triple framework of moralization (mental illness is caused by sin), sanctification (such as the notion of "God's fool"), and diabolization. A mad person, if subject to what Laharie calls "demonopathic manifestations" or possession could thus become an object of competition in the "fight between God and Satan."[13] As in Kroll's arguments, we find here the idea of discernment that was so central to Churchmen in Ermine's era. Was a person "possessed" by a demon or chosen by God for special experiences? The crucial point is that throughout the middle ages multiple frameworks were available for the interpretation of extraordinary mental states, and consequently it was far from clear to Ermine's contemporaries how a case like hers should be interpreted.

Jean le Graveur and his superiors were thus aware that the kinds of behavior Ermine exhibited and the ways in which she reported the relentless demonic torments inflicted on her could be considered from a number of different perspectives: Ermine could suffer from demonic possession and/or mental illness or else enjoy a divinely sanctioned state of grace. In late nineteenth-century France, Jean-Martin Charcot, the famous psychiatrist, faced a similar interpretive dilemma. Charcot was treating women whose symptoms and behavior recalled that of their medieval sisters, but as Cristina Mazzoni observes, "With Charcot, then, phenomena that had previously been regarded (though not always without suspicion) as manifestations of the supernatural—be it the divine supernatural, as in the case of mysticism, or the demonic supernatural, as in the case of sorcery or possession by the devil—were systematically reinterpreted with a new and powerful hermeneutic tool: the concept of neurosis and, preeminently, of hysteria."[14] Charcot thus faced the same quandary as Ermine's contemporaries had faced and found the solution in a new definition of hysteria and the invention of what he believed were appropriate treatments.

Ermine's confessor chose the framework of divine intervention for his account of Ermine's experiences. For him, God's will became manifest through this simple and pious woman. How and why Jean le Graveur and his superiors chose to adopt a mostly positive stance toward Ermine will be explored in this book. Thus I resist the temptation to put Ermine on the couch or submit her to tests and scans, but rather aim to place her into the multiple frameworks in which her medieval contemporaries would have seen her. I choose to subscribe to Glucklich's cautious approach; speaking of the sixteenth-century Italian saint Maria Maddalena de' Pazzi, whose self-inflicted torments he analyzes, Glucklich states: "The broadest problem in the application of psychotherapy to saints such as Maria Maddalena is the monumental methodological reduction it entails. The assumption that a single culture-bound clinical theory can explain vast amounts of cases across cultures and centuries is tenuous."[15] In order to illuminate the many facets of Ermine's experiences and Jean's record of them, I have divided this study into chapters that treat different aspects of her "strange case" from perspectives that were available to people in late fourteenth-century France.

The Plan of This Book

I first explore the world Ermine lived in: the city of Reims at a time of great political and religious turmoil; her state of widowhood and the economic constraints she experienced; the religious landscape of France at the time and especially of the city of Reims. I also define her status in view of the existence of different groups of "quasireligious" women. Chapter 2 examines the notion of the "holy couple" that consists of a confessor-biographer and a holy woman. I place Jean le Graveur and Ermine in the context of other such couples to highlight both similarities and differences. Ermine's devotion and ascetic practices are at the center of Chapter 3, while the next two chapters analyze two different kinds of demonic apparitions and their effect on Ermine: demons in human and animal shape and demons masquerading as saints ("counterfeit saints"). The epilogue takes a brief look at Ermine's afterlife and explores what the manuscripts can tell us about the reception and judgment of Ermine. The English translations of large parts of Jean le Graveur's text that appear as an appendix to this book give a flavor, I hope, of the drama and unusual structure of the *Visions*. Since the manuscripts of the *Visions* have no illustrations (except for a much later touchingly inept sketch of her grave plate that I reproduce as Figure 10), I chose images that I hope will enrich and illustrate the arguments of this book.

CHAPTER I

Ermine and Her World

When Ermine and her elderly husband, Regnault, approached the city of Reims with its magnificent cathedral and impressive fortifications, they knew that they were entering a new kind of life. At home, in Lucheux, a small town in rural Vermandois, just west of the northern French city of Arras, Regnault had labored on his rented plot of land until the weakness and infirmity of old age forced him to admit that he could no longer provide for himself and his wife in this way. The decision to leave their home and friends must have been a difficult one, especially since there was no new career awaiting either of them in the big city. They had not been destitute in the country: at one point we learn that in Lucheux they had been dues-paying members of the confraternity of Saint Léger, who had been martyred in 680 C.E. in that very town. But now their future was uncertain, and it was up to Ermine to provide for both of them. Ermine was only thirty-seven to her husband's sixty-three in 1384, but as a rural migrant few opportunities were open to her. Migrants, and female migrants in particular, most often had to content themselves with the lowest-paid positions in urban settings. Such women could become laundresses or wool carders, or they could try to eke out a living by selling simple things, such as pickled fish or herbs.[1] Ermine decided to sell merchandise she could pick up for free in the marshes outside of Reims: herbs and straw that could be used for the roofs of thatched houses. With their income, however meager, assured, the couple settled in the rue Neuve (today rue Gambetta) near the priory of Saint-Paul du Val-des-Ecoliers. The proximity to this religious institution proved providential, for the couple's confessor, the subprior Jean le Graveur, would turn out to play a major role in Ermine's life after she was widowed in 1393. Indeed, if it were

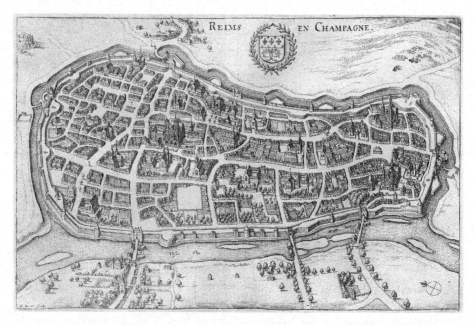

FIGURE 1. A seventeenth-century view of Reims by Merian. The Val-des-Ecoliers where Ermine and her confessor lived used to be in the northern central section of Reims. Author's collection.

not for Jean le Graveur, we would know nothing about the strange and often frightening events that occurred during the last ten months of Ermine's life. Ermine, like the vast majority of ordinary people of little means, would have left no trace in any official record, and we could not now attempt to resurrect her and her remarkable experiences.

When the French historian Michel Mollat published his important study on the poor in the Middle Ages in 1986, he bluntly stated that the poor are "people who left no records and who remain largely unknown."[2] More recent studies of such sources as records of charitable institutions, wills, and miracle collections have brought to life many aspects of poor people's existence. We can also find ideas about the function of poor people in pious treatises where, as the potential recipients of rich citizens' acts of charity, they could help their benefactors along on the path to heaven. But we rarely hear the voices of the poor themselves. Indeed, even those people who were not desperately poor, but what we would today call middle class, left few traces, except perhaps wills or contracts of various kinds. Women left even fewer traces than men. Only rarely do we get a glimpse of what Peter Biller dubbed the "Common Woman," that is, a laywoman who had no religious affiliation. While scholars have paid lots of attention to nuns of various orders as well as to more informal religious groups, such as the beguines—that is, a tiny percentage of all medieval women—the common women are much harder to grasp because they do not have many clearly defined characteristics that unite them. Many of these common women were indifferent to religion, while others "being quite pious, at the same time also wanted the world, human love, and sex."[3]

Ermine de Reims forms part of this second category since she was married and widowed before her disturbing career as a visionary began. Because we learn about so much of her life in addition to the demonic torments and the heavenly visions she experienced, Ermine can become for us an expert witness of life as a simple or "common" woman in late fourteenth-century France. We will try to enter into her heart and mind and make an effort to understand her emotions, fears, and ambitions by listening to what Ermine lived through and how she spoke of her adventures to her confessor, Jean le Graveur. Living with Ermine and Jean le Graveur for ten months in late medieval Reims will allow us to understand a whole range of issues central to late medieval religious and political thought and life, from repercussions of the Great Schism of the Western Church to devotional practices and ideas about demonic possession, from ideals for female sainthood to incipient notions of witchcraft.

A Time of Crisis

Ermine and her husband were born into a "calamitous century."[4] Regnault entered the world around 1321; he was thus in his teens at the beginning of one of the great crises of the fourteenth century, the Hundred Years' War that intermittently pitted England against France between 1337 and 1453.[5] When in 1337 the French king Philip VI annexed the Guyenne region, which had been an English fief and for which the English king owed homage to the French king, Edward III retaliated by laying claim to the French throne. His argument was that through his father's marriage to Isabelle of France, the daughter of the French king Philip IV le Bel (d. 1314), he was in fact more closely related to that king than was Philip VI, a descendant of one of Philip le Bel's brothers, Charles de Valois. This was the beginning of over a hundred years of hostilities that ebbed and flowed through the reigns of a number of French and English kings.

Early on in the conflict Edward III established the base of his operations at Antwerp in Flanders, where the duke of Brabant aided the English cause. Not too far from the border with Flanders lay the city of Reims whose sacred status and wealth made it a target for the English troops. [6] According to the legend the ninth-century archbishop of Reims, Hincmar, had created in his *Life* of Saint Remigius, the Merovingian Clovis, the first Christian king of France, had been baptized and crowned by Saint Remigius in Reims in 496 C.E. Thus people believed that the city had been elected by God to be the site of all future royal coronations or *sacres,* a ceremony that required the holy chrism for anointing the king. For Clovis's *sacre,* Hincmar claimed, this ingredient had been transported from heaven by a miraculous dove so that Saint Remigius could complete the king's baptism. And indeed, all French kings had been crowned in Reims.[7] In the last decades of the war, in 1429, it was again in Reims that Joan of Arc crowned Charles VII, the king who had been disinherited by his parents in favor of the English king Henry V in 1420. No wonder that Edward III set his sights on that city early on in this conflict.

In 1339 the English troops took Cambrai and overran the area north of Reims, including the Vermandois, home to Regnault. One of the most notorious events of this military campaign took place in the small town of Aubenton: English soldiers burned it to the ground while massacring its citizens. Desperate refugees fled to Reims. It was during this time that serious efforts began to strengthen the city's fortifications in order to make it impregnable. This enterprise cost the city vast sums and was finally completed in 1358. The citizens' investment paid off: Reims remained a safe city and was never conquered by the English.

Most of Regnault's life was overshadowed by the war. When he was twenty-five, in 1346, the English decisively defeated the French forces at the battle of Crécy, a town about 250 kilometers northwest of Reims. Then the English took Calais, an event commemorated in Rodin's famous 1889 sculpture of the burghers of Calais, a group of wealthy men who, clad only in their shirts and with halters around their necks, were willing to sacrifice themselves so that Edward III would spare the town's population. About to be beheaded by the wrathful king, they were saved when Edward's pregnant wife Philippa of Hainault intervened. A truce that lasted until 1355 followed this extreme expenditure of military might and cruelty.

The year 1356 saw another bitter defeat of the French at the battle of Poitiers, which resulted in the French king Jean II le Bon being taken prisoner and held for a huge ransom. This unprecedented disaster plunged the citizens of Reims into despair.[8] Two years later the Jacquerie, or peasant revolts, unsettled the region further. In the aftermath of the defeat of Poitiers and the huge ransom demanded for the king, ever greater taxes were extracted from the peasants. The political instability caused by the king's absence and the rivalries between the dauphin and his relative Charles the Bad of Navarre (who was eyeing the royal throne) added to the turmoil. The area around Reims was one of the centers of the Jacquerie. The archbishop of Reims, Jacques de Craon, was so frightened by the roving bands of peasants approaching Reims that he fled the city and took refuge in his fortress outside of town. But soon, with the help of Charles of Navarre, the uprising was suppressed. Was Regnault, by now in his mid-thirties, part of the Jacquerie? Unfortunately we know too little about his life to answer this question. Ermine, born around 1347, was still a child during the revolts, yet it is very likely that this period of extreme violence in her home region left a mark on her psyche.

In the winter of 1359–60 the costly fortifications of Reims were put to a serious test. On December 4, 1359, Edward III began a siege of the town that was intense but unsuccessful; after about five weeks the English king gave up and moved on to Burgundy. The Rémois were safe for the moment but not home free: to demonstrate their civic and royalist spirit they had to pay their share of 20,000 écus of the 600,000 total to redeem king Jean le Bon, still a hostage held by the English. The burghers of Reims had to borrow most of this sum from Italian merchants and remained in debt for many years.

It was not until 1369 that the armies of Charles V, Jean le Bon's son, began to retake areas that had been lost to the English. Charles reigned from 1364 to 1380, a time of relative peace in the kingdom. His son Charles VI took over in 1380 and for the next forty-two years was king, albeit the "mad king," for in 1392 his first bout of mental instability announced the chaos into which he was to plunge France: first the civil war that raged between the Burgundians and the Armagnacs from 1411 on, then the English invasion after Agincourt in 1415. Not until 1453 did the war between the French and the English come to an end.

Ermine was born ten years into this seemingly endless war and just a year before the Black Death, another great calamity of the fourteenth century, decimated Europe's population. The plague had arrived in Europe via the

Asian trade routes. Moving westward to the Crimea and further, the plague bacillus, borne by fleas hidden within rodents' fur, quickly approached Europe through the Mediterranean ports. In 1346 the Near Eastern countries were infected; in October 1347, carried by Genoese merchant ships, the disease appeared in Sicily and began to move north.[9] The Italian poet Giovanni Boccaccio in his *Decameron* described its spread and effects in gruesome detail. In 1348 the plague reached northern France where the mortality rates in some areas reached 40 to 50 percent.

While some of its neighbors were spared, Reims took the full brunt of the epidemic. The canon of Reims, Pierre de Damouzy, had composed a medical treatise on the disease just before it arrived in Reims.[10] His confidence in medical science quickly proved to be unfounded: no known remedy had the slightest effect against this fast-moving scourge. Quarantine was the only weapon against the plague's spread, a strategy adopted by the famous poet and composer Guillaume de Machaut (1300–1377), also a canon in Reims, who gave a dramatic account of the outbreak and its portents in the prologue to his love debate poem *The Judgment of the King of Navarre*. He witnessed "horrible, uncanny things," such as eclipses and comets, and interpreted them as signs of the growing menace of the plague.[11] He bemoaned the moral decay of his world where lords pillage their subjects and even murder them. His special wrath was reserved for the Jews whom he referred to as "Judée la honnie," shameful Judea. The Jews had been expelled from France in 1306 but were allowed to return in 1315, only to be expelled again in 1396. At the time of the plague Jews lived in many medieval communities. For Machaut they were "evil and disloyal" people who lent much money to Christians and then set about poisoning streams and wells that until then "had been clear and healthy; and thus many lost their lives."[12] But God, so Machaut claimed, saw to it that their crimes were revealed, and "all the Jews were destroyed—some hung, others burnt alive, one drowned, another beheaded." The contemporary chronicler Jean le Bel also reported that Jews were said not only to have poisoned wells but also to have been striving for world domination and riches (*avoir la seigneurie et l'avoir de tout le monde*), eerily foreshadowing anti-Semitic tracts like the Protocols of the Elders of Zion. According to Jean Le Bel the Jews' actions enraged everyone to such an extent that the Jews were put to death and suffered a "joyful martyrdom."[13]

Machaut saw the poisoning of the waters as a crime against Nature who, as a personified entity, was so offended by this transgression against her that she unleashed raging whirlwinds and stones that killed scores of people. The aftermath of this disaster consisted of haze and filth: "The air which had been clear and pure, was now vile, black and hazy, horrible and fetid, putrefied and infected," and quickly people became ill; "they had large swellings from which they died" (vv. 313–15; 323–24). Five hundred thousand died, Machaut dramatically claimed. The dead were thrown into trenches as the cemeteries overflowed. People no longer dared to leave their houses as friends infected friends and families were decimated. The social fabric disintegrated, fields were left unplowed, and cattle roamed free. Wages went up as the workforce dwindled. The breakdown of civic and family ties, described by the Greek historian Thucydides during one of the ancient outbreaks of the plague in the fifth century B.C.E., gripped cities again in the fourteenth century. Machaut, for his part, locked himself in his house until he could be certain that the city's air was no longer infected. His strategy worked: he died in 1377 at the age of seventy-seven.

Like Machaut, many people considered the plague a scourge sent by God. In many areas, particularly in Germany, processions of flagellants made their way through the countryside, singing and praying for an end to the plague while castigating themselves, their blood flowing down their backs. The flagellants, along with the rumors of the Jews' role in the spread of the plague, fanned the fires of anti-Semitism that resulted in many pogroms, particularly during Easter week in 1349. This was also the moment when the citizens of Reims organized several processions to ward off the disease, as did countless other Christians elsewhere. Solemnly chanting, they carried around the shroud of the city's patron saint Saint Remigius—but in vain. From August to October the plague ravaged the population. The dead included members of all social classes. The city's administration and justice system collapsed.

Ermine and Regnault survived the epidemic of 1348–49. The mortality for rural regions is harder to gauge than that for cities because urban record keeping was more extensive and accurate than that of the countryside. We do not know whether Ermine and Regnault lost any family members to the disease. Eventually the Black Death caught up with Ermine, however. In 1396 a particularly virulent plague epidemic returned to Reims, and in August of that year she was killed by that terrible disease. She most likely contracted the infection by caring for a sick neighbor. For Ermine the plague did not bring out the worst but the best: instead of abandoning friends and neighbors in need as so many citizens did during the numerous medieval plague epidemics, she came to their aid, even at the risk of her own life.

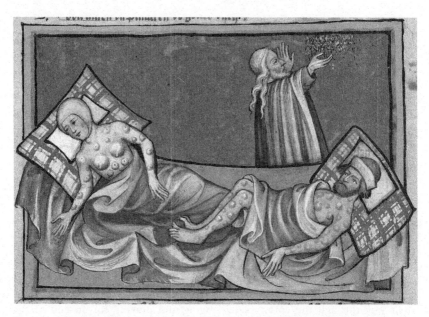

FIGURE 2. Plague sufferers in the so-called Toggenburg Bible (1411), which contains a late copy of the *World Chronicle* of Rudolf of Ems (c. 1200–1254). This image illustrates the episode in Exodus 9 when God allowed Moses to call down the plague on the Egyptians. The victims' plague buboes are very visible. Berlin, Kupferstichkabinett Cod. 78 E 1. Bpk, Berlin. Art Resource, NY.

Yet another major crisis of the fourteenth century was the Great Schism of the Western Church (1378–1417), which saw two and finally three popes engaged in almost forty years of frequent hostilities and endless mutual excommunications.[14] During most of the fourteenth century the popes, the majority of French origin, had resided in Avignon. In 1377 Pope Gregory XI (1370–1378) was persuaded to return the papacy to Rome. After his death in March 1378 the conclave of cardinals had to elect a new pope. A Roman mob surrounded the conclave and threatened the cardinals unless they elected an Italian pope. Confusion and fear spread among the cardinals, but they finally agreed on a new pope: Bartolomeo Prignano, who took the name of Urban VI. He soon showed himself to be autocratic and unsympathetic to some of the luxurious habits the cardinals had developed. They went so far as to describe him in a letter to the French king as a rabid monster. Only a few months after Urban's election the cardinals left Rome and, in the more pleas-ant Italian countryside, proceeded to elect another pope, the Frenchman

Robert of Geneva, a relative of the French king, who took the name Clement VII. Their justification was that they had elected Urban under duress and that therefore the original election was invalid. Almost immediately the European rulers had to take sides: France, not surprisingly, opted for Clement VII, while England never wavered from Urban VI. The Italian regions went for Urban, as did the Empire, while the Spanish kingdoms after a long inquiry sided with Clement VII. Thus Europe was divided by what the fourteenth-century chronicler Jean Froissart called a "great pestilence."[15] In addition to the plague bacillus the population now suffered from an epidemic of division and hatred created by human ambition and intransigence. The Schism outlasted the original two popes and even extended to three popes after the Council of Pisa in 1409. Not until the huge Council of Constance, sponsored by Emperor Sigismund, did this division of Christendom come to an end in 1417.

When Ermine first became aware of this crisis that cut the church into two warring factions, the powerful and wily Spaniard Pedro de Luna had succeeded Clement VII as Pope Benedict XIII in 1394. The Italian Pietro Tomacelli had become Pope Boniface IX upon the death of Urban VI in 1389. Right after Clement VII's death the French had tried to intervene with the Avignon cardinals in order to prevent a new election, hoping that the Roman pope would then abdicate and a new unified election could be held. Their hopes were quickly destroyed, though, when they learned that Pedro de Luna, who as a cardinal had supported the abdication of both popes, had managed very quickly to get himself elected pope. The displeasure of the French monarch and the University of Paris finally led to a withdrawal of obedience from Benedict XIII in July 1398, a situation that for a while left France basically without any pope at all.

The crisis leading up to the removal of French obedience from the Avignon pope was brewing in the last years of Ermine's life, and we will see how it entered into her visions and how it influenced her thinking about the Church. Although Ermine was an illiterate peasant woman, she showed great interest in the Schism, particularly its effects on Reims and the surrounding countryside. She was especially fascinated by one actor in the drama of the Schism: Jean de Varennes (d. 1396?), a charismatic hermit and former official of the Avignon papal court, who had settled in a small sanctuary at Saint-Lié, a few miles outside of Reims, and who attracted large crowds through his preaching.[16] He was a controversial figure who had turned against his pope, Benedict XIII, by calling for his abdication. In 1392, by divine command (as

Varennes claimed), he styled himself as a second Moses who was called by
God to end the Schism and reform the Church. On Palm Sunday 1396 the
hermit preached a powerful sermon against the Avignon pope, who was then
still supported by the French monarchy. Varennes was swiftly arrested and
probably died in prison. Ermine's preoccupation with Jean de Varennes and
his fate surfaces frequently in her visions and in her discussions with her
confessor. Thus, despite her simplicity she was aware of the political life of
her region and beyond.

Regnault and Ermine lived in a time that saw great calamities, both man-
made and natural. Regnault's voice has not come down to us (he will, however, appear in a demonic and ghostly shape in Ermine's visions), and we
cannot know how his life was shaped by the conflicts and epidemics I just
recounted. For Ermine we will see that political and natural events affected
her life in many, sometimes unexpected, ways.

Living in the Big City

A beautiful and enormous cathedral, one of the crown jewels of French
Gothic architecture, dominates the city of Reims to this day. As we saw
above, very early on in French history Reims had become the city of the
sacre of the French kings and had thus gained a special status in the French
imagination. In 1328 the city had a population of about 16,000 to 18,000, not
a huge number compared with Paris, which at that time is estimated to have
had a population of close to 200,000, but certainly much larger than the
village of Lucheux that Ermine and Regnault had left behind. Reims had
grown steadily throughout the twelfth century, and by the beginning of the
thirteenth century the city had expanded beyond the ancient walls and almost
tripled its urban area. Situated at the heart of the Champagne region, it was
a major commercial center. At several lively market areas in the city people
traded wine, wheat, cattle, and especially textiles. The Rémois cloth trade
sent its wares all over Europe, including to England, Scandinavia, and Spain,
and as far away as North Africa, Syria, Turkey, the Black Sea, and Persia.[17]
This highly developed commercial activity—Reims was one of the great
foires, or markets, of the Champagne region—may have encouraged Ermine
and her husband to try their luck in the big city.

In the period that Ermine and Regnault lived in Reims, the city was
under Burgundian domination, and relative peace reigned in the region. The

countryside, however, was in poor shape; this fact, in addition to Regnault's advanced age, may explain the couple's migration. In the post-plague years, from 1351 to 1360, more than 1,800 rural migrants arrived in Reims and joined the ranks of the bourgeois.[18] The newcomers had to pay a fee of five sous, a sum that represented about two to three days of a worker's salary at the time. Were Regnault and Ermine able to pay this fee? Most likely they were, for they found quarters in the rue Neuve and began attending services at their neighborhood church.

Reims was the center of a large ecclesiastical province that comprised eleven dioceses.[19] In the second half of the fourteenth century more and more confraternities and other pious institutions appeared in the city. Reims's numerous religious institutions spanned the whole range of monastic orders, priories, chapels, oratories, and two beguinages. The Benedictines alone had three monasteries in Reims, one of which was a nunnery that in 1354 housed twenty-five nuns.[20] There were eleven parish churches, among them Saint Etienne where Ermine and Regnault worshipped. The Mendicant Orders, that is, the Franciscans, the Dominicans, the Carmelites, and the Augustinians, began to arrive in the thirteenth century. Following the rule of Saint Augustine, another order formed part of the vast religious panorama of Reims: the canons regular of the Val-des-Ecoliers.[21] Like some other orders, the Augustinians had started out as hermits but soon moved into the cities where they became involved in pastoral care, often in conflict with the parish priests. There were only so many donations to go around, after all.

The congregation of the Val-des-Ecoliers of which Jean le Graveur was the subprior saw the light of day at the dawn of the thirteenth century in the area of Chaumont in the Haute-Marne in northern France.[22] From its very beginning it was a scholarly order: it was founded in 1201 by Guillaume Langlois, a doctor of theology from the University of Paris, and three of his colleagues. Soon a number of students joined them, and because of their passion for intellectual pursuits they named themselves Val-des-Ecoliers, the valley of scholars. The order was approved by Pope Honorius III in 1219. The canons could thus pursue the pastoral and mendicant roles that resembled those of the Dominicans and Franciscans. They could preach, and they were to renounce property, an ideal they could never quite fulfill in an urban setting. Unlike the strict rule of Saint Benedict, the Augustinian rule was more of "a collection of exhortations and precepts." Frances Andrews characterizes it as follows: "From its opening words it focuses simply on the need to share life in the monastery and 'to have one heart and soul seeking God.'

Its essence is the idea that the common life, based on shared property and common prayer, will promote fraternity and love, allowing religious of different abilities and economic backgrounds to live together in a spiritual community." While fasting, chastity, and "humble clothing," as well as obedience and discipline were mentioned, the rule did not address specifics of communal organization. The friars could thus "devise their own observance."[23] For the members of the Val-des-Ecoliers this meant among other things that they were never allowed to sit down in the cloister without a book. The new order was so successful that its members created a number of sister houses, among them the one in Reims (the order's "eighth daughter") and one in Paris, Sainte-Catherine du Val-des-Ecoliers, founded by the French king Saint Louis in 1230. At the time Ermine and Regnault came to know Jean le Graveur, Hugues de Nizy served as the sixth prior of the house in Reims. Jean became the couple's confessor, and he must have felt very close to Ermine, for when she was widowed in 1393 in her mid-forties, it was Jean who took care of her both practically and spiritually. He arranged for her to move to a room overlooking the courtyard of his priory and took charge of her religious instruction. At that point he probably did not yet realize that he would also become the chronicler of the horrific demonic assaults and the occasional consoling divine visions that would mark the last ten months of her life.

Living as a Widow

How should we imagine medieval widowhood? For women of the aristocracy and even of the merchant and professional classes the loss of a husband could often mean a gain in independence, sometimes even a second career. A noblewoman might take over the control of her late husband's estate, and middle-class women who were barred from some professions were allowed to engage in them once they were widowed. A number of female surgeons, for example, were able to practice only as successors to their husbands. Widows also had legal rights, rights that grew in the later Middle Ages. In the registers of Paris law courts we find many cases of widows fighting against what they considered unjust inheritance practices or arguing their cases against fraudulent debt payments demanded from them after their husband's death. In her didactic work *The Book of the Three Virtues* (1405) the famous writer Christine de Pizan (c. 1364–c. 1430) counsels widows to avoid lawsuits if at all possible. A woman, she reminds her readers, cannot appear in court at all hours as can a man. In order to be successful in court a woman must have a man's heart—and deep pockets because a lawsuit can ruin a woman very quickly. She speaks from experience. In her allegorical and in part autobiographical work *Christine's Vision*, dating from the same year, Christine recalls the financial and legal troubles that followed her husband's death in 1387, when she was twenty-three and had to care for her three young children and aged mother:

> Now I had fallen into the valley of tribulation. . . . For as I was not present at my husband's death . . . I could not establish the precise state of his finances. For it is the common habit of men to say and explain nothing about their financial affairs to their wives. . . . And this does not make sense when the women are not stupid but prudent and good administrators. . . . Then troubles arose from all sides, and, as is the common fare of widows, lawsuits and legal disputes came to me from everywhere. . . . Ah, when I think of the many winter mornings I spent standing around the palace, dying of cold, waiting for the counselors to remind them or to charge them with my case; or how often I heard there various decisions and strange conclusions that brought tears to my eyes; but worst of all was the expense that was beyond my means.[24]

In part because of these financial problems Christine de Pizan decided to become a professional writer, a decision that changed not only her own situation but also the face of medieval literature.

But very often the second career for widows was a religious one. Margaret Wade Labarge, a pioneer in medieval women's history, has shown that for some well-known medieval holy women the pursuit of their saintly vocation had to wait until after their husbands' death. Some of them, like Loretta, the widowed countess of Leicester, became a recluse in 1221; others, like Ela, the countess of Salisbury, founded an abbey that she then entered as a nun in 1232. The most famous of the women Wade Labarge brings to life in her article is Saint Birgitta of Sweden (1303–1373), a mother of eight who was widowed at age forty-one.[25] Her revelations, recorded by a number of different clerics, were of a profoundly mystical nature but also dealt with political issues. She insisted that her warnings and messages be transmitted to the pope and several European kings.[26] In 1349 Birgitta moved to Rome and in 1371 traveled to the Holy Land as a pilgrim. She was canonized no fewer than three times (in 1391, 1415, and 1419), a strategy designed to make sure that the aftermath of the Great Schism did not wipe out her initial canonization.

Even young widows, for example, Yvette of Huy (1158–1228), a Flemish mother of three who lost her husband when she was eighteen years old, often chose the life of recluse over remarriage. When her children could fend for themselves, she moved into a leprosarium, a small leper hospital, which she then expanded and directed with great skill. Far from becoming a martyr by contracting leprosy (as she had hoped!), she became a skilled and useful administrator, a career that would not have been possible for her as a married woman.[27]

Christine de Pizan, whom we just encountered battling various lawsuits, is the most celebrated example of a woman whose career began when she was left alone with a family to raise. She started most likely as a copyist but soon became one of the most successful and sought-after writers of her time. She composed almost two dozen works of poetry, political, and religious texts. Her best-known work today is *The Book of the City of Ladies* (1405) in which she strove to give women their rightful place in the intellectual and political development of human history. Her last work of 1429 dealt with one of the most celebrated women of all time: Joan of Arc.[28] Christine did not write about Ermine, although it is possible that she had heard of her. Jean Gerson (1363–1429), the famous and powerful chancellor of the University of Paris, had contact with Christine and may even have been her friend. It was to his authority that Jean le Graveur appealed after Ermine's death by sending him the text of her *Visions* with a request for his expert opinion on their orthodoxy. In his reactions to this strange woman's experiences Gerson waffled over the next few decades, as we will see in Chapter 5. Christine herself was rather skeptical of visionaries in general. In *The Book of the Three Virtues* she does exalt the contemplative over the active life, but when she describes the ecstasies and levitations of contemporary mystics (who, she observed, seemed to be spending a lot of time in bed!), her tone suggests that visions and an exclusively contemplative life smack of self-indulgence and pride. Gerson as well was suspicious of too much "joy and pleasure" in spiritual experiences and hinted that true humility was not compatible with these forms of self-centered mysticism.[29]

Christine de Pizan certainly was a proponent of the active life. Her career was one of astonishing productivity, and while she showed immense grief over her husband's death, she also admitted openly that she would never have become a writer had she remained a wife. Some women of high achievement were clearly conscious of the opportunities that the widowed state could offer them. But what about widows who were illiterate and poor? Poorer women would have to find a way to earn a living after their husbands' deaths or else become the charges of a hospital or almonry. Old age and poverty went together in medieval society as they often do today. [30] Fears of becoming destitute as she was getting older surely haunted Ermine when her husband died. When they had moved to Reims, Ermine had to become the breadwin-ner. Regnault, as Jean le Graveur informs us, "was feeble and old and could do nothing anymore but go to church" (50). But however useless Regnault was in practical terms, he did give her the status of a married woman. Widow-hood would add another layer of vulnerability to her precarious existence. Furthermore, the couple had no children in their old age (we do not know whether they never had any children or whether perhaps their offspring had died, certainly a possibility given the high infant mortality rates in the Middle Ages), depriving Ermine of a family network that could have cared for her.

What kind of options did Ermine have then in her newly widowed state? Could she become a nun like many aristocratic women at the time? Or could she join a beguinage, a community of pious women that remained in the world while leading a religious life? The main obstacle to either of these choices was the dowry that convents and even beguinages required. While earlier in the fourteenth century the beguinages in Reims had admitted women of all social classes, including the poor, at the time of Ermine's bereavement women who needed to work for a living were no longer wel-comed by the Rémois beguine houses.[31]

Other strategies for survival in old age existed in the late Middle Ages. Of course, there was no Social Security, no long-term care insurance, and yet many people lived a long if often infirm life. One solution for the aged who had no immediate family and who were not completely destitute was to arrange for a move into the house of younger people who could care for them and eventually become their heirs. Let us see how this kind of arrangement worked out for Beatrice Bocheta in fifteenth-century Switzerland.[32] She left extensive traces in the notarial records of Sion, a beautiful town in the Alps. Married and widowed three times, childless, she had to face old age alone. In 1469, as a notarial contract shows, she decided to adopt a distant relative, Jean Sartor; she moved in with him and his wife in the fall of 1471. While Beatrice had promised to make Jean her heir, for the moment she only con-tributed clothes and food to his household. Her empty house in the center of Sion seemed to be waiting for the young couple. But less than a year later things deteriorated: Beatrice annulled the arrangement because of conflicts with the household, as she put it, and moved out, taking her furniture and other belongings with her. Three years later she appeared again at the notary, claiming to be alone and in need of aid. This time she arranged for the notary to deed all her belongings to another notary and his wife, hoping that they would care for her until her death. Of all her property she reserved only twenty sous that she bequeathed to a local chapel. But in 1479, we encounter her again: now about seventy-two years old, she is mentioned as a witness to testify about her elderly half-witted nephew who was found dead in an orchard. We can see how this resourceful woman, over a period of at least ten years, tried to provide for what she knew would be a solitary and helpless old age. Given her rather prosperous financial circumstances, she could experiment with a number of different arrangements.

Another example from Switzerland, this time from the northern city of Basel, can help us imagine how older city dwellers tried to plan for the future. The title of Gabriela Signori's study contains a number of key terms that define what can happen to an aging population—and not only in the Middle Ages:[33] Signori illustrates a potential social descent linked to one's life cycle. She further analyzes both formal and informal strategies that people developed when confronted with the possibility of this descent. Informal strategies could involve children who were called upon to alleviate their parents' problems caused by illness and old age. Many moralistic treatises of the period hammer this obligation into the minds of their readers. But more formal strategies were also employed: in 1486 an elderly couple declared before the court in Basel that they were too old and infirm to take care of themselves. They did not want to move in with their daughter and son-in-law; they preferred their grandson and his wife, with whom they made a contract that promised him their goods in exchange for taking care of them for the rest of their lives. This contract disinherited their son, but this was the right of the burghers of Basel and other European areas.

A transaction like this was quite common for people who could trade their possessions for future care. The great fear that marks a number of these contracts is that of the moment when one can no longer work. A baker from Basel testified to this situation in court in 1500, stating that he was now too weak to practice his craft and he feared that everything he had worked for would slip away and he would no longer be able to afford food and drink. He therefore decided to buy what was called *Notpfründe*—a contract regulating funds for emergencies or long-term care—from his son-in-law. The idea of a retirement age was unknown in the Middle Ages (and beyond), and people basically had to work until they became too decrepit to continue. In documents of late medieval Norwich, widows as old as seventy-nine and eighty-two were referred to as "almost past work"![34]

We know that when Ermine and Regnault moved to Reims, Ermine was working because Regnault no longer could. The migration of older childless couples, many of them described as sickly and lame, to an urban center was not uncommon in the later Middle Ages.[35] Often the women continued to work, mostly in unskilled jobs that would never allow them to belong to a guild or even earn a decent living. Ermine's at-best marginal occupation of gathering reeds and selling straw was typical of this class of female workers. In late medieval Florence we find a large number of working women who "on their own could not live from their labor unless it was supplemented by other resources or included, in the case of domestic service the additional benefit of board and room." Some women rented out rooms or had small plots of land that brought in some income.[36] Ermine did not have these options: if her meager earnings were to become insufficient, the only direction she could turn was to charitable institutions.

Confraternities and other charitable establishments often ran "poor tables" for the needy, where alms were distributed.[37] Others offered hospices for the destitute, including widows. But entering such a hospice still meant working: even the old and infirm were expected to work at such jobs as washing and mending or to do other menial tasks around the hospice. It also, most often, meant giving up one's independence. The statutes for the mid-fourteenth-century Parisian hospice the Haudriettes, for example, specified that the women sheltered there could never leave again. They were not allowed to dispose of their property as they wished but had to designate the owner of the hospice as their heir. Any immoral behavior (including drinking or cursing) or failure to follow the strict religious regimen could result in expulsion and loss of their belongings.[38] Would an institution like this have been suitable for Ermine? Would its directors have put up with the horrible visions and dreadful experiences Ermine had to suffer every night and sometimes even during the day? Fortunately for her, she did not have to find out, for her confessor made her an offer that was quite unusual: she was to come and live in a house adjacent to the priory, where she could look out into the courtyard of the Augustinians' church and lead an existence that Jean le Graveur likened to that of a monk: she was to obey him "comme fait un religieux a son souverain" (as does a monk his superior).[39] Triply vulnerable

as a poor, aging widow without a family (although she did have friends who
offered help), Ermine was thus rescued by her confessor, who enabled her to
embark on what one could call a "second career." Could this career lead to
sainthood as her confessor undoubtedly hoped? Could this simple peasant
one day join the ranks of holy women? To ponder these questions we have
to take a brief look at the religious life in Ermine's time as well as the kind
of templates or models that were available to aspiring saints and their
biographers.

Religious Life and Saintly Models in Late Medieval France

The Gregorian Reform, named after Pope Gregory VII (1073–1085), of the
eleventh century had as its goal to reform and purify the clergy, taking aim
at such abuses as simony and concubinage. Laypeople were often aware of
the clergy's corruption. In mid-eleventh-century Italy, for example, both men
and women "were involved in what was called at the time a liturgical strike,
refusing to accept the sacraments from impure priests."[40] They thus adopted
the position of the Donatists of the fourth century who had claimed that a
sacrament dispensed by a corrupt priest lost its efficacy. We will see that even
in Ermine's time the age-old question of whether a sacrament is efficacious if
dispensed by an unworthy member of the clergy resurfaces.[41] When describing Ermine's miraculous visions of a small child in the communion Host,
Jean le Graveur stresses that Ermine had these blessed experiences even when
mass was being celebrated by priests "rumored to live with women" (138).
Ermine's vision is thus used to confirm a point of dogma.

After the Gregorian Reform that, among other rules, insisted on clerical
celibacy, religious life in Europe had become more sharply divided between
the clergy and the laity. But laypeople hungered for participation in religious
ritual and spiritual activities. In 1215 the Fourth Lateran Council began to
regularize lay participation in religious practices by issuing a number of
decrees on such issues as confession and baptism. Annual confession and
communion now became obligatory for both men and women.[42]

The thirteenth century brought other great changes to religious life in
Europe. Saint Francis of Assisi and Saint Dominic founded the mendicant
orders. These orders were much more involved in urban life than the older
orders, such as the Benedictines or Cistercians. The Franciscans in particular
began to compete with parish priests for the pastoral care of city and country

dwellers. These orders also gave rise to new forms of lay religiosity, such as Third Orders and confraternities that offered opportunities for the participation of laypeople. We saw above how quickly these orders and other organizations spread in the city of Reims. New forms of religious life emerged, such as the beguines, associations of pious laywomen of whom some continued to live in the world and others lived in beguinages, both small and large, that sprang up especially in the Low Countries and in France, including in Reims.[43] Women showed great inventiveness in developing new models for a devout life, often even staying at home and adopting a penitential way of life that could involve extreme fasting or bodily castigations. Frequently these women also had visionary experiences (as did Ermine) and lived lives that did not have "formal markers of profession," that is, they did not join an established order, were not enclosed, and did not wear a nun's habit. These "common women" disregarded the traditional borderlines between lay and religious lives. As Barbara Newman rightly observes, "It was this very liminality that vexed their critics, who did not like anomalies in the orderly scheme of things."[44] Indeed, in 1312 the Council of Vienne issued a decree, known as *De quibusdam* (Since certain women) that condemned all quasi-religious movements, such as the beguines or secular canonesses, but the groups continued to flourish nonetheless. One reason for their continued existence was the varied interpretation of the end of the decree, which constituted a kind of "escape clause" and which stated, "Of course, by the preceding we in no way intend to forbid any faithful women, whether or not they promise chastity, from living honestly in their dwellings (*in suis hospitiis*), doing penance, serving the Lord in a spirit of humility (*humilitatis*), this being allowed to them as the Lord inspires them."[45] Elizabeth Makowski explores three kinds of responses to this decree, highlighting the "disjunctions between normative literature and popular religious practice": academic commentaries by canonists; *consilia*, that is, opinions issued by consulting jurists for a specific case, such as questions on wills, inheritance, or the right to make donations; and *decisiones*, opinions written up by jurists involved in litigating specific cases.[46] Strikingly, while the academic commentators with one exception disregarded the escape clause and issued a blanket condemnation of all beguines, the jurists never questioned the beguines' right to exist and were only concerned with their legal status, such as the question of whether they were subject to secular or ecclesiastical courts.

Among the academic commentators the most important influential was the famous canonist Johannes Andreae (1270–1348), who set the tone for the condemnation by labeling all beguines "deceitful and deluded," seeing them as women who claim to fly on the backs of animals and who dare to comment on Scripture, a form of insanity according to him. The idea of "flying on the backs of animals" harks back to the *canon Episcopi*, a decree supposedly dating from the late ninth century, that inveighed against the superstitious beliefs of certain women who claimed that they could travel by air and at night as servants of the goddess Diana, "an image that powerfully influenced fifteenth-century notions of witches flying to diabolical Sabbaths."[47] Since this canon became part of the most important Decretal, that of Gratian dating from around 1150, the idea of women's night flights continued to be discussed. Even though the *canon Episcopi* clearly stated that these women's accounts of flying around at night were delusions, later commentators did not exclude the reality of demons transporting women, and eventually the concept of women flying to witches' Sabbaths took hold—with deadly consequences.[48] In Chapter 4 we will explore how Ermine being transported by demons to a diabolical meeting in the woods outside of Reims fits into these thought patterns.

Johannes Andreae linked the idea of women's delusional air travel with their desire to explicate Scripture, thus equating exegetical desires with the madness of diabolical illusions, but what most of the commentators seemed to be afraid of was something more mundane, that is, that women forming quasi-religious communities "might lead others to presume erroneously that they are true religious."[49] The one exception of this negative attitude of the commentators was Alberic of Metz, also known as Albericus Metensis (d. 1354), a papal chaplain and auditor at the Roman law court called the Rota. In 1323 he pondered what was meant by the term *hospitiis*, or dwellings. Does it refer to a communal or a private lodging? He arrived at the conclusion that the escape clause referred to women who live in private accommodations and not in group homes. Therefore, a woman who lives a quasi-religious life at home is not subject to the condemnation of the Vienne decree.[50] Charles de Miramon defines a quasi-religious person as someone who "exists outside but not too far outside, an institutionalized and legally recognized model for religious life."[51]

How can we define Ermine's status in light of these opinions? Ermine's way of life after her husband's death was liminal in several ways. First, the house in which her room was located stood on the border between an urban street and a religious establishment, the Val-des-Ecoliers. Second, although she was not an enclosed nun, Jean le Graveur expected her to take one of the three monastic vows (chastity, poverty, and obedience) that the true religious were obliged to take: she pledged obedience to him, as we saw above, "as does a monk to his superior" (51). Thus, both her living arrangements and her relationship to the Augustinian male community that welcomed her were unusual and defy easy classification.

Once Ermine had moved in, Jean le Graveur set about shaping her into a holy woman. In order to write about her and construct her holiness, Jean le Graveur needed to draw on some existing models, none of which, however, corresponded precisely to his experiences with Ermine.

A variety of female saintly models were available for emulation in medieval France. The early Christian martyrs and ascetics like Saint Catherine of Alexandria or Saint Margaret were still popular and their *Lives* continued to be read, both in Latin and in the vernacular. Saints in the medieval period came primarily from the upper classes, but in theory the road to sainthood was open to everyone. In twelfth-century France, for example, Alpais of Cudot (c. 1150/55–1211) began her life helping her father in the fields and herding swine but then gained a saintly reputation through her extreme illnesses, miraculous abstinence from food, and innumerable revelations (which included a cosmological vision of the earth in the shape of a ball, with a huge sun near it). Soon, archbishops, royal officials, dukes, and even kings clamored to visit her and pay homage to her saintliness. Her deeds became the subject of a saint's *Life* and were recorded in numerous chronicles.[52]

The situation regarding female sanctity was quite different in France compared with other parts of Europe, such as the Low Countries, certain areas of Germany, or Italy. Between the late twelfth century and Ermine's time one can find only about a dozen women who were considered holy in their own time. And while other northern European regions featured clusters of mystical activity, such as those in the city of Liège in Belgium or the convent of Helfta in Germany, in France there were no discernible patterns of holiness. Some women, like Isabelle of France (c. 1223-c. 1269/70) came from the highest aristocracy, were part of the efforts to create a *beata stirps* (blessed lineage) for the Capetian dynasty, and lived in religious institutions without becoming professed nuns.[53] Others were connected to a Franciscan milieu. Douceline of Digne (1214–1274), for example, although responsible for the creation of a beguine community in southern France, was closely linked to the Franciscans, not least through her famous brother, Hugues of Digne. Delphine of Sabran (1284–1360) and Jeanne-Marie of Maillé (1331–1414), two famous examples of women who realized the ideal of chaste marriage, also became, respectively, a Franciscan Tertiary and a Poor Clare. Marguerite of Oingt (d. 1310) was the only Carthusian woman who became known during her lifetime as a mystical writer and holy woman. As for these women's social class, the majority of those just mentioned came from the nobility. This all-too-brief sketch shows that most of these holy women had a religious affiliation, even if they were not necessarily enclosed nuns, and that the Franciscan influence dominated.

But during the time of the Great Schism a new kind of holy woman emerged, the layperson whose visionary and prophetic gifts allowed her to try and intervene in the political events of her time.[54] One contemporary of Ermine is especially noteworthy here: Constance of Rabastens (d. after 1387), a widow living between Toulouse and Albi, who over several years had dramatic visions of which a large number concerned the Great Schism.[55] Her confessor Raimond of Sabanac, a law professor from Toulouse, transcribed her revelations. But since her visions championed the Roman pope Urban VI, who was not supported in the Languedoc region, which favored the Avignon pope Clement VII, the ecclesiastical authorities in Toulouse soon tried to silence her. Her confessor at one point refused to write down any more of her revelations, fearing persecution himself. Constance's Church-political views as expressed through her visions thus strained the relationship between visionary and confessor, a strain that will also become apparent in the relationship between Ermine and her confessor, Jean le Graveur. Eventually Constance of Rabastens vanished in an inquisitorial prison in Toulouse; no cult ever developed around her, and the text of her revelations survives in a single manuscript, written in Catalan.

For Constance as for Ermine contemporary politics entered into the very fabric of their lives and religious experiences, which distinguishes them and the texts about them from the majority of thirteenth- and fourteenth-century works by and about holy women. This is the context, then, in which we have to place Jean le Graveur's efforts to shape Ermine into a holy woman during the time of the Great Schism, a holy woman who would lend authority not only to Jean himself but also to his institution.

Jean le Graveur's Book

Ermine's *Visions* is a very strange book. It is not overly long but quite repetitive: again and again demons invade her bedchamber in hideous animal or semihuman shapes; again and again she is fooled by demons disguised as saints; again and again she sees Christ appear in the communion Host as a human child or adult. In the modern edition the text runs to over 120 pages; in the manuscript, to 78 folios.[56] Jean wrote these folios after Ermine's death, but nonetheless they have a journalistic quality. He must have kept a notebook where he penned every day what happened to Ermine and what she told him about her visions. Jean himself keys us in on his method when he reproduces an early conversation he had with his pious charge. He tells Ermine that he thinks both her soul and body are in great danger and that he, a simple man, may not be able to counsel her all by himself but may have to seek advice from other people, such as the prior of Saint Denis. Therefore, he urges her to remember every morning what she saw during the night, to think about it diligently, and to report everything to him. Ermine is very apprehensive since she does not want him to tell anyone in town. She clearly considers what is happening to her embarrassing. Jean reassures her: he will write down what she says and only reveal it to those men whose counsel he seeks. But he also thinks of later readers with whom he intends to share Ermine's experiences for the profit of their souls—which is what he is now doing, as he tells us in the prologue (53–54). Ermine's story, he insists, will be "a mirror," a form of instruction that will "teach us how to guard against the falsehoods and deceptions of this perverse Antichrist, who is filled with the devil, and his minions" (49). It will show the truth of the Christian faith and the deception of the devil. This is a tall order for the adventures of a simple peasant woman, and it will be up to Jean to shape her experiences so that their telling can fulfill the mission he sets for himself: to contribute to the salvation of his fellow Christians.

The *Visions* has a very unusual form—a daily journal or logbook of demonic assaults and a few divine visions—that is unique in medieval literature. Each entry in this journal is precisely dated, from October 31, 1395, to Ermine's death on August 25, 1396, with a postscript for January 1397, recounting a miracle attributed to Ermine. It is not a dry account of events but features many dialogues between Ermine and her confessor as well as between Ermine and the demons (when they attack her in human form and can therefore speak French!).

To see just how unusual the text is, we can take a quick look at other religious works composed in the late Middle Ages. One popular form religious literature took from antiquity on was the saint's *Life*, which chronicles a saint's youth, spiritual development, and achievements; his or her saintly death; and posthumous miracles. For potential saints who lived in the Middle Ages a *Life* was normally written in Latin with the purpose of using the text in a canonization trial. The *Visions* bears no resemblance to such a text: written in French, the book lacks all biographical aspects of the typical *Life*. We learn nothing about Ermine's youth; we do not know whether she had a saintly vocation before she met Jean. In fact, her past life surfaces only when demons take on the shape of former friends from the countryside and try to lure her away from Reims and Jean's care.

Some holy women—and men—put together *rapiaria*, scrapbooks of spiritual sayings or thoughts, while others kept diaries, but their structure and content were quite different from what Jean noted down for Ermine. Often these diaries were elaborated from notes recording pious readings; these books could then become spiritual guides or personal exempla books.[57] One example of a late medieval diary is that of the Viennese beguine Agnes Blannbekin (d. 1315) who, in 235 chapters gives an account of her stunning visions and experiences (including her using Jesus's foreskin as a ring on her finger), but here the structure is determined by specific aspects of her faith and devotions and does not resemble the blow-by-blow accounts Jean le Graveur offers us in the *Visions*.[58] In fifteenth-century Nuremberg, Katharina Tucher kept a diary of her mystical experiences, but again there is no resem-blance to the *Visions* since Katharina meditates on various aspects of Christian mysteries without giving us any chronological signposts.[59] What unites these kinds of diaries is of course the fact that their authors were the holy women themselves, who were literate in their own vernaculars and often in Latin as well. (Ermine's complete lack of education will become evident in our next chapters.) In any case we can see that the diaries of holy women concentrated on the spiritual aspects of their lives and were organized by literary principles that do not apply to Jean's breathless day-by-day accounts. While demonic assaults and heavenly visions were certainly a staple of medieval religious works, the fascinating tidbits of daily life and the constantly repeated drama of Ermine's nightly tribulations that we find in Jean le Graveur's book are absent from other texts. There truly is no work that could equal the *Visions* in its detailed narrative centering on a woman caught between demons and saints and yet continuing with her daily existence in medieval Reims, doing laundry and some gardening while waiting for the next demonic assault or heavenly vision.

Sometimes a vision can tell us more about the earthly realm of medieval life than about the heavenly one. I will close this chapter with one amusing example. Throughout the *Visions*, Ermine's confessor vituperates against the exaggerated female fashions of his day. We will see in Chapter 4 that female demons have a great fashion sense when they appear to Ermine in low-cut black dresses with trailing sleeves and push-up bras. But women saints also want to be fashionable, as countless medieval paintings demonstrate. And they do not like a male confessor's criticism of their carefully designed outfits. Thus, on April 9, 1396, three young women enter Ermine's bedroom (just after a demonic raven had stolen her supper, a little piece of cheese) and identify themselves as Saint Catherine of Alexandria, Saint Agnes, and Saint Mary Magdalene.

> They were dressed in dresses of red velvet with little birds in shining
> gold scattered all over, and their hoods were just like their dresses.
> Their sleeves were pointed and almost touched the floor, lined with
> ermine inside and out. Some of them had their sleeves hanging
> down, others had swept them back over their shoulders. And their
> dresses were cut tight at the waist and more ample at the hips and
> they hugged their breasts so that one could see the cleavage of their
> round breasts. The dresses also had a rich white fur appliqué, about
> half a foot long, and their hoods were lined with fur. (107)

Ermine, needless to say, is stunned and inquires whether the young women are thus outfitted when they are with God. Of course not, they answer, but "we show ourselves to you this way so that you will tell the subprior that he is trying in vain to blame women for their beautiful outfits, because when a woman can afford it, she dresses honorably, and this is not a sin. A queen dresses like a queen, a duchess like a duchess, a knight's wife like a knight's wife, a *bourgeoise* like a *bourgeoise*, well and honorably, each one according to her wealth, and this is not something that displeases God" (107). Thus fashion is not a sin as long as women dress according to their social status, a concern of the sumptuary laws of this era. For an hour the three fashionplates parade around Ermine's room, insisting again and again that the subprior should stop blaming women for their beautiful dresses. After they leave, a dazzling light stays behind that prevents Ermine in the morning from seeing what color her own simple cloak is.

This display provokes Jean le Graveur to add one of his rather infrequent direct addresses to the reader. He is not convinced by this saintly fashion show: "You who listen to or read this book should believe firmly that extravagant clothes please the devil and that therefore they displease God. For, according to Scripture, one cannot serve two masters [Mt. 6:24], and all those who are lovers of worldly things are enemies of God, and he who seeks worldly honor loses that of heaven" (107). Several things are striking in this scene. First, Jean le Graveur's mastery of a sophisticated vestimentary vocabulary and his knowledge of what constitutes cutting-edge fashion in late fourteenth-century Reims surprise us in an Augustinian friar. Second, the saintly ladies believe that Ermine can influence her confessor's religious anti-fashion stance. But no confrontation between Ermine and Jean le Graveur takes place over this contentious issue. Yet we can see that for the saintly apparitions the two form a kind of "couple" where one partner has influence over the other.

Both in the production of the text and in the dramatic events of Ermine's life, Jean le Graveur and Ermine form a team. She lives through her often horrific experiences and talks about them; he writes them down. But Jean, of course, is also an actor in the story he writes. A complex dynamic necessarily develops between two human beings in such a situation. This dynamic is the subject of our next chapter.

CHAPTER 2

Ermine and Her Confessor, Jean le Graveur

Life Choices

Let us imagine the moment when Jean le Graveur suggested to Ermine that she could "move in with him." Of course, he did not mean this in the modern sense: they would not cohabit as a couple, but nonetheless she would be very near him at all times, just a stone's throw from the Augustinian priory he called home. Here is how Jean describes the crucial moment that occurred in 1393:

> And it happened that Regnault passed away and he was seventy-two at the time of his death, and Ermine was forty-six. After her husband died, Ermine's friends came to Reims several times and wanted to take her back to the countryside, saying that she was now all alone and a poor woman, and that for that reason she would live alone in Reims in great poverty for she had no friends there; and that if she did not want to return to her region, then they would not be able to take care of her for the rest of her life. So she came to me, the subprior of the Val-des-Ecoliers, for advice because I had been her and her husband's confessor when he was still alive. I told her not to go back to her hometown and that she had begun to serve God, and that she must persevere in this all her life and that she should put her trust in God for He would not fail her. She believed me and sent back her friends without them achieving what they had hoped

FIGURE 3. A Dominican friar and a Dominican nun here evoke the notion of the "holy couple," c. 1520, from *Roman de la Rose*. Pierpont Morgan Library, New York, MS M. 948, f. 118r. Gift of Beatrice Bishop Berle, in memory of her father, Cortlandt Field Bishop, 1972. This image shows False Seeming and Constrained Abstinence, characters in the second part of the *Roman de la Rose* by Jean de Meun (c. 1270) that represent religious hypocrisy. According to the *Roman*, Constrained Abstinence is a beguine, but the illustrator, Master Girard of Acarie (active 1516–1540), chose to depict both of them as Dominicans. I like to imagine Jean and Ermine's encounter through this image.

for. And I made her live in a little room of about sixteen feet square near our priory whose windows looked out on the courtyard of the church of the Val-des-Ecoliers and from which one can hear our masses day and night. And I commanded Ermine to get up every night to hear the matins we chanted in the church and she answered that she would do so gladly. . . . And she asked my permission as a monk would ask his abbot.[1]

Several warning bells go off if we read this passage with some skepticism and not completely through Jean le Graveur's eyes. Ermine, a poor and vulnerable widow recently bereaved but not without generous offers of support from friends, turns to her confessor for advice. In response he estranges her from her friends, prevents her return to her hometown, and invents a devotional and ascetic program for her that, as we will see in the next chapter, is full of contradictions, oscillating between extreme penitential practices and repeated calls for moderation on Jean's part. That such a program could be a step toward sanctity was not lost on Jean: after Ermine's death he submitted the *Visions* to Jean Gerson for an initial vetting. Did Jean le Graveur sacrifice Ermine's mental and material well-being to his own goals of producing a saint for the glory of his order? Perhaps. If we put on more sympathetic lenses, however, we can see Jean as coming to Ermine's rescue at the very moment when she most needs it. Both perspectives have their validity, as we will see throughout this chapter.

The living arrangement proposed by Jean le Graveur was, to say the least, unusual. Women who wanted to begin a religious life had a number of options in the late Middle Ages. If they were wealthy enough to pay a substantial dowry, they could join one of the established nunneries, such as the Cistercians or the Benedictines.[2] As we saw in Chapter 1, by the fourteenth century Reims boasted a large number of religious houses that adhered to the traditional dowry scheme. The beguines as well required a dowry by the time Ermine was widowed, an expense she was not able to afford. Could she have become an urban recluse? Contrary to what we may think after watching the harrowing film *Anchoress* in which a young woman digs her way out of what looks like a prison cell attached to a church in the open country,[3] for the most part anchoresses did not live in walled-up cells but in urban, more open anchorholds that allowed for their participation in city life. Indeed, in order not to be considered "hypocritical frauds," they had to live in "full view of the people." An anchorhold also provided "women protection from intrusive relatives or lustful men."[4] The anchoresses portrayed by Anneke Mulder-Bakker were for the most part not shrinking violets but energetic women, literate, and certainly not as destitute as Ermine appears at the moment of her husband's death. They chose enclosure most often after an active life of charity.

There are a number of theoretical treatises that give advice on how to live the life of an anchoress; the most famous of these is the *Ancrene wisse* or *Ancrene riwle*, composed in England around 1220. This rule spells out the qualities an anchoress must possess as well as her prescribed occupations and daily schedule. A glimpse into the life of Dorothea of Montau (1347–1394), the patron saint of Prussia (who was not canonized until 1976) and an almost exact contemporary of Ermine de Reims, gives us a vivid picture of a woman's entry into a medieval anchorhold. Dorothea, after being widowed, ardently desired a life of enclosure, and Johannes of Marienwerder, her confessor and biographer, gave his consent. He tells us, "The Lord provided Dorothea with a rule she was to observe in her cell and said 'You shall have a glass window that can be opened and closed according to your physical needs. A crucifix shall be suspended from it so that everyone who comes to you will be reminded that your cell is the home of the saints, for it is a good sign when I stand at the door. Once you have moved into your cell, you shall not extend your hand to anyone, touch anyone's hand, or accept any gift without your confessor's permission.'"[5] Christ then exhorts Dorothea to forget about all earthly belongings and to concentrate only on spiritual wealth. But the Lord also regulates her relationship with her confessor: asked by Dorothea whether she can receive the sacrament as often as her confessor (for example, three times on Christmas Day since he will celebrate three masses), Christ answers, "No, you must be content to receive me just once daily" (151).[6] He continues: "You shall put yourself entirely into your confessor's care, just as you have given yourself entirely into mine. . . . Thank me for thus being separated from all other people" (151). Dorothea's enclosure thus will separate her from anyone but her confessor; their relationship will be exclusive and governed by the obedience owed by Dorothea to Johannes, the same kind of religious obedience Jean le Graveur evokes in his account of Ermine's move into his proximity.

We do not know exactly how Ermine envisioned her life after her husband's death. Even though she was not without friends—who after all did offer to provide for her—they resided in the countryside and would not be able to support her if she stayed in Reims. Most of the options available to pious widows were closed to her for financial reasons, and we should therefore not be surprised that she accepted Jean's offer.

That the living arrangement proposed by Jean le Graveur could lead to scandal must certainly have occurred to both Jean and Ermine. Not even the holiest woman and her confessor could escape suspicion, as we can see in the *Life of Christina of Markyate* (c. 1096–c. 1155), the story of an English noblewoman, anchorite, and eventual Benedictine prioress. Having managed a dramatic escape from her home and her parents' marriage plans for her, she was aided by a group of male and female hermits whom she joined. After she began living at Markyate, rumors began to fly about her and the abbot Geoffrey of St. Albans. She was accused of being attracted to him by "earthly love" and being a "loose woman," while the abbot was being "slandered as a seducer."[7] The author of Christina's *Life* of course did not believe such rumors, as evidenced by his use of the term "slandered" (*diffamabatur*); he also suggested that the rumors were spread by the devil who was jealous of all the good that could spring from the abbot and the holy woman's association. Later we will see that for Ermine it is also a demon who suggests that Jean le Graveur has sexual designs on her.

What kinds of interaction between religious men and women were permissible in the Middle Ages? If both partners were educated and witty, as were the eleventh-century abbot Baudri of Bourgueil, one of the famous Loire poets, and his noble correspondent Constance of Angers, who resided in the convent of Le Ronceray, erotic banter was not unheard of.[8] In one of his epistles to Constance, Baudri assures her that although his feelings are ardent, "You can safely open this letter, and you can safely put it in your lap." In the same milieu we find Robert of Arbrissel, founder of the monastery of Fontevraud, which sheltered both monks and nuns. Baudri of Bourgueil wrote Robert's *Life* after his death in 1116 at the request of Petronilla, the abbess of Fontevraud.[9] Headed by an abbess, this early twelfth-century experiment in male-female cohabitation proved successful, although Robert was reprimanded by his superiors for his habit of sleeping next to women in order to test the strength of his asceticism. Bishop Marbode of Rennes laid out the dangers women present to male ascetics in a letter to Robert, which condenses dozens of stereotypical depictions of women's status as sexual predators, ending with "by their appearance alone they pour seductive poison into the marrow and rouse the dark places of the soul with insatiable lust." Marbode reproached Robert about his lack of discretion in his dealings with women and, in fact, accused him of being "reckless" by exposing himself to the very danger he tried to avoid through his asceticism. But apparently Robert succeeded in staying chaste since Marbode does not go so far as to accuse him of actual sexual transgressions.[10] The male-female cohabitation at Fontevraud thus posed risks but also constituted a huge advantage when it came to the *cura monialium*, or the pastoral care, of nuns. As Jacques Dalarun astutely observes,

In setting up a body of religious men, clerics, and lay converts, all
pledged to serve the nuns and totally under the authority of the
abbess, Robert resolved in one action and for the next seven centuries the problem of the *cura monialium*, the sacerdotal care of nuns.
The matter would tear other communities apart, for we know that
in most religious movements with both masculine and feminine
branches, the men grumbled about having to concern themselves
with the women, thinking that they had more noble things to
accomplish than dedicating themselves to the service of nuns. At
Fontevraud, Robert solved the problem before it ever arose.[11]

This "grumbling" attitude was not necessarily the norm, however. Rather,
"diversity, negotiation, and dialogue" characterized the complex relationships
between religious women and men.[12] Some of these relationships flourished
in double monasteries that existed throughout Europe from the earliest centuries of monastic foundation, although they never became the norm. Thus,
for many religious women the question of how they could receive the sacraments remained problematic. Obviously, religious women could not do without male pastoral care since to this day women are not allowed to be ordained
in the Catholic Church and can therefore not celebrate mass, hear confession,
or dispense any other sacrament.[13] In an all-female monastic setting priests
would regularly visit nunneries for this purpose. The pastoral care of nuns
was often a controversial subject for medieval male clerics and monks.[14] Many
monastic orders did not want to establish female branches and tried to resist
the pressure of women eager to join their orders. In 1228, for example, the
Cistercian order issued a statute that stated that no nunneries were allowed
to attach themselves to the order and that existing communities no longer
had any rights to pastoral care. Saint Francis and Saint Dominic, founders of
the Franciscan and Dominican orders, respectively, did not endorse female
versions of their orders, although during his lifetime Francis did support
Clare and her nuns at San Damiano. But once the two founders were dead,
that is, from 1227 onward, the papal curia approved the creation of female
mendicant orders. Since both orders, and especially the Dominicans, had a
strong preaching mission—which of course included a female audience—the
female orders became very visible and therefore attractive to many pious
women. In order to give some structure and supervision to groups of women
seeking a religious life, the papacy thus felt forced to act against the two
saints' explicit wishes and approve the creation of female Franciscans (the

Poor Clares, named after Clare of Assisi) and Dominicans.[15] Nunneries thus flourished: from the year 1000 to the end of the thirteenth century in England and France, their number grew from about 70 to more than 650.[16] Male clerics, whether they wanted to or not, had to provide the pastoral care for these women: they had to hear their confessions, dispense the sacraments, and celebrate mass in the convent.

Pastoral care in villages and towns had a different character. In an urban environment people could choose which church to attend and who was to be their confessor. In the late Middle Ages, as lay piety developed, the role of the confessor became more complex. Very often he now played the role of a spiritual advisor, and when a woman with religious aspirations met a confessor who recognized her potential as a visionary or mystical writer—and who for a variety of reasons decided to "promote" this woman—a "holy couple" was born. Often the relationship resulted in a confessor turning himself into the woman's biographer or collaborator in the composition of pious and visionary texts.

Holy Couples

How They Met

Several fascinating studies explore the complex interpersonal dynamic between holy women and the clerics who supported them and profited from the women's spiritual experiences. The male half of these couples was frequently not only confessor to the female half but also "confidant, arbiter of orthodoxy, director, disciple, and promoter." These men functioned as "mentors, . . . spiritual friends, patrons, symbolic (and sometimes biological) kin, and coworkers in the vineyard of the Lord."[17] These couples could exist in monastic settings, as did, for example, the famous twelfth-century visionary Hildegard of Bingen (1098–1179) and her collaborators Volmar and Guibert of Gembloux, and Elisabeth of Schönau (1128/1129–1164) and her brother, the monk Ekbert, who helped disseminate her revelations. Their common home, the Benedictine double monastery of Schönau, made this collaboration possible.

But many of the holy couples can be found in an urban milieu, and we have to ask ourselves how these two people came to know each other and recognized that each could respond to the needs of the other. Sometimes it

was the holy woman who sought the assistance of her confessor in making
known her visionary experiences or spiritual revelations. In other cases one
gets the feeling that a male cleric set his sights on a woman whose religious
charisma he might want to share and promote by becoming her scribe or
biographer. However this dynamic worked, each partner in this arrangement
clearly got something out of it: the woman would receive the help and support of an authoritative male figure while the cleric would gain more direct
access to the divine.[18] But since it was almost exclusively the men who set
pen to paper, we always have to be cautious when reading these types of texts:
many of them have an agenda, such as the woman's eventual canonization or
the enhancement of a religious institution's reputation. While some of the
polemic goals are obvious, others are not always easy to tease out.

The holy couples got together in a variety of ways, ranging from chance
encounters to carefully planned collaborations. Scholars studying them sometimes use phrases like "a spark must have been ignited" between the two or
even "love at first sight" when they describe the meeting of a male cleric with
the holy woman who was to become his subject and often his collaborator.[19]

A "spark" sprang from Jacques of Vitry to Marie of Oignies (c. 1177–
1213) when he first spotted her in 1208. A prominent churchman, Jacques (c.
1160/1170–1240) was born in Reims, studied in Paris, spent more than a
decade as bishop of Acre in Palestine, and became one of the foremost crusade propagandists of his time. But before this brilliant career he had settled
in the small town of Oignies (in modern-day Belgium) where he encountered
a pious recluse named Marie. She lived in a cell near an Augustinian priory
after having served in a leper colony with her husband, with whom she had
agreed on a celibate marriage. Marie, like Ermine, was a laywoman, but
unlike her later sister, she lived the communal life of a beguine. Jacques,
fascinated by her copious shedding of tears—requiring several cloths that she
wrung out during mass—which he saw as a manifestation of extraordinary
spiritual gifts, decided to become her protector and promoter. He felt that
such a woman could be a useful tool in his fight against heresy. In his *Life* of
Marie he not only chronicled her experiences but also tried to analyze them,
that is, to become the interpreter of phenomena that he himself could not
experience but that he considered crucial for spiritual "completeness," as
Brian McGuire puts it.[20] Despite Jacques' efforts Marie was never canonized,
although Goswin of Bossut wrote a liturgical office for her. The wide circulation of her *Life* as well as the veneration of her relics demonstrate that in the

thirteenth century the development of a cult did not necessarily depend on official papal endorsement. Indeed, there was little papal support for the case of a charismatic laywoman whose piety manifested itself outside of the sanctioned channels, such as enclosed nunneries. The newly elected pope Honorius III granted Jacques nothing more than permission for the holy women of the diocese of Liège to continue to live together in their urban settings.[21]

Another beguine who became the object of interest and devotion for a male cleric was Christina of Stommeln (1242–1312), from a small town near Cologne.[22] Peter of Dacia, about twelve years older than Christina, was a Swedish Dominican who was studying in Cologne when he heard about the remarkable events—demonic attacks and vexations quite similar to those of Ermine—surrounding this woman; he was intrigued and decided to get to know her. They became what Christine Ruhrberg calls an *Arbeitspaar*, a couple who worked together. Their friendship and collaboration were predestined, as Peter makes clear in his *Life* of Christina, where he tells how the heavenly bridegroom spoke of him to Christina in a vision: "Look at this man carefully, for he is your friend and will remain so and he will do much for you; but you will do things for him that you would do for no other mortal. And you should know that he will enter with you into the eternal life."[23] This prediction crystallizes all the important elements of this type of relationship: the salvific dimension linked to exclusivity and mutuality; both of them will gain in this relationship and will enjoy eternal life together. From a textual perspective their collaboration was extremely fruitful, for in the end Peter composed an extensive, multilayered codex about her that included details from a notebook containing her life story as told to a priest, several narratives about her, and numerous letters. With these extensive and detailed writings that offered a theological interpretation of Christina's vexations, Peter hoped to promote her sanctity, a difficult and, as in so many other cases, finally futile goal.

The Italian mystic Angela of Foligno (c. 1248–1309) met her future scribe and confessor, Brother A., during a dramatic scene in Assisi, the birthplace of Saint Francis who had also died there in 1226.[24] Angela, who had been married and had several children, was finally liberated from earthly cares by the deaths of all her family members. She joined the tertiary order of the Franciscans and in 1291 embarked on a pilgrimage to Assisi. On the way she was visited by the voice of the Holy Ghost and arrived at the church of San

Francesco in ecstasy, a heightened state not even dampened by the ample luncheon meal she consumed. Still, eventually she emerged from her rapturous state and was so upset that she sat at the gate to the church and began to wail and scream. This performance summoned several horrified friars from the nearby Franciscan house, among them Brother A., who also happened to be a kinsman of Angela's. Brother A. makes it clear that the dramatic scene of Angela sitting in front of the church screaming initially caused him to be ashamed and embarrassed; in fact he ordered Angela never to return to Assisi. But he was also intrigued and went to Foligno to learn the cause of her extraordinary behavior. When Angela began to explain what happened, he stopped her to warn her that an evil spirit may have inspired her rather than the Holy Spirit. But finally, she got to explain the reason for her screaming: on the way to Assisi she had been taken over by the Holy Spirit, who eventually left her when she sat in front of the church.[25]

Between Brother A.'s eyewitness account and Angela's explanation there is a description of the crucial moment he becomes her scribe: "Here then is the starting point of my redaction, the very first step which I began to write after the screaming and shouting episode by Christ's faithful one in church of St. Francis, as mentioned in the preceding narrative."[26] Brother A. then describes in great detail how he became Angela's scribe for the book now called the *Memorial* and how he went about ensuring the truth of this work. This description of his working method (to which we will return in a moment) and his interactions with Angela in the composition of the text sheds some fascinating light on the relationship between a confessor and the holy woman in his charge.[27] The nonlinear narrative, constantly backtracking and foreshadowing, shows that Brother A. gave a structure to his remarks to heighten the tension and create suspense around their initial meeting. Angela and Brother A.'s first moments together were marked by high drama and uncertainty (was Angela mad? divinely inspired?), and by both shame and desire for Brother A.: shame at Angela's display of unbridled emotion and the desire to know more about it, to find its cause. This intense first meeting triggered the symbiotic relationship between Angela and Brother A., between seer and scribe.

Sometimes the themes of the *coup de foudre* and conversion come together, as they do in the story of Margaret of Ypres (1216–1237) and the Dominican friar Zeger of Lille.[28] Here the confessor and the biographer are not identical since it was Thomas of Cantimpré who penned Margaret's *Life*. But the biographer creates an atmosphere in his writing of their first meeting

that is as intimate and passionate as if he had witnessed it himself. After a
pious childhood Margaret fell in love with a young man, "although without
the filth of lustful desire." Still, she believed that her love for Christ should
not be shared with a human lover and would not entertain any thoughts of
marriage. At this crucial moment in her young life, which Thomas presents
as a crossroads between worldly and heavenly aspirations, Friar Zeger
appeared and converted her back to a religious life. As he heard people's
confessions after mass, "by chance he cast his eyes on Margaret, who was
dressed in secular clothing among other women, and saw with a kind of
divine instinct—for he had never seen her before—that she would be apt to
receive God's grace and become a chosen vessel, as Christ revealed to him."

This election by Friar Zeger made her "abandon the world"—although
she continued to live at home in a frequently contentious relationship with
her family. In the following months Margaret developed such an ardent love
for the friar that she began to "fear that this was against the Lord in some
way" and could arouse the suspicions of their superiors. Her appeal to Christ
to tell her whether her relationship with Zeger could cause a diminishment
of Christ's love for her was answered quickly by Christ "in spirit: Do not
fear to trust him in my stead. Nothing he commands will harm you in flesh
or in spirit." Thus reassured, Margaret continued to rely entirely on Zeger
for her spiritual comfort, to such a degree that when he absented himself to
return to his friary in Lille, she had a vision of him with her "bodily eyes."
Thomas tried to find a scientific optical explanation for this vision, but some
medieval readers could have understood it as a kind of lovesickness where
desire brings forth a vision of the beloved.[29]

Not all first encounters between confessors and holy women were quite
this dramatic, but most of them occupy a special place in the texts chronicling
them. Johannes of Marienwerder, the confessor of Dorothea of Montau, presents their first meeting in a remarkable way: he waits until chapter 27 of the
second book of the *Life*, almost the middle of the text, to tell "how she came
to Marienwerder to the man who had been recommended to her" and then
switches from the third person to the first person by having Dorothea recount
in her own words how the two met. After describing that Dorothea was now
a widow (after over twenty-six years of marriage) and how, after she arrived
at the cathedral church of Marienwerder, she sat down behind a portal and
received an order from the Lord to speak, Johannes appears to cite the words
Dorothea was commanded to utter.[30] This narrative technique allows Dorothea to speak directly about the consolation she received from the Lord,

about the ardent desire she had for the Eucharist at that moment, and, most important, about the feelings she instantly developed for Johannes:

> So I went to that man on whose account I had come and begged him to hear my confession and give me the body of my dear Lord on the feast of Corpus Christi. As he heard my confession for the first time, I immediately conceived a greater love for him than for any other person. At once I loved him as sincerely as a brother and trusted him so explicitly that then and there I would have revealed all the secrets of my heart to him had the Lord taught me how to phrase them properly at that very moment. I remained there for a week in his pleasant company and revealed to him in perfect confidence what was in my heart, as much as my dear Lord allowed me.[31]

The tale of their first encounter is thus mediated multiple times: Johannes presents Dorothea as the mouthpiece for the Lord; it is the Lord who tells her how to describe the event and the feelings that accompanied it. Dorothea expresses her love for Johannes in neither her own words nor Johannes's but rather in Christ's words that are channeled through Dorothea. But then it is again Johannes who reports these words. Johannes's rhetorical precautions here suggest that a confession of exclusive love on the part of a mature widow could perhaps be seen as suspect. Dorothea's love for Johannes is indeed exclusive and durable, as becomes clear when she pledges perpetual obedience to Johannes a few days later. This vow is again the result of the Lord's command: "During this time the Lord drove her and ordered her to swear to him that she should remain with B [as Johannes now refers to himself] for the rest of her life, never to abandon him" (128). Johannes then went on to write Dorothea's spiritual biography in three books, followed by a fourth on the thirty-seven degrees and names of divine love. In the biography Johannes's persona is a constant presence, but his description of their relationship never again reaches the intensity of their first encounter and Dorothea's declaration of love for him.

The account Jean le Graveur gives of how he met Ermine and became her confidant is much less intense and perhaps signals that he wants to forestall any kind of suspicion that his interest in Ermine was anything but clerical, a precaution that however does not prevent these suspicions from flourishing, as we will see below. Jean is careful to introduce Ermine as part of a married couple when he insists that he had been the confessor of both

Ermine and her husband, Regnault, for some years before Regnault's death. It is only at this point that Ermine and Jean become closer because Ermine seeks his counsel when her friends from the countryside try to persuade her to go back with them to the region of the Vermandois. This request, as we saw at the beginning of this chapter, results in his offer of a room and the constant attention on his part that goes with this new living arrangement. We also saw that Jean describes their new relationship as that of a monk to his superior: "She asked my permission as does a monk from his superior" (*elle prenait congié a moy comme fait ung religieux a son souverain*; 51). It is certainly striking that he uses the masculine term *religieux*, thus insisting that their relationship will not be marked by any kind of sexual tension that could result from male-female proximity—a stance that will be undercut multiple times throughout the text, however. He also establishes a clear hierarchy, insisting on the obedience she owes him as her superior. He thus envisions their relationship in traditional monastic terms, a framework that quickly explodes when Ermine's life begins to be dominated by demonic intrusions into what Jean apparently conceived of as a kind of cell that could become part of the priory.

How They Worked Together

Once the "holy couples" were formed, they set about their collaboration, which could take a variety of forms, each of them fraught with risks: "Danger lay not only in the development of excessively close relationships between confessors and holy women penitents, but in the threat such women offered to the authority of the confessor. Women who spoke with the voice of God, especially from outside the walls of a convent, challenged the authority of the clerical establishment even as they sought it. Though they needed the support of respected confessors and the orthodox church, their authority to speak, if it was established as divinely inspired, superseded the very authority that validated it."[32] Our holy couples confronted these dangers in different ways, depending on the nature of the holy woman and that of her biographer, confessor, or scribe. Many of these collaborations involved not only literate clerics but also literate and educated women. The most common scenario was that of a woman dictating accounts of visions and revelations to a male confessor or secretary, who then assembled all the different parts into a spiritual (auto)biography or a collection of revelations.[33] Hildegard of Bingen's

collaboration with her scribe Volmar and later her collaborator Guibert of
Gembloux is the prime example of an unusually educated woman who transmitted her visions to male clerics. Hildegard, a nun in the Rhineland from
an early age, a skilled abbess, and a correspondent with powerful men of her
time, was the author of a number of important theological and medical
works, most of which were inspired by visions.[34] Throughout her long life
she managed to have complete control over the transcription of her visions:
while Volmar, for example, is always cited as an eyewitness to Hildegard's
visionary experiences, it was Hildegard who had the power of final approval
of anything that was written.[35] The *Life* of Hildegard by Gottfried of Disibo-
denberg and other monks incorporates a memoir by the seer that describes
how her collaboration with Volmar began: feeling a "great burden of my
sorrows" because she could not speak openly about her visions, she finally
approached her "teacher" Volmar who was "astounded" and told her to write
down what she saw so that he could try and understand it. Convinced that
Hildegard's visions were sent by God, he cleared them with his abbot and
became her scribe: "With great desire he worked on these things *with me*."[36]
Hildegard here avoids any notion of hierarchy but stresses the equality and
companionship she perceived in their working together.

Visually, their collaboration is depicted as Hildegard receiving divine
inspiration from God through a kind of fiery wave and writing on a wax
tablet while Volmar sticks his head through an opening in Hildegard's cell,
his manuscript pages at the ready.[37] Alternatively, the scribe is shown in a
separate space (Fig. 4).[38] In these images it is clearly Hildegard who had
the direct access to the divine. Hildegard's visions resulted in sophisticated
theological writings that were approved by the archbishop of Mainz and
could thus be disseminated.[39] Even her assumption of what was essentially a
priestly function, namely, to preach in public, was accepted by the Churchmen of her time. The normal attitude in this era was to forbid women to
preach by citing Saint Paul's injunction against women's teaching, but in
Hildegard's case clerics "actually *invited* her to preach and then wrote to her
afterward, begging for transcripts of her sermons."[40] The wonderful film
Vision, directed by Margarethe von Trotta in 2009 and starring Barbara
Sukowa as Hildegard, unfortunately stops before the main character goes on
any of her travels along the Rhine to prophesy and preach.

Hildegard's authority was such that we have not much sense of her
scribes' possible anxieties over writing down her divine visions. For Angela
of Foligno and Brother A. the case is quite different: Brother A., who is along

FIGURE 4. Hildegard of Bingen transcribes her divine revelations, shown as a red flood flowing from heaven's window, on a wax tablet. On the left Volmar writes them on parchment. A nun stands demurely on the right. From Hildegard's *De operatione Dei*. Lucca, Biblioteca Statale, Cod. Lat. 1942, thirteenth century. Gianni Dagli Orti, The Art Archive at Art Resource, NY.

with Angela the major character in his book, was extremely anxious about the authenticity of Angela's revelations, the literary form he should give them, his frequent loss of contact with Angela, his lack of time and precision for the kind of writing her revelations deserve, and the hostility he encountered from his colleagues and superiors. He describes his method as follows: "I began briefly and carelessly jotting down notes on a small sheet of paper as a sort of 'memorial' for myself, because I thought I would have little to write. Later, after I had compelled her to talk, it was revealed to Christ's faithful one that I should use a larger copy book, not a small sheet of paper. Because I only half believed her, I wrote on two or three blank pages I found in my book. Later, of necessity, I made a copy book of quality paper."[41] It would be difficult to find a more intriguing description of the writing relationship between a cleric and a holy woman. Several details stand out: that Brother A. "compelled" Angela to talk; that he initially just took informal notes until "it was revealed" that he should use a larger notebook, finally ending up fabricating a book from better paper. In a similar way, Johannes of Marienwerder listened to Dorothea of Montau, took notes, and then worked from these notes on the composition of the book.[42]

For both Brother A. and Johannes of Marienwerder there seems to be a clear evolution from notes to finished book, an evolution that we do not find as such for Jean le Graveur and Ermine. Jean's text rather seems to reproduce a notebook without any further elaboration, with its daily immediacy and the consequent repetitiveness intact. Jean also does not state that his superiors tried to prevent him from writing, as does Brother A. here: "What caused me no little pain and concern was that many of her words which seemed to me worthy of being written I had to omit in my haste, because of my inadequacy as a scribe, and out of my fear of my brothers who opposed my work. They murmured so strongly against me that as a result the guardian and the provincial [his Franciscan superior] strictly forbade me to write and later even reprimanded me. It is true that they did not know what I was writing and how good it was."[43] Despite this interdiction Brother A. continued to write, of course.[44] He continuously strove for accuracy in his transcriptions of Angela's words, knowing full well that he could never achieve it. He presented himself as a "sieve or a sifter" that retained only the coarsest flour; he stated, "I would add nothing of my own, not even a single word, unless it was exactly as I could grasp it just out of her mouth as she related it." Despite these efforts, when he read the text back to Angela, she often told him that she did not recognize what he had written, that "his words were dry and without any savor" and even "obscure" because they could not reproduce the true meaning of what she had heard and seen. She reproached him with harsh words: "You have written what is bland, inferior, and amounts to nothing; but concerning what is precious in what my soul feels, you have written nothing."[45] This scene dramatizes perfectly the gap between a holy woman's charisma and the male cleric's efforts at transcription, which are depicted here as laborious and yet always inadequate. The inexpressibility of the mystical experience is at the heart of Angela and Brother A.'s conflict and the saint's nastiness toward her scribe.

About a century later in the south of France, Raimond of Sabanac, a cleric and lawyer from Toulouse, also struggled with the transcriptions of a seer's revelations. Constance of Rabastens, whom we encountered already in Chapter 1, was a widow who between 1384 and 1386 had visions of a political nature about the Great Schism of the Western Church that pitted two popes against each other; she received divine commands to have them written down and persuaded her confessor Raimond to do just that.[46] Constance's visions showed her Pope Clement VII, the pope who had been accepted by the authorities in her region, in hell, being punished by demons. Her visions were deemed dangerous and eventually landed her in jail. All along, Raimond was her reluctant scribe until he and Constance consulted the inquisitor of Toulouse, who called a council to examine the visions and then forbade any further transcription of them. Raimond then asked for a divine sign and promptly fell ill but soon recovered. But he still did not want to write and asked for another sign: his eyesight got so bad that he needed glasses; and although he saw this as a positive sign, he still did not want to write. Nonetheless the text got produced, at the end with the help of Constance's son, a monk at a nearby monastery. No documentation on how the text survived has come down to us, and only one manuscript of the text in a Catalan translation survives. In the text itself Raimond presents himself as a character whose ability to write is curtailed by the ecclesiastical authorities but who seeks divine guidance that would allow him to circumvent the inquisitorial interdiction. This scenario of the relationship between holy woman and male cleric has a context that is absent from almost all the other accounts of holy couples: concrete political situations and the resulting pressures that shape and ultimately end the relationship between the two. As we will see, the Great Schism also hovers in the background of Jean le Graveur's work, with the appearance of the charismatic hermit and former church official Jean de Varennes.

In many saintly biographies the working relationship between a holy woman and her confessor-scribe-biographer is thematized, as we just saw. But in some cases the identities of the woman's collaborators remain vague even as the creation of the text becomes a major theme. The prime example of this scenario is *The Book of Margery Kempe*. Margery Kempe (c. 1373– c. 1440) hailed from Lynn in England and is probably one of the most written-about medieval women; her fascinating spiritual autobiography has been the subject of hundreds of scholarly analyses.

The mother of many children, Margery experienced a kind of postpar-
tum mania after the birth of her first baby, a trigger for her career as a
visionary and pious pilgrim. After her father's death she became an inveterate
traveler; leaving her husband behind in England, she went on a number of
pilgrimages, including to Rome and the Holy Land.[47] Throughout her travels
and after her return she had very tense relationships with the people surrounding her and at one point was even accused of being a heretic. Margery's
story is one of the most fascinating in medieval culture, but here we have but
one limited interest, namely, what Laurie Finke terms moments of "dialogic
writing" in the *Book of Margery Kempe*—scenes that dramatize the relationship between the female visionary and her male priest-scribe.[48] Margery does
not present herself as the author of her text in the modern sense—that would
be too prideful. Rather, she refers to herself in the third person as "this
creature." But she does control the production of her text. She explains that
events are not recorded in a chronological order but in the order in which
she remembers them. A gap of twenty years between her experiences and
their recording caused a host of problems of recollection and accuracy, but
the main problem for Margery was to find a willing and competent scribe.
The first scribe may have been her son (although she only refers to him as an
Englishman who married in Germany, as did her son); this book she gives to
a priest to read, who can make no sense of it, promises to rewrite it, then
refuses, then restarts. Finke summarizes the multiple obstacles to the creation
of Margery's text as "bad penmanship and spelling, poor eyesight, language
barriers, fear of ostracization, punishment and censorship," obstacles that can
disappear only through a "miracle." Eventually we do have the text but with
many layers of transcription and retranscription separating us from Margery's
voice: "The reader encounters 'Margery' at three removes (at least); the presence of her voice—of mystical experience—cannot be recuperated." In the
end we cannot really know whose language we are reading.[49]

Thus we encounter a number of quite different scenarios that can lead
to the production of a visionary text, but all of them dramatize in one way
or another the relationship between the visionary woman and her scribe.
Anxieties surface in almost all cases, anxiety about accuracy, chronological
gaps and incomplete recollections, insufficient understanding, and even a
possible lack of grace that would impede the faithful recording of a holy
woman's revelations; there were also anxieties about real-world situations:
political risks and fears of accusations of heresy. All these elements enter into

the production of the texts that strive to reveal women's immediate experiences of the divine and almost as often of the demonic.

Ermine and Jean

How do Ermine and Jean le Graveur fit into these varied scenarios and traditions? We already considered the question of genre at the end of Chapter 1, where we saw that Ermine's *Visions* is an unusual type of text, really the only one of its kind. It is not a saint's *Life* since there are no details about Ermine concerning her life before she arrived in Reims. This is a crucial omission on the part of Jean le Graveur, for a saint's birth, childhood, and youth are indispensable elements in any saint's *Life*. Nor is Jean's text a collection of meditations or a didactic dialogue, another common form of religious works at the time. But there are some parallels with other works produced through the collaboration of female visionary and male confessor. One of these is the thematization of the couple's relationship; that is, the confessor stars in his own narrative, sometimes referring to himself in the third person or, as in the case of Ermine's *Visions*, in the first person. What is also striking in our text is the frequent use of dialogue, giving a distinct voice to Ermine herself. A close reading of the Prologue shows how Jean envisioned their collaboration and how he tried to guard against the dangers of deception.[50]

He begins by defining the purpose of the text, which is to alert Christians to the devil's myriad deceptions (he lists the devil's many "disguises," which we will explore in Chapters 4 and 5) and to help protect his readers from these deceptions. He, a poor and unworthy sinner, subprior of the church of Saint-Paul of Reims of the Order of the Val-des-Ecoliers, has written down the adventures (*aventures*; 47), which he "has heard from the mouth of a simple little woman . . . who had confessed herself to me for several years." He assures us that he has written them down as best he could, according to what she had told him every day. And because this may be hard to believe, he evokes a conversation he had one day with Ermine after hearing her confession. Here he switches to the dramatic mode of the dialogue: "'Ermine, you have told me many things that are difficult to believe, are they the truth?' At that point she put her hand in mine and said, 'Believe, my dear sir, that, in the name of the Savior whom I will soon receive, I have never lied to you and there is no oath that I would not take to that effect, and I would rather have my head cut off than that I would knowingly commit perjury before God'" (47). On the very next page appears another dialogue where Jean warns Ermine that any lies told in confession will lead to eternal damnation, and he commands her again to affirm the truth of what she tells him every day. She again responds that everything she says is the pure truth but that it may not be the whole truth because she cannot retain all her experiences owing to the troubles (she uses the word *mechiefs*, meaning the demonic vexations she suffers every day) she has and also because of her simplicity (*simplesce*; 48). It is this self-confessed simplicity that reassures Jean: because Ermine is so simple-minded, she could never invent all the things she tells him.[51]

To buttress his truth claim even more, Jean now mentions that he, the other Augustinian friars, and the people Ermine shared a house with also witnessed Ermine's trials and tribulations, mostly by hearing the noise the demonic visitors and Ermine herself made almost every night. Jean names one of the witnesses, Marie d'Aubenton, as a special proof of Ermine's veracity because Marie frequently saw the traces of demonic assaults on Ermine's body. Finally, he states that on her deathbed, in front of six notable personages, Ermine reaffirmed the truth of everything she ever told him. This multilayered, repetitive opening section signals Jean le Graveur's worries over Ermine's trustworthiness. Because what happened to her was so excessive, doubts as to her veracity would necessarily arise. He tries to forestall these doubts through a number of techniques, of which the most effective is the dialogues between himself and Ermine on the topic of her truth-telling. He makes her speak "in her own voice," trying to win his readers over to his conviction of her absolute truthfulness.

Jean's method of transcribing Ermine's experiences was apparently simple: "You will tell me every day what you have seen, what you were told and how you responded, as accurately as you can. And make sure to think over everything diligently as soon as the adventure is over so that you can tell me about it the next day, so that I can give you some advice in case there is something that is not quite clear" (53–54). Their collaboration thus consisted of Ermine reporting her tribulations to Jean, who then wrote them down. Jean seeks the advice of his superiors in this matter, who counsel him to take notes (*que j'en feisse aucune memoire*; 54) that he should then make public after Ermine's death. Thus, the text we have is a later redaction of these notes that Jean strives to make as accurate as possible by incorporating the very words (*les propres paroles*) that were spoken to Ermine by various demons and a few saints, as well as her responses, the "forms" she saw, and the actions (*les fais*) she experienced (55). Jean acknowledges that completeness is impossible and that he will therefore choose to report only the most remarkable or marvelous happenings. And indeed, throughout the text we find Jean's use of the brevity topos. For the days just before Christmas 1395, for example, he gives only a kind of summary of the beatings and other attacks by demons Ermine experienced and adds that other things happened that he will not mention in order to keep his account brief (66).

But Jean does not only transcribe what Ermine told him; he also inserts scenes into the text that dramatize the collaborative relationship they developed. In addition to being Ermine's counselor and the interpreter of some of these demonic and saintly apparitions, he was a day-to-day presence in her life and shared in her experiences in a very direct way. Early on in their relationship, on November 24, 1395, Ermine tells Jean about the horrific night she had just spent being tormented and propositioned by enormous black, hairy demons with huge horns and ears. She managed to fight back by getting her tablet with a depiction of the *arma Christi* out of a coffer but in doing so fell backward down the steps. After that, she was so confused and upset that she felt "filled completely with the demon" and did not want to see her confessor; she literally fled from him (*elle me fuioit*; 56). Jean thus inscribes himself into this scene in multiple ways. First, he identifies himself by his position and by the relationship he has to Ermine by stating that she swears an oath "to me the subprior, her confessor" (*a moy supprieur, son confesseur*; 56) that any other torment would be preferable to this one. Jean then affirms that in the wake of the demonic attack Ermine was so perturbed that she fled from him, again bringing the narrative back to himself. Thus, even though he is not present at the nocturnal assaults, he is intertwined with Ermine in their aftermath.

Jean is an actor in his own and Ermine's drama, and the demons recognize his importance by disguising themselves as him and by impersonating him as the individual who cares most about Ermine. On December 19, 1395, the Sunday before Christmas, for example, Jean goes up to Ermine's room where she is still in bed at Vespers because of the horrible beating the demons had given her the night before (65). He sets the scene through a number of small details:

I, the subprior, went to see her and ascended the steps to her room. I lifted the latch of her door, greeted her, and sat down next to her, and she said her confession. Afterward, she said to me: "I am sure

that tonight there will be another assault, for my whole body trembles
and my hair stands on end. But don't bother to come and see me in
the morning, for I will send for you if I need you." And when the
next day arrived, the demon knew very well what she had said and
took on my shape through clothes and speech and ascended the steps
to her room, lifted the latch of her door, greeted her, and said: "You
told me last night when I was here that you would be attacked and
that your whole body trembled and your hair stood on end, and that
I should not bother to come and see you, but that you would call for
me if you needed me. But, my beautiful daughter, I did not stick to
this arrangement for I was worried about you and therefore I asked
your leave last night to come and see you this morning." (65)

Needless to say, Ermine realizes that the personage is not Jean but a demon
and tells him that he cannot be the subprior because he is still at home. Thus
unmasked, the devil uses his fist to give her cheek a brutal beating and then
leaves. Jean offers no comment after this elaborate scene of demonic masquer-
ade. As critical readers we are struck by a number of implausible details, most
important the phrase "the demon knew very well what she had said." How
can Jean know this? Did the demon tell him? Jean offers no explanation
about how he obtained this bit of information. The episode serves to highlight Ermine's extraordinary capacity of discernment, and it also shows their
great intimacy (he sits by her bed) and the trust that Ermine feels for Jean.
Conversely, in our skeptical mode, we could interpret the fact that demons
take on Jean's shape as a manifestation of Ermine's conflicted feelings toward
her demanding confessor.

In early March 1396 Ermine is the victim of a particularly brutal demonic
attack by huge black flies, even as she prays in the chapel of Saint Catherine,
part of the Augustinians' church. In his typical mixture of realistic detail and
supernatural events, Jean describes that Ermine was on her knees in the
chapel in a location where one could see "God" (that is, the Eucharist) elevated "through a hole in a wooden board." A huge fly zooming around the
church enters through this very hole and bites her in the eye. Ermine cries
out, and Jean specifies that "I and the entire convent saw everything, that is,
the red and black stain and her eye that cried" (96). In the evening the flies
attack Ermine in her room, surrounding her from head to toe. When she
gets up for matins prayers, flies move under her dress and torment her even
more. She cannot sleep; in fact she has not slept for days. Her brain "is

boiling, and for good reason for she had two demons in the shape of flies in her head." In despair she runs over to the convent where the whole chapter of brothers comforts her, and then they find Jean in the church and bring him to Ermine to give her special consolation. That very night a fake angel appears to her, reassures her that he is telling the truth and is not an impostor, and urges her to prefer his help over that of Jean who, though a good man, is not capable of helping her (97). This is a rather mild attack on Jean's competence, certainly milder than the one a month earlier when a demon emerging from the head of a huge cat with flaming eyes had told Ermine that only he, the demon, could protect her from all the terrible things that are happening to her and that Jean will not only abandon and hate her but will drive her mad: "You will become crazy and will not know anymore where to turn" (83). But Ermine remains steadfast, stating firmly that she will continue to trust Jean and that even if the demon tried for a hundred years to convince her otherwise, he would just be wasting his time. At that the demon shuts up. But the possibility of an incipient mental illness has been evoked.

No demonic impersonator can shake her faith in her confessor. And yet this is exactly what the demons try to achieve: to make her distrust Jean and abandon him. This theme is what makes Jean le Graveur's account of Ermine's experiences unique in the literature featuring holy couples. Jean weaves it like a kind of leitmotif through the entire text: demons make continuous efforts to destroy Ermine's relationship with her confessor and to wrest her away from him. These demonic attempts to separate the two define their interactions in a special way.

From the very beginning, that is, October 31, 1395, the first day for which we have an entry in this peculiar diary, demons strive to deceive Ermine by speaking in Jean's and other friars' voices. The French word Jean uses for these instances is always *hucher,* which suggests an eerie scream. Jean convinces her that this is the devil's voice, not his own. This demonic opening gambit sets up the tug of war between the influence and dominion of her confessor and other desires and possible life choices that appear to exist within Ermine. Awakened by these voices at the beginning of her tribulations, Ermine witnesses what will become her nightly horrors: a black dog with fiery eyes sitting on the windowsill and a huge head with enormous eyes but no mouth or nose. From this point on, the demons do not only impersonate Jean; they begin a concerted campaign against him. One demon, pretending to be one of her friends from the countryside, reproaches her with abandoning her friends and urges her to leave Jean (57). This particular demonic message appears again and again during the ten months chronicled by Jean. It is possible, of course, that Ermine's friends really appeared at her doorstep and that she, by now completely in her confessor's orbit, could or would not recognize them. At one point a few months later a demon masquerading as one of her countrymen—although in this case the fact that this man had been dead for thirteen years alerts Ermine to the demonic impersonation—even offers money to Ermine if she "stops talking" to Jean. "The demon counted the money in front of her and she heard the clicking sound it made," but Ermine remains steadfast: "I will not go back to my country, I will not take your money, and I will not leave Jean. Rather, I will tell him everything you said to me as soon as I see him." She then paces around her room, and a voice tells her, "Believe the subprior; don't leave him, and confess yourself often" (69).

On November 30, 1395, we find her lying on her bedroom floor, on her naked stomach because the demons rolled up her gown and hair shirt. Jean's description of this compromising posture sounds sober and detached, yet one cannot help wondering what he might really have thought of this potentially provocative scene. The demons taunt her efforts at asceticism, which are prescribed, as they claim, by Jean who is nothing but a deceiver (*ung trompeur et ung bourdeur*, 60). They urge her not to tell Jean anything else, but of course Ermine refuses. A day later another demon, taking on the form of Saint John the Baptist,[52] accuses Ermine of monopolizing Jean, a grievous sin, and thus keeping his much-needed pastoral attentions away from other people. Paradoxically the demons also call Jean ignorant and claim that his offers to "help" are in vain (109). They predict that Jean will die ten years before Ermine and that therefore he will not be able to provide confession for her at her death. This claim is obviously false, as all Jean's readers will know, since he wrote the text after Ermine's death in 1396. But even after a real saint, Paul the Simple, appears to her and explains that what she hears and sees are demons and that what she should do is believe in Jean and trust him no matter what (113), the demonic attempts to separate them continue; just a few days later a counterfeit Saint Mary Magdalene again wants to woo her away from her confessor (122).

As both a true saint and a counterfeit or demonic saint, Paul the Simple plays a special role for Ermine during the last ten months of her life. Who was this saint? Relatively unknown in medieval France, Saint Paul the Simple (d. c. 339 C.E.), a disciple of the desert saint Saint Anthony, had been a married man who at the age of sixty was so disgusted by his wife's infidelities that he begged Saint Anthony to give him shelter in his hermitage in the desert—which Anthony did after a series of trials for poor Paul. His docility equaled simplicity in the ancient monastic context and earned him the sur-name "the simple." This kind of simplicity is akin to that of Ermine and may explain his special role for her. Indeed, Saint Paul the Simple himself tells Ermine that it was not his *grant sens* (great intellect) that got him into paradise but his obedience to God's commandments and his avoidance of sin (150). Ermine's simplicity emulates these virtues.

It is in his demonic form that Paul the Simple appears to Ermine on July 18, 1396, uttering the most serious accusation against Jean: he will make sexual advances toward Ermine (*il te requerra de ribaudie*; 149). The word *ribaudie* has very negative connotations linked to sexual debauchery and prostitution. The demonic Paul draws on these connotations when he adds that both Ermine and Jean will be damned. Ermine of course rejects this accusation and states that she will believe in Jean for the rest of her life. And she finally calls this insinuating voice (which has no human or other shape) Satan (*sathenas*) and orders it to leave her in peace.

What are we to make of these incidents? The account Jean gives of them in many ways articulates the fraught relationship between confessor and holy woman. Several aspects appear again and again: the question of trust; Jean's advice to her concerning her piety; and especially the suspicions about a possible sexual attraction that must have accompanied any relationship as close as Jean and Ermine's.

When Ermine was widowed and began to live in Jean's proximity, she was about forty-eight years old. Was she still a sexual being? We will see in Chapter 4 that many aspects of the demonic hauntings Ermine suffers are of a sexual nature and that she is accused by various demons of being a whore. She has multiple "ugly dreams" and is even visited by exhibitionist demons (black, like people from "overseas") who fornicate on her bedroom floor, fill it with a horrible stink, and punctuate their pleasure with trumpet sounds (88, 113)—quite a sexual environment for a middle-aged widow! Jean at one point addresses his listeners directly with an explanation of Ermine's "ugly dream," of the fact that the demons showed her their *ordure* (literally "gar-bage," but here a reference to their genitals) and of "the things" they did: all this happened to "give the woman evil pleasure," but sweet Jesus protected her as he protected her from other dangers. Jean is thus very well aware of the constant sexual dangers that surrounded Ermine, but is he also aware of the possible role he may have played in generating these sexual visions?

In Christian Europe widows were in a precarious position when it came to sexual activity. The Church Fathers Saint Augustine and Saint Jerome believed that conquering the libido was one of the most important tasks for a widow and that the remembrance of former sexual joys could easily lead widows into temptation.[53] In sermons and conduct manuals families were urged to keep an eye on widows and marry them off quickly if possible. Medical experts believed that a widow's uterus would clog up with unused "semen" and that consequently widows would desire sex for relief. These kinds of beliefs gave rise to satirical views of the ever-unsatisfied, rapacious widow who would stop at nothing to seduce young, potent men. The only weapon against this kind of sexual depredation would be a life of devotion and asceticism.[54] Ermine's relentless battle against the demons' exhibitionist behavior and sexual innuendo thus reflects traditional views on the risks husbandless women ran in medieval society, but, at the same time, the very excess of the demonic attacks sets her story apart from those of most other holy women, where sexual aspects certainly appeared but not in quite the same manner.[55]

What about the jealousy and possessiveness that characterize the relationships of so many couples? While Ermine seems to have a monopoly on Jean's attentions, other Churchmen had to spread themselves thinner. Jacques of Vitry, whom we encountered already as the champion of Marie of Oignies, parceled out his time to various women. The example of Lutgard of Aywières, another thirteenth-century holy woman from the Low Countries, demonstrates how the competition for the male cleric's attentions could manifest itself. Thomas of Cantimpré, who also wrote a version of the *Life* of Marie of Oignies, tells us in a chapter of Lutgard's *Life* entitled "How she delivered Master Jacques de Vitry from a certain very grave temptation" that "it happened that he loved a certain religious woman who was languishing in bed, not with a lustful love but with an excessively human love. As a result he was too assiduously intent on consoling this woman and became indolent and laid aside his office of preaching. Therefore the righteous Lutgard, sensing in the spirit the fetters of his heart and the deceit of the devil, set to the task of interceding for him to the Lord with many tears."[56]

A cynical reader might see jealousy disguised as holy intervention at work here. Thomas denies that Jacques might be motivated by "lustful love," but by evoking the term at all he floats the possibility of a notable cleric's lustful yearning after a woman. It is Lutgard who then sees demonic influence in Jacques's devotion to this woman in need of consolation and manages to wrest Jacques away from her so that he can attend to his duties in a more communal manner. This example immediately brings to mind the reproach the demon in the shape of Saint John the Baptist leveled at Ermine: that she monopolizes Jean and thus endangers his virtue, which would consist in fulfilling his pastoral duties by devoting himself to a wide range of people.

The most telling detail is undoubtedly the demons' claim that Jean lusts after Ermine. Since Jean himself wrote the text, we can interpret this intriguing passage as a kind of implicit disclaimer: because the accusation was uttered by "demons," it is by definition untrue. Just as Johannes of Marienwerder wrapped Dorothea of Montau's declaration of love for him into multiple textual layers, so Jean's words about his own possible sexual attraction to Ermine are put into the mouth of a demon whose words Ermine then reports back to Jean, who transcribes them. Of course, we cannot know what really transpired between these two people, but the textual contortions Jean goes through in order to present and then efface a possible scenario of sexual desire on his part are certainly noteworthy.

Jean le Graveur, Ermine, and Jean de Varennes

The intertwining of the personal and the political makes Ermine's *Visions* stand out in the religious literature of the late Middle Ages. That Jean le Graveur's opinion of a controversial religious figure should become another touchstone for his relationship with Ermine is one of our text's astounding and intriguing features. In fact, Jean le Graveur's attitude toward Jean de Varennes (1340/45–1396?), a former papal official of the Avignon popes Clement VII and Benedict XIII who seemed to be able to fascinate large crowds, becomes a major element in the demons' campaign to separate our two protagonists.

After leaving Benedict XIII's court under a cloud of dissent (he doubted the Avignon pope's legitimacy), Jean de Varennes set himself up as a hermit in the woods of Nanteuil about sixteen kilometers from Reims, where his preaching attracted large crowds.[57] There this controversial preacher agitated against his former master, the very pope he had formerly served, in large public assemblies. Jean de Varennes, as Brian McGuire observed, was "a dangerous critic for the clergy of Reims" for he attacked clerical abuses and in his sermons showed himself to be a strong advocate of the poor—as did Jean Gerson.[58] After his arrest in May 1396 Jean de Varennes wrote a document in which he listed the accusations against him and responded to them. He did indeed, he admitted, preach against the wealthy lords "so that they stop devouring the people and then the people would stop rising up in rebellion," and he further conceded that he believed that all evils in this world can be attributed to Churchmen.[59] As McGuire points out, Gerson did not participate in de Varennes's prosecution; indeed he shared many of the preacher's convictions. But there was a crucial difference between the two: Jean de Varennes preached publicly and in French while Gerson stated his most critical opinions in the confines of the university and most often in Latin.[60] At the time that Jean le Graveur wrote his text, then, he must have been aware of Gerson's attitude, especially since he was planning to submit Ermine's *Visions* to Gerson for vetting. The somewhat indecisive attitude toward the hermit, the many conflicting opinions on his preaching bandied about by demons and humans, thus dramatize the bind that Jean le Graveur found himself in: depending on the source, Jean de Varennes could be a dangerous revolutionary or a champion of the poor.

Word of the meetings organized by Jean de Varennes reached Ermine, and before long the hermit played a special role for our pious heroine. In fact, the historian André Vauchez believes that Jean de Varennes "is at the center of the spiritual crisis lived by this pious laywoman."[61] In some way Jean le Graveur had to deal with Ermine's interest in this influential preacher, and he decided to frame his own and Ermine's attitude toward de Varennes in a very original way: as a touchstone for the relationship between himself and the woman he had taken under his wing. Thus, Jean le Graveur interweaves the story of his wavering belief in the hermit's mission to reform and unify the Church with his personal relationship with Ermine. There are more than a dozen instances throughout the text where demonic voices argue the cause of Jean de Varennes, accuse her confessor of abandoning his faith in de Varennes, and urge her to leave him because of his lack of support for the hermit.

It is in January 1396 that Ermine first becomes interested in Jean de Varennes, inquiring of one of the voices that constantly surround her whether he is doing good things (72). The voice is very evasive and refuses to answer. In May, Jean le Graveur addresses the issue of Jean de Varennes head-on: in a direct address to his readers he explains why he decided to report Ermine's interest in de Varennes. Basically, he wants to help his fellow Christians who may have been misled by de Varennes (115–16). Right after this lengthy explanation of why he will report anything that touches upon Ermine and

Jean de Varennes, a demon in the shape of a lady dressed in white and clutching a lily appears in Ermine's room one night as she is praying, just before the feast of Ascension. The demonic lady accuses Jean le Graveur of having changed his mind on Jean de Varennes's saintliness, which for the demon is not in doubt. "I tell you," the demon declares, "that Jean de Varennes is a saintly man and a place for him is prepared in paradise, and there will be no peace in the Church if it is not through him and he will become pope" (116). This prophetic pronouncement gets Ermine thinking, and she begins to believe that the lady told the truth. And all night long and the next day as well, Jean le Graveur tells us, "she was tempted to leave me and to go and beg for bread throughout the region for God's love. The demon had persuaded her that she had too easy a life and that she did nothing for God's love" (116). The demon here connects several issues: the argument that Ermine should leave her confessor is linked with his attitude toward Jean de Varennes but also with the oft-repeated reproach that by living in Jean's orbit her life has become too cozy.

A couple of months later, on July 8, 1396, a demon in the shape of Saint Paul the Simple, weaves yet another theme into his exhortation to Ermine to leave Jean le Graveur. He repeats what the lily-carrying demon had stated in May, namely, that the fact that Ermine's confessor now has a negative opinion of Jean de Varennes is reason enough for her to abandon him. He reminds her that she is now old and feeble and has nothing put her away for her old age, thus voicing anxieties that surely must have tormented Ermine frequently. The demon suggests that she marry a good man (*ung bon preudhomme*; 145) who would take care of her. Here, Jean le Graveur adds the commentary that at that time Ermine had a number of marriage proposals, although why she would be so desirable in the marriage market remains unclear. Perhaps Jean invented these suitors in order to underline again Ermine's devotion and fidelity toward him. In any case marriage is not a bad thing according to the demon, who makes the cogent argument that marriage is one of the seven sacraments and that many married people have in fact attained paradise. When Ermine retorts violently that she will never marry again, the demon suggests she go to work instead. But Ermine is undeterred: first of all, she claims, it is all the same to her what her confessor thinks of Jean de Varennes; she does know, in any case, that he does not actually hate the hermit. Second, she will never leave her confessor; on the contrary, she hopes that God will grant her to be with him even after death.

As Jean de Varennes's preaching becomes more and more known, the net of royal persecution starts to tighten around him. A sermon against Pope Benedict XIII that de Varennes had pronounced on Palm Sunday 1396 resulted in his arrest on May 30, his disappearance, and most likely his death in prison. Thus, when the demonic Paul the Simple addresses Ermine in July, speculation was rife as to what had happened to de Varennes, and many people hoped he would return. The demon that speaks to Ermine on August 6 plays with these hopes when he claims that while Ermine's confessor hates the hermit, the king and the scholars of the University of Paris love him and will enable him to return to his former haunt. When Ermine states that she does not care that much anymore about the hermit and that he, the demon, should go and speak to the clergy, the demon responds that he wants her, a simple woman, to know the truth so that she will not perish together with the clergy (158). Finally, on August 15, ten days before Ermine's death, another demon claims that Jean de Varennes is preaching at this very moment in Paris and has converted the king and the queen as well as many other people. Only the archbishop of Reims and his disciples continue to resist conversion. The demon urges Ermine to no longer listen to the clergy in order to save her soul. Needless to say, she refuses and the demon leaves after emitting a horrible stink.

Most likely, the demonic voices express popular sentiment in favor of Jean de Varennes. People captivated by this charismatic preacher did not want to accept his disappearance and continued to hope for his return. This is undoubtedly why Jean le Graveur feels compelled to explain to "you who read or listen to this book" (vous qui lisez ce livre cy ou escoutez; 163) that Jean de Varennes never preached in Paris in mid-August, as most people know well. He adds that the voice that told Ermine on August 6 that de Varennes would soon return to Saint Lié was lying, as did all the other voices that predicted the hermit's liberation. This explanation closes the matter of Jean de Varennes. Over many months the demons' evocation of Jean de Varennes's importance for Ermine was linked to their program of alienating her from her confessor. But it is clear that the repeated attempts by satanic voices to discredit Jean le Graveur's s role in Ermine's life—based on de Graveur's lack of support for the contentious hermit—fail dismally. Through the multiple and controversial appearances of Jean de Varennes that punctuate Ermine's Visions, Jean le Graveur dramatizes one of the important underpinnings of their relationship: Ermine's trust in her confessor cannot be shaken even if they find themselves on opposite sides of a church-political divide. In these passages, then, contemporary history enters into what otherwise could be a timeless story of demonic vexations and the complicated dynamics of a "holy couple."

In all of the episodes we just explored—and which could be supplemented by even more examples—Jean shows us a wide array of demonic attempts to undermine the trust of the couple Ermine-Jean, only to reaffirm the steadfastness of their faith in each other. Their union and their collaboration thus appear to be divinely sanctioned.

Compared with the other couples we encountered in this chapter, the collaboration between Jean and Ermine was different: Ermine did not strive to create a holy text, nor did she seem to perceive any meaning in her experiences other than torments that required her steadfastness and some joyful visions that gave her relief. It was Jean who provided the didactic framework and who gave some shape to the text. But he did not choose to present a coherent narrative; rather, he dramatized the excessive and repetitive demonic attacks interspersed with a few divine visions through a blow-by-blow account whose only structure is chronology. And it was Jean alone who finally, after Ermine's death and thus the end of their "couple," began to promote her holy reputation through his text. What Jean attempted to do in Ermine's lifetime was to try and shape Ermine into a pious woman whose devotion and ascetic practices approximated those of other holy women of the time. How difficult this particular task was will become evident in our next chapter.

CHAPTER 3

Ermine's Piety and Devotional Practices

Endless prayers and fasts, copious tears and intense sufferings imitating Christ's Passion, an almost frenzied devotion to the Eucharist, hair shirts and hard beds, self-inflicted torments with chains and nettles, fights with demons and angelic visitations—these were some of the hallmarks of late medieval piety and devotion as practiced by the most fervent women and men.[1] But at the same time, these Christians were also part of a community, be it religious or lay, that followed prescribed rules and rituals, communicated to them by their superiors or parish priests. The tension between the moderate religious practices championed by most Churchmen and the strange and unsettling events so characteristic of much of late medieval devotion lies at the heart of Ermine's *Visions*. As Jean le Graveur struggles to make sense of Ermine's tribulations, he also tries to contain them in some way by educating her and making her adhere to Christian teachings and rituals.

Ermine's piety and devotion are in many ways typical of late medieval lay religious culture. She tries to follow the precepts offered by her confessor Jean le Graveur, and she adopts some ascetic practices that then are deemed excessive and dangerous by her confessor. What distinguishes her from most ordinary Christians of her time is the subject of her *Visions*, namely, the continuous demonic attacks and much rarer heavenly visions that God grants her. As a woman of humble origins, she is uneducated and lacks the literate culture that defined so many of the woman mystics of the thirteenth and fourteenth centuries. In this chapter we will explore Ermine's religious practices and see how she fits into established patterns of devotion and asceticism and how she diverges from them.

Jean le Graveur designed the *Visions* not overtly as a devotional hand-book but as a "mirror," that is, a didactic text whose function it is, as he clearly states, to instruct us on how to guard against the deceptions of the Antichrist and his minions (49).[2] And although Jean adds that we should not trust "dreams, visions, or other revelations" because we are not worthy of them, we will see that many lessons on the Christian faith are contained in the very visions, namely, the demonic ones, Jean discredits here in the pro-logue (49). Even more intriguingly and paradoxically, we will see that most of the definitions of Christian dogma are actually proffered by demons whose challenges to accepted Christian beliefs and practices pursue Ermine relent-lessly. The contours of Christian beliefs and acceptable devotional practices are blurred by the continuous presence of demons in Ermine's life, but they do emerge nonetheless—and often because of these demons.

Ermine's Religious Education

On the evening of January 17, 1396, Jean le Graveur calls Ermine to him in order to make her recite her Pater Noster, her Creed, and her Ave Maria, just to see, he states, whether she knows how to say them (71). He notices that she mispronounces some syllables in the Pater Noster, so he corrects her and makes her say it again. She also omits four articles from the Creed; Jean wants her to learn it once more and to that end reads it to her again: that is, she is expected to memorize the words that Jean transmits to her orally, without necessarily understanding them, for they are in Latin, as we can see from the titles Jean assigns to the prayers and the Creed (*patenostre* [*sic*], *Ave Maria, Credo*; 71). Ermine is clearly troubled by her imperfections for when she prays later that night, she cannot concentrate on her prayers. Were these prayers in French or Latin? Did Ermine try to reproduce at night what Jean had taught her during the day? Jean does not tell us explicitly, but the use of the terms *lecon* (reading or lesson) and *oroison* (prayer) is revealing: "And when she was praying (*en oroisons*) at night in her room she was so troubled by her *lecon* that she could not think of her prayers (*oroisons*) and could not say them as devoutly as she usually did."[3] *Lecon* most likely refers to the reading Jean had offered her earlier in the day and that she now tries to recall. That she cannot do so accurately troubles her so much that she cannot focus on her own personal prayer. Ermine was not alone in her anguish over a lack of concen-tration while praying. Jean Gerson addressed this question—and also the

distinction between liturgical (*lecon*) and personal prayer (*oroison*)—in a treatise dating from 1416–1417, *De valore orationis et de attentione* (On the value
of prayer and on paying attention). Here he forgives people for losing track
when performing liturgical prayers—implying a kind of automatic attention
that will allow them to return to the required words after a momentary
distraction—but does reprimand them for wandering off mentally when saying their personal prayers: in that case the content was not canonical and
thus had to be attended to with the utmost concentration.[4]

At the moment of Ermine's anguish over a lack of attention and over
her inability to recall Jean's *lecon*, "the voice" (*la voix*) begins to whisper to
her that she should serve God as she always has and that the subprior, that
is, Jean le Graveur, should not go too deeply into the issues of her religious
knowledge. Ermine believes the voice to be that of a demon, but the voice
denies this and exhorts her to tell all her troubles to Jean. The next morning
Ermine reports all this to her confessor, who suggests a compromise: if she
learns her Creed well, he will not reprimand her for her mispronunciation of
some syllables in the Pater Noster because "this is not a grave sin." Jean
expected Ermine to recite the prayer in Latin by sounding out the syllables,
most likely without her necessarily understanding the separate words she was
uttering, a kind of "phonetic literacy."[5]

What we witness here is pastoral care at its most basic level. The Pater
Noster and the Ave Maria were the minimum a Christian needed to know;
indeed, for the English abbot Thomas of Walsingham (d. 1422) "the illiterate
are those who know only their *paternoster* and ave."[6] Jean helps Ermine with
her pronunciation of these prayers and makes sure she knows all the articles
of the Creed. Ermine's anxiety about her inadequacy results in an auditory
visitation by "the voice," which essentially puts limits on what Jean can and
should expect from her. And what he can expect is indeed very little, for
Ermine's education is practically nonexistent. Coming from a rural background, she, unlike many other holy women of her time, seems to have had
no access to any kind of education.[7] Nuns and monks received their education in monastic institutions. Nuns were expected to master reading and to
a certain extent writing (these two skills were quite separate in this period),
music, grammar, and in some cases Latin versification, as well as acquire a
knowledge of the Scriptures and the writings of the Church Fathers. By the
fourteenth century, however, in many places, especially England, the vernacular played a prominent role in religious literature.[8] Literacy, both in Latin
and the vernacular, was also linked to class, of course. Noblewomen in both

nunneries and the secular world advanced further than lower-class women, and one should not be surprised that a woman like Isabelle of France (1225–1270), the sister of the French king Saint Louis, was capable of correcting the inadequate Latin of her clergy.[9]

Public schools did not exist in the Middle Ages, although there may have been some informal schools for both boys and girls as early as the ninth century. But it is not clear where they were set up and who the teachers were. For the most part nonmonastic medieval schools were associated with cathedrals. In Liège, for example, there were external schools for boys and girls that were run by the cathedral chapter; and for the time Ermine lived we find references to more than twenty small schools under the authority of the chancellor of Notre-Dame of Paris, where female lay teachers labored to instill the basics of grammar and reading into girls.[10] But having the ability to read did not necessarily mean that the individual could understand what she or he was reading. Most people had some knowledge of letters and numbers and were not what one would call today completely illiterate. In the Middle Ages the term *illiterate* usually referred to a lack of knowledge of Latin.

Reading was most commonly taught through the Psalter, a collection of the Psalms. In fact *psalterium dicere* (to say the Psalter) came to be a synonym for learning to read. People learned to sing the Psalms, helped by the mnemonic devices of melody and rhythm, but did not necessarily fully comprehend everything they were reciting.[11] The case of Lutgard of Aywières (1182–1246) illustrates this discrepancy between reading or reciting and true understanding of the Psalms.[12] Thomas of Cantimpré, her biographer, reports that the Lord had given Lutgard the gift of curing the sick. Overrun by needy crowds of suffering people—and thus prevented from "dallying" with Christ—Lutgard prays for a different gift. Asked by Christ which grace she would like to receive, Lutgard replies, "I wish that I might understand the Psalter through which I pray, so that I might be more devout." The Lord does grant her better understanding, but it is still not enough. Lutgard complains, "What use is it to me to know the secrets of Scripture—I, an unlettered, uncultivated, and uneducated nun?"[13] But rather than asking for even more education Lutgard now asks for Christ's heart, a request He grants her through a "communion of hearts." Lutgard makes no further educational requests; on the contrary, she prays to the Virgin to "avert the fate" of her learning French because if she did, she would have to become an abbess in one of the French-speaking convents in her region. The Virgin consents to this request, thus supporting the opposite of the miraculous xenoglossia that occurs in a number of lives of holy women.[14] Yet, as Barbara Newman astutely observes, the account of Lutgard's variegated linguistic competencies in Flemish, French, and Latin has been shaped by her hagiographer and is filled with paradoxes.[15] Nonetheless, Lutgard's type of differentiated literacy in three languages undoubtedly reflects the medieval reality of a whole spectrum of different abilities of medieval religious women that could range from the theological sophistication of a Hildegard of Bingen and the poetic beauty of the writings of a poet like the Flemish Hadewijch to the apparently shaky literacy of women like Lutgard and the even shakier literacy of Ermine.

Lutgard's contemporary Christina the Astonishing (ca. 1150–1224), whose *Life* was also written by Thomas of Cantimpré, managed to advance further than Lutgard: although she had been completely illiterate from birth, she understood all Latin and fully knew the meaning of Holy Scripture. When she was asked very obscure questions by certain spiritual friends, she would explain them very openly. But she did this most unwillingly and rarely, for she said that to expound on Holy Scriptures was a task belonging to the clergy and not to the ministry of such as her.[16]

Thomas here puts his finger on one of the most contentious issues related to women's Latinity: they would be allowed to compete with male clerics in the interpretation of the Scriptures only if they had received this ability as a grace directly from God.

Saint Clare of Montefalco (d. 1308) also made the transition from knowing nothing "but the seven psalms and a morning lesson" to reciting and even teaching the Divine Office. Like Lutgard, she was giving "exhaustive answers to readers and to theologian-preachers regarding doubtful points and profound questions." Her biographer Berengario di Donadio assured his readers that Clare had acquired this knowledge and authority by divine intervention—and could therefore pose no threat to male clerical superiority.[17]

This cautionary note even holds true for one of the most famous medieval female saints, Catherine of Siena (1347–1380), now celebrated as a Doctor of the Church. Her biographer Raymond of Capua described how Catherine gained miraculous literacy, although before that she did make an effort herself by studying an alphabet with a friend. As did Lutgard, Catherine—impatient with her own progress at learning to read—implored the Lord to help her read the Psalms so that she could praise Him better. The Lord complied. Raymond was amazed that Catherine now could read the Psalms quickly, although, he added, she would not be able to spell out the words.[18] He said nothing about her ability to write and thus emphasized the modesty of her achievements in gaining Latin literacy. Yet in Italian, Catherine had different abilities: Tommaso Caffarini, her other biographer, highlighted Catherine's skills as a writer. In her penetrating study of Catherine's place in medieval Italian vernacular literature, Jane Tylus shows that for Raymond, Catherine was a "figure of orality" but for Caffarini she was "without question a writer."[19] Both representations of her literacy, whether oral or written, apply to the realm of the vernacular and show Catherine far removed from her early and futile struggles to learn Latin by herself. In fourteenth-century Italy, then, sophisticated religious and other types of literature had made the move from Latin to the vernacular, as it was doing in other European countries.[20] While Latin remained the lingua franca in educated circles for many more centuries, a vibrant vernacular literature flourished alongside it.

But Latin remained at the center of the trope of miraculous literacy, a trope that focused attention on the importance of a core of such devotional texts as the Psalter, for when illiterate women prayed for literacy, it was most often because they wanted to understand their daily devotions as distilled in the Psalter. And at the same time, divinely sent xenoglossia reduced the risk of women being accused of wanting to usurp a priestly function by reading and interpreting the Scriptures.

Given the availability and widespread use of this trope by biographers of holy women, it is all the more striking that Jean le Graveur chooses to depict his daily struggle with Ermine's lack of even the most basic education. We can certainly observe a level of realism here that is absent from many medieval texts of this sort. Who could invent, for example, the fact that Ermine mixes up the words *seraphim* and *Saracen*? In this passage, taking place on May 22, 1396, a counterfeit Saint Mary Magdalene visits Ermine and tells her, "I have with me two seraphims," but when Ermine recounts this experience to her confessor, "she said that the two red angels that approached her were Saracens, because she did not know the word *seraphim*" (122–23).[21]

With the scene of Jean le Graveur correcting Ermine's reciting of the Creed and trying to improve her pronunciation, we are at ground zero of what it meant to be a pastor to the people Jean Gerson called *les simples gens*, that is, those who lacked a knowledge of Latin and often of even the most rudimentary tenets of the Christian faith. It is quite rare to see a pastor in such close-up, depicting his own struggle to instill in one of his parishioners the most basic devotional practices as they were enshrined in such instructional texts as Jean Gerson's *Doctrinal aux simples gens* of 1387. The *Doctrinal* belongs to the genre of *pastoralia,* handbooks for priests that had existed for centuries but that became even more popular in the wake of the Fourth Lateran Council of 1215. The many penitential manuals meant to guide priests in hearing confessions and assigning penances had been composed in Latin.[22] But with increasing participation of the laity in religious life and the fact that some parish priests' knowledge of Latin was less than stellar, *pastoralia* in the vernacular began to appear as well.

The landscape of lay piety in Christian Europe changed substantially after the Fourth Lateran Council in 1215, as we saw in Chapter 1. Canon 21 of the council's decrees stated that men and women who had reached the age of reason have to confess their sins at least once a year to their priest and to do the penance, as far as possible, that is imposed on them. Further, they should take communion once a year at Easter. Whoever does not follow this decree will be excluded from the Church and will not be buried within the Church.[23] This decree was repeated by many subsequent councils, which sometimes changed the frequency of confession and communion to three or more times a year. The implementation of these new practices imposed complex and wide-ranging burdens on parish priests, who were often ill equipped to minister to their flock and their new needs. To help priests with their new duties, educated clerics composed concise pastoral handbooks, many of them in the vernacular, like Gerson's *Doctrinal aux simples gens* (Teachings for simple people).[24]

Composed in September 1387, this booklet was copied and distributed in Reims by the archbishop Guy de Roye for the benefit of the simple laypeople.[25] The archbishop ordered that every parish and diocese belonging to Reims should get a copy and that every priest and chaplain should read two or three chapters every Sunday to whomever may want to listen. Gerson explains that he wrote the text in French so that "simple" priests who know little Latin as well as the "simple people" can understand it; and it is rather short so that one can understand it clearly. We are thus in the rare position of knowing exactly what was expected at a minimum from the pastors working in Reims just at the time when Ermine and her husband arrived there. A brief look at Gerson's text enables us to understand the contours of lay piety in late fourteenth-century Reims. The *Doctrinal* distills, in French and in a very concise manner, centuries of Christian teaching.

The *Doctrinal* begins with the Creed (*articles de la foy*) that crystallizes the fundamental tenets of the Christian faith: belief in the Trinity; in Christ's incarnation, birth, death, and resurrection; and in the Last Judgment.[26] Here

Gerson adds that some people in their simplicity may believe in some other articles of the faith. If this is the case, they need to return to those articles held by the Holy Church. Gerson then goes on to speak about charity, supplying some edifying examples from the Bible and early Church teachings. A brief treatise on the "works of mercy" is followed by the Ten Commandments; a section on how we can serve God with our five senses; and a description of the Seven Deadly Sins. Then come the Ave Maria and an explanation of the Seven Sacraments. Noteworthy are his remarks on the Eucharist, the "superlative" sacrament, which Gerson advises to "celebrate willingly and often." He then analyzes what makes good and bad priests (these sections were probably meant for silent reading by the priests and not for public consumption). Gerson then returns to the issue of communion, adding remarks on confession. All adults have to confess at least once a year, men starting at age fourteen, women at age twelve, which are the ages when they can marry. Saint Augustine favored weekly communion (every Sunday), and Gerson agrees that frequent confession and communion can profit every Christian's soul.

Returning later again to the issue of confession, Gerson tells his readers that some simple people claim not to know how to say their confessions and expect the priest to spell out their sins for them. This is not how confession works, Gerson makes clear. You need to remember your sins "nakedly and purely" (*nuement et purement*):[27] when and how often, on feast days or not, on fasting days or in holy places, with whom (without naming names, however), whether you sinned of your own volition or were incited by someone else, and how long you remained in sin. This is one of the most detailed sections in the *Doctrinal* and provides a kind of blueprint for efficacious confessions. Modeled on medieval handbooks of penance, this part of the text abbreviates and translates into French many of the items of advice and guidance that were transmitted over the centuries in Latin exclusively to clerics. The *Doctrinal* ends with graphic descriptions of purgatory and hell (even transcribing the lamentations of those stuck in the horrible contradictions of hell's icy waters and burning fires) and of the Last Judgment and paradise, a place that Gerson deems indescribable in its beauty and joyousness. This—in a rather capacious nutshell—is what both priests and laypeople in late medieval Reims were supposed to know and practice.

Ermine exemplifies the kind of simple Christian whose knowledge of confessional practices was minimal. But Jean le Graveur does not merely tell us but rather *shows* us the kinds of anxiety that could accompany the universal

obligation to formulate a convincing confession. In the following dramatic
scene we again find Ermine assaulted by a demon (this time masquerading as
Saint Peter) who lifts her dress and kicks her in the chest hard enough to
leave a painful blue mark (71). Immediately after the attack a voice appears
"next to her head" and identifies itself as the "voice that has always comforted
you." The voice reassures her that while the demons will continue to "tempt"
her, they will not return in their "ugly shape" because she is now "absent
from their writings," an intriguing reference to a kind of demonic notebook
or to-do list in which attacks on poor Ermine must have been listed. Medieval
miracle tales often reassured people that after absolution the record of their
sins vanished and demons could no longer remember them. "Now," the
voice continues, you need "to guard against sinning, believe the subprior and
do what he tells you to do, lead a virtuous life and confess yourself often."
Ermine replies, "I am a simple woman and do not know my sins well and do
not know what I should confess," thus articulating exactly the kind of quandary Gerson foresaw in his *Doctrinal*. The voice reminds her that she once
insulted a sick woman and should confess that transgression. When Ermine
states that she has already confessed this sin, the voice urges her to do so once
more and do "God's service" as she is accustomed to do. This event takes
place on January 8, 1396, and in the text of *Visions* is followed by the passage
on Jean's January 17 examination of Ermine's knowledge of the Creed we
looked at earlier. Thus nine days pass between Ermine's instruction on confession and Jean's reviewing the basics of the faith with her, but the text as
Jean constructed it juxtaposes the two events.

The two entries in what seems to be a faithful diary of Ermine's experiences thus come together as a mini-handbook that shows how the minimum
requirements articulated by Lateran IV play out in the life of a simple but
pious woman. Jean's account illustrates Ermine's religious education, on the
one hand through the unidentified voice and on the other through his staging
of a private lesson for Ermine, starring himself. Jean thus offers essential
lessons on Christian practice through a multilayered, dramatic didacticism
centered on Ermine's experiences but applicable to all medieval Christians.

Ermine's Devotional Practices

Prayer is a requirement for every Christian. Ermine spends an enormous
amount of time praying, usually kneeling, sometimes at an open window,

and often the entire night. Her prayers, as we saw earlier, were of both a liturgical and a personal nature. Ermine owns a rosary, as did most Christians, that is frequently snatched away by demons (and then returned) and a small tablet on which are painted the *arma Christi*, or the instruments of the Passion. These objects were some of the mainstays of Christian devotion in the Middle Ages. The *arma Christi* were linked to communion through the widespread pictorial tradition of the mass of Saint Gregory. The original story, first told by Paul the Deacon in the eighth century, gives an account of a woman who doubted the Host during mass, whereupon the Host transformed itself into a bleeding finger. Eventually, the bleeding finger gave way to the Man of Sorrows, and the story gained prominence through Jacobus de Voragine's *Golden Legend*, an immensely popular collection of saints' legends of the thirteenth century as well as through sermons and collections of exemplary tales.[28] In countless images Pope Gregory kneels before the altar on which the Host has been transformed into the suffering Christ who sometimes fills the eucharistic chalice with blood from the wound in his side. In the woodcut reproduced here (Fig. 5) Christ is holding the scourge and around him are grouped the instruments of the Passion (the column where he was scourged, a bowl and a sponge with vinegar, a blindfold, the crown of thorns, a ladder with Christ's bloody footprints) as well as Mary and Saint John. We also see the Judas kiss, Saint Peter's rooster (who crowed when Peter denied knowing Jesus), and the cloak the Roman soldiers played dice for next to Christ's open grave.

Through this schematic rendering of objects associated with Christ's last days, the *arma Christi* functioned as pictorial shortcuts for the meditation on the suffering of Christ, and they were depicted not only in images of the mass of Saint Gregory but in countless paintings and manuscripts (and later in printed books). A devotional booklet from fourteenth-century Germany, for example, shows on facing pages three large nails, a hammer, pincers, the cloth used to cover Christ's eye, twenty-nine gray roundels (representing the thirty pieces of silver Judas took for his betrayal of Christ), and three bloody footprints, signifying Christ's walk to Golgatha. On the right page we see the coat the Romans threw dice for, a stick, a scourge, a ladder, a lance, and a rectangle representing Christ's tomb from above.[29] In similar images one also finds sneering faces denoting the mocking of Christ, heads with "Jewish" hats, and frequently Christ's wound, sometimes in what was believed to have been its natural size. These images were popular in both monastic and lay milieus. The small size of the booklet just mentioned and the protective ivory

FIGURE 5. Mass of Saint Gregory with instruments of the Passion, fifteenth-century single-leaf woodcut. Kupferstichkabinett, Berlin. Bpk, Berlin, Art Resource, NY.

covers suggest that this object was meant to be carried around and opened up at moments of prayer and meditation.

Ermine's *arma Christi* were in the shape of a painted little tablet "where the name of Our Lord Jesus Christ and his arms appeared: that is, the cross, the lance, the nails, the column, and the scourge" (56). For Ermine, at least in this instance, the *arma Christi* are not so much an aid to meditation as a true weapon that she means to use against the demons. Alas, the first time she tries to pull the tablet out of a chest where she keeps it so that she can brandish it against a horrible horned demon who tries to kiss her, her hand gets stuck in the chest, she falls over backward and down the stairs, and becomes so disoriented and upset that she avoids Jean and feels and sees "nothing but the demon." The first attempt at self-defense via the *arma Christi* is thus a complete failure.

The second time she is more successful. While Ermine is praying on the evening of December 1, 1395, with her tablet before her, thus using it for meditation, "someone" (60) snatches it from her and takes it away. But she continues her prayers, and a short time later a counterfeit Saint John the Baptist appears in her room, clothed *comme il faut* in a long, hairy outfit; he returns her tablet with his "beautiful white hands." He praises her devotional practices (her fasts and hair shirt) but reproaches her with taking up too much of Jean le Graveur's time. He advises her to spend less time with Jean in order to free him for other obligations; then he vanishes. Of course, Ermine discerns immediately that this Saint John was a demon. Unperturbed, Ermine grabs her tablet and is overjoyed to have it back for she "trusts in it as does a knight in his shield, and she put it in front of her chest at every assault as does a knight with his shield" (*comme fait le chevalier son escu*; 61). Thus Ermine uses the *arma Christi* for both meditation and protection. Through the use of the terms *chevalier* and *escu* Jean spells out the connection to the *locus classicus* of the notion of spiritual militancy, Paul's Letter to the Ephesians 6:11: "Put on the whole armor of God that you may be able to stand against the wiles of the devil." This exhortation could apply both to men and women, a gender equality that is often depicted in images of armed women, including the Virgin Mary, taking aim at the devil with swords, lances, and other deadly weapons.[30] Didactic and devotional texts, such as the thirteenth-century *Ancrene wisse* (also extant in a medieval French translation), made this imagery widely available to the faithful. In part VII, for example, the author develops at length the parable of the knight and the shield, which can signify Christ's body, among other things, that all Christians can use as a defense against the evil one.[31]

The *arma Christi* thus formed part of a twofold imaginary: they stood for the spiritual weapons that could be used by any Christian and at the same time were linked to the Eucharist through their appearance in images of the mass of Saint Gregory.

Ermine and the Eucharist

Along with confession the Fourth Lateran Council regulated communion or the taking of the Eucharist; annual confession was to be followed by communion. The same Council also proclaimed the dogma of transubstantiation, stating that Christ's body and blood are substantially changed into the bread and wine of communion. Thus by the late Middle Ages belief in the transubstantiation of the Host—its literal transformation into Christ's flesh—was accepted, or as the philosopher William Ockham (d. 1347) put it, "[Christ's body] is truly contained in the whole host and in every one of its parts at once."[32] The idea that a piece of bread should transform itself invisibly into Christ's flesh necessarily stirred people's imagination. Visions and miracles around the Eucharist became a staple of late medieval culture. While earlier eucharistic visions—like the famous one by King Edward the Confessor, who saw a little child in the Host, or the one of Pope Gregory that we just discussed—had been granted mostly to religious or holy men, in the later Middle Ages this kind of "liturgical realism" became a grace afforded to women, religious and lay alike.[33] As Caroline Bynum observes, "In the eucharist Christ was available to the beginner as well as to the spiritually trained."[34] Ermine falls into the first category, but we would not know it given the quantity and variety of her eucharistic visions, especially in the last few months of her life.

Eucharistic miracles and visions could take different forms, and many of them appeared in exemplary tales, or *exempla*, that were repeated again and again in sermons and edifying collections of religious and moral teachings. Miri Rubin divides the Host's miraculous properties and behavior into three categories: first, a vision of the real substances contained in the bread and wine offered during communion, that is, flesh and blood (these visions were either a reward for exceptional piety or sent by God to quell doubts among Christians);[35] second, "unnatural behavior" of animals or the elements in the presence of the Host; and third, "the appearance of Eucharistic properties, usually flesh, blood, or the Man of Sorrows, to a knowing abuser—a Jew, a witch, a thief, a negligent priest—and the ensuing punishment."[36] The Host could also serve as miraculous nourishment, a theme that has been explored in depth by Caroline Walker Bynum in her classic study *Holy Feast and Holy Fast*.[37]

The humanity of Christ was reflected in the physical properties of the Host during communion that were revealed in a variety of visions: a child, an adolescent, a grown man, the Man of Sorrows, all of these appeared to people in eucharistic visions. These were consoling visions that we will explore for Ermine in a moment. But there is another type of supernatural experience linked to the Eucharist: the Host transforming itself into a lump of flesh, sometimes with the appearance of a dismembered human body, a phenomenon that for some could produce anxiety and even terror, although others seem to have accepted this potentially disquieting experience with equanimity. Thus we have no reports that Ida of Louvain (d. ca. 1300), who reacted to the reciting of John 1:14 ("and the Word was made flesh") with a taste of flesh in her mouth, was terror-stricken; nor was Jeanne-Marie of Maillé (1331–1414), a noble French lady under Franciscan influence, when she saw a profusely bleeding Christ child during communion.[38] Colette of Corbie (1387–1447), the great reformer of the Franciscan order, who, when she was praying to the Virgin, had a vision of "a dish completely filled with carved-up flesh like that of a child," also accepted this vision as divinely sent.[39] These kinds of experiences and visions combined the ideas of the Christ child and of Christ's bloody sacrifice in the most physical way, that of bloody human flesh.[40] These two elements, appearing together here, could also occur separately, as was evidenced in the dramatic spiritual experiences of Beatrice of Ornacieux.

Beatrice of Ornacieux's (d. 1303) *Life* was written by the famous mystic Marguerite of Oingt, who served as prioress of the Carthusian order where Beatrice was a nun. Given to extreme self-mortification, such as driving nails through her hand in order to replicate Christ's torments, Beatrice suffered intensely when she felt that Christ had withdrawn His grace from her.[41] Here we find splendid eucharistic visions followed by a dreadful experience also linked to the Eucharist:

> For a long period of time every day at the elevation she saw the
> Body of our Lord in the form of a little child. Thus she saw a great
> brightness between the priest's hands, so vivid and so bright and of
> such wonderful beauty that in her opinion it could not be compared

to anything the human spirit could imagine. It seemed to her that
this brightness had a circular shape and that in the brightness there
appeared a great red brightness, so resplendent and so beautiful that
it illuminated with its great beauty all of the white brightness. And
in that white brightness appeared a little child; she could not
describe nor make anyone understand the great beauty of this child.
Above this child there appeared a great brightness which looked like
gold; it gave off such a vivid brilliance that it enfolded all the other
brightnesses into itself and entered itself into the other brightnesses.
. . . And it appeared to her that the beauty and splendor they had in
common appeared united in that child.[42]

Marguerite's account of Beatrice's spectacular vision has a clear theological
message centered on the Trinity, where Son, Father, and Holy Spirit are three
yet one. Margaret also emphasizes Beatrice's special grace in receiving a vision
that no human can truly imagine or express. But all was not well for Beatrice:
she tormented herself over some sins she believed she had committed and felt
that Christ had "forgotten her because in her prayers she had no longer her
habitual fervor and devotion." On Christmas Day, even after her confession,
she felt unworthy of taking communion but finally approached the altar in
agony because on Christ's birthday she wanted to commune with Him.
Driven by a strong desire for the Host, she received it, but a small piece
remained in her mouth causing a frightening "bitterness in her heart"; then
"the Host that she still had in her mouth began to grow until her mouth was
completely filled by it." She tried to pull it out, "but some unknown force
held it back, and she tasted flesh and blood." Beatrice in her terror prayed
for death, fainted, and then "swallowed what she had in her mouth without
noticing it until the moment when she felt it penetrate her heart." The joy
and comfort she now felt almost made her faint again.[43]

   This sequence of events illustrates the emotional charge associated with
the Eucharist in medieval culture: it could be a source of extreme anguish
and physical suffering (such as choking on a piece of raw human flesh!) and
of equally extreme joy. Joy predominates in accounts of eucharistic visions of
the Christ child, while a vision of the Man of Sorrows incites sorrow and
makes the viewer share Christ's suffering. Thus in different periods and in
different countries Christ granted the grace of His varying visual presence in
the Host to fervent believers.

One of the most widespread eucharistic visions was that of the child in the Host, well known to theologians of the time. Thomas Aquinas addressed it directly when he asked "whether Christ's body is truly there when flesh or a child appears in this sacrament."[44] Thus, the Flemish holy woman Marie of Oignies "happily accepted the Lord under the appearance of a child,"[45] and in Italy, Angela of Foligno (ca. 1248–1309) felt joy at the different manifestations of Christ in the Host.

Angela's vision, as told to her scribe, Brother A., shows that within the same vision Christ can take on multiple forms:

> On another occasion she said she had seen the Christ Child in the host. He appeared to her as someone tall and very lordly, as one holding dominion. He also seemed to hold something in his hand as a sign of his dominion, and he sat on a throne. But I cannot say what he was holding in his hands. I saw this with my bodily eyes, as I did everything I ever saw of the host. . . . Christ was so beautiful and magnificently adorned. He looked like a child of twelve. This vision was such a source of joy for me that I do not believe I will ever lose the joy of it. I was also so sure of it that I do not doubt a single detail of it. Hence it is not necessary for you to write it.[46]

But write it he did, of course. This vision—a bodily one, not a dream vision—conjures up three different images of Christ in one and the same Host: a child, a lord, and a boy of twelve. The German Dominican nun Adelheid Langmann (1312–1375) received the Host and then "saw the Christ Child playing in her heart, which, like a radiant monstrance, became as bright as the sun."[47] And Ida of Louvain (d. 1300), in addition to often tasting the Host's "flesh" in her mouth "occasionally washed, hugged, and played with the Christ child after first seeing him in a wafer."[48] Here the child steps out of the Host into the woman's life, and she can lavish the love and care on him that, as a nun, she could not give her own child. In all these examples of eucharistic visions intense joy is the dominant emotion.

Ermine is also blessed with numerous eucharistic visions, but it is quite stunning that the very first time she sees the child in the Host is during a demonic mass celebrated by a counterfeit Saint Augustine.[49] The anxiety Ermine feels over communion first manifests in early February 1396, when Jean describes Ermine's desire for taking communion in her room because "she wanted to keep herself more closed in" (*se vouloit tenir plus closement*;

83). And in fact, Ermine had received permission to take communion in her room until the *dimanche des Brandons*, that is, the first Sunday of Lent that was celebrated with a bonfire and a procession of lit torches, or *brandons*. She now wants to extend this permission. At that moment the *corneur*, the mocking voice, appears and predicts that her confessor will not grant this permission but that he, the voice, will: it will be private, he promises, just us and God. Ermine immediately recognizes the voice as that of a demon and throws him out of her room. In this passage Jean places Ermine's reclusionary desires into the context of private communion, not something that was easily granted to Christians except in cases of extreme illness. The fact that it is a demon who proposes a communion with "just us and God" makes it clear that the desire of private communion is unacceptable and, even more than that, dangerous to a person's spiritual health.

The next day the *corneur* comes back while Ermine is praying after communion in the friars' church, clearly having agreed to take communion outside of her room again. The demon challenges the transubstantiation of the Host by claiming that it is—and will remain—nothing but a piece of bread (84). The voice repeats the same challenge on Easter Sunday, adding that it is heresy to believe that the Host is anything but plain bread (102). Later that same day, when Ermine is back in her room, the fake Saint Augustine appears with great pomp in her room; he is attended by angels and dressed magnificently. He accuses her confessor of preaching false doctrine to her by claiming that the Eucharist is more than mere bread. The demonic priest begins to celebrate a mass with all the usual elements; he puts a Host into the mouth of one of his minions, then elevates another Host destined for his second companion: "The Host formed itself into the shape of a very beautiful small child and such a great brightness shone forth from this child that the woman thought her eyes would give out. . . . And the priest put it into the mouth of the other one who was kneeling; and the child howled a bit, thus demonstrating that it was a living thing" (103). The counterfeit Saint Augustine then explains what happened: "The one who received the bread received only bread, but the one who received the child received his savior." "I believe," Ermine retorts, "that he has received a devil from hell" (104). She then rushes to the friars' chapter house to report this strange event to Jean. Ermine admits that had she not seen this "mass" with her own eyes, she would not believe it, and she swears to the truth of her vision.

The framework of a demonic mass gives a special significance to Ermine's very first "child in Host" vision. The overwhelming message is one of caution: the demon wants Ermine to believe that the only way to receive the true savior is when the Host is in the shape of a child. Given the popularity of these types of visions in the thirteenth and fourteenth centuries, this demonic message seems to raise a warning flag against a proliferation of this type of vision. But this message is complicated by another passage where Saint Paul the Simple, this time in his counterfeit demonic form, cautions Ermine that it is demons—acting like magicians (*enchanteurs*; 148)—who send eucharistic visions. Demons mock her, he insists, by showing her a little child in the Host and other unusual things, visions that, if they were real, she would not be worthy of. That this demon echoes precisely the lesson that Ermine's confessor had given her about six months earlier (January 6, 1396) should give us pause. At that moment Jean had urged Ermine to pray against a vision of the child in the Host. "You should receive Christ simply," he said, "in the shape of bread and spiritually and not in any other form" (135). Jean anticipates here arguments that were later used in anti-Catholic propaganda, where the apparitions of a child in the Host or other visible manifestations of the human Christ proved, to the Protestants, the idolatrous nature of the Catholic mass.[50]

Yet, despite Jean's admonitions Ermine's eucharistic visions continue unabated. Jean is so troubled that he seeks counsel from some "notable people with whom I was friends, very learned and devout" (138). They concede that such revelations are possible, but they advise that each time Ermine sees the Host in "an unusual shape," she should focus on what the priest elevates. If she still sees a child, she should think of the Christ child and Christmas; and if she sees the column where Christ was whipped, she should think of Christ's sufferings and Good Friday.[51] In other words, the eucharistic visions should be fitted into the liturgical calendar and should be used for meditations on approved topics—exactly what the Virgin Mary advised the monk Abundus of Villers to do in response to visions more than a century earlier, as we will see below.

The feast of Corpus Christi was the day in the liturgical calendar most closely associated with the Eucharist, and it is on that day in 1396 that Ermine receives another lesson regarding communion. This feast day was inspired by a dream Juliana of Cornillon, a holy woman from Flanders, had in 1208. She, together with Eve of Saint Martin, began a campaign for the creation of this feast that culminated in its approval as a universal feast by Pope Urban IV in 1264. It became an official feast day for the Catholic Church at the Council of Vienne in 1311.[52] The celebrations consisted of processions, often with guilds and other civic groups, during which the Host was carried through the street in often magnificent monstrances and then displayed for another eight days, the octave of Corpus Christi, in the city's churches. As Leah Sinanoglou observes, "By the late fourteenth and fifteenth century, veneration of the host was a cult of fanatical proportions."[53]

The city of Reims followed the custom of staging elaborate processions. Thus, on June 1, 1396, we find Ermine proceeding solemnly through the streets of Reims as part of such a procession. But all is not well, for Ermine is kicked brutally by a demon—but then manages to concentrate on the monstrance in which a priest is carrying the Host. She sees it first as bread, then as a living child, then as bread, then again as a child. As a result she falls into ecstasy (129). In the days following the feast demons relentlessly torment Ermine until finally Saint Paul the Simple appears and instructs her that the Church celebrates the feast for eight days and that God had given permission to the demons to torment her during this octave, but that at the end of this octave the demons would stop tormenting her—a promise that turns out to be false. Thus Paul the Simple links the central feast of the Eucharist to divinely sanctioned demonic attacks and at the same time offers a lesson on the liturgical calendar.

A eucharistic vision can also serve as a touchstone for doctrine and at the same time make a political point. On June 12, 1396, for example, Ermine again sees the child in the Host, but this time Jean le Graveur adds a commentary on the question of whether the celebrant of the masses that trigger Ermine's visions of the child needs to be pure. This question had been debated as far back as the fourth century when the Donatists claimed that a sacrament offered by a corrupt priest would be invalid. Jean hastens to specify that of course "priests rumored to live together with women" (138) did not celebrate mass in "our" church;[54] but the important doctrinal point he makes is that even unworthy and sinful members of the clergy cannot destroy the efficacy of the sacrament. And during the time of the Great Schism it was also important to affirm, as Jean does here, that it did not matter which pope had appointed the bishops who ordained the priests offering the Eucharist at mass: the fact that Ermine's divinely sent visions happened regardless of who was the celebrant proves that the sacrament exists independently of its dispenser.

But there is another aspect to Jean's commentary. We saw how anxious Ermine is about the rebellious hermit Jean de Varennes, how Jean le Graveur tries to navigate his own conflicted views of this personage, and how the demons use this conflict to try and separate Ermine from her confessor. Jean de Varennes embraced a reformist spirit: that is, like so many others before him, he wanted to purify a corrupt and unchaste clergy. He thus preached against priests who kept concubines and sternly doubted that sacraments dispensed by such people could be efficacious.[55] Thus, Jean le Graveur, by rejecting the hermit's position, offers an implicit critique of Jean de Varennes. While he does not state clearly his own attitude toward de Varennes when Ermine repeatedly implores him to do so, here he provides an indirect answer in his interpretation of Ermine's eucharistic visions.

It would be tempting to simply follow Ermine's visionary trajectory here and accompany her as she has countless visions of the child in the Host, the Man of Sorrows, and huge red Hosts, thus taking a trip through the landscape of extreme eucharistic piety in late medieval Europe. But this is impossible, for Ermine's visions accelerate and multiply in the last months of her life at a frenetic pace. Linked to these visions are emotional outbursts of crying and screaming that exhaust Ermine and alarm her confessor. Fears of demonic deception torment Ermine as she continues to see the child in the Host and the Man of Sorrows, but she is also truly happy with what she calls the "simple Host." It becomes clear that devotion to the Eucharist—and anxiety regarding visions of the Host—is the central theme of Jean's account of Ermine's last months. And since his book is meant to be a "mirror," a text that teaches us something, we must look for lessons. The first one is that we must be extremely suspicious of eucharistic visions. With this lesson Jean inscribes himself into the current of moderation and caution regarding visionary experiences represented by such eminent theologians as Jean Gerson.[56] The second lesson is clearly presented as such: if such visions occur, they must be used as occasions for meditation; this is a central tenet of late medieval spirituality. Here it is spelled out doubly: once by Saint Paul the Simple in his saintly incarnation and once by the Virgin Mary.

Before his apotheosis on July 19, 1396, in the shape of a luminous little "sun," Paul the Simple has one last lesson for Ermine. He instructs her that when she sees the child in the Host to think of the Virgin Mary and her child, who "is even more beautiful than the one you see." And when Ermine sees in the Host Christ being beaten, carrying the cross, and then being nailed to it, she is to think of Christ's sufferings and should meditate "in peace" (151). Paul the Simple here attempts to direct Ermine's overwrought experiences into the safer channels of focused meditation, a "peaceful" meditation that avoids the emotional excesses Ermine—and many other late medieval women—has become known for. The saint stresses a kind of meditation that can involve the imagination but not literal imitation of Christ's suffering. Thus Paul the Simple would not endorse what the hagiographers of Saint Francis and Marie of Oignies did: they presented them as literally *becoming* Christ on the cross. As Caroline Walker Bynum observes, "Some male descriptions of holy women explicitly stress that *imitatio* is fact, not memory or imagination."[57]

It is the notion of memory that is the focus of the second lesson, delivered on August 15, the feast day of the Assumption of the Virgin, by no less a personage than the Virgin Mary herself. Mary often appears in visions as a theologian or legal advisor; she can resolve thorny exegetical issues for troubled Christians.[58] The thirteenth-century monk Abundus of Villers in Brabant (modern-day Belgium), for example, was extremely troubled by a sermon he heard on August 15 in which the priest claimed that for Saint Jerome the Assumption of the Virgin was a "matter of opinion." The Virgin appeared and, speaking of her own Assumption as a theologian would, assured him that Saint Augustine once preached a sermon in which "he clearly asserts my complete glorification, in body and soul." Abundus then questioned a preacher about this sermon who is not sure whether and where Augustine said this and "relayed the question to the masters in Paris" who confirmed that Augustine had indeed made that point.[59] The Parisian university scholars thus confirmed what the Virgin herself had already conveyed to Abundus or, as the modern poet Paul Valéry famously said, "tout finit à la Sorbonne."

Abundus's vision was rather simple: the Virgin appeared to him as a "bride-like," beautiful woman. For Ermine the heavens open and Mary appears in a grand celestial vision clothed in gold with a golden crown to remind her that contrary to what the demons claimed, it was Christ himself who sent the visions of the child in the Host and the Man of Sorrows to Ermine. And why? So that Ermine will retain in her memory his Passion. Thus the Virgin Mary defines the function of eucharistic visions as mnemonic and not as an invitation to literal imitation or even self-mutilation. The vision should be treated as an image but not as an idolatrous one: to forestall idolatry in medieval devotion, images must only represent what one prays to and not themselves be the object of prayer. In the same way, Mary cautions against adoring the images visible in the visions rather than what they represent. Conversely, images and other works of art can inspire visions, as has been shown in a number of interesting studies.[60] Ermine herself clearly knew paintings that showed the suffering Christ, for when she has a particularly detailed vision of Christ tied to a column and being scourged, Jean observes that "his hair and beard were somewhat red, not at all black as the painters make them when they paint their crucifixes" (144). If we ever needed additional proof of the interaction of devotional art and devotional practice, here it is.

After addressing Ermine in the teacherlike fashion we just saw, the Virgin vanishes, the heavens close, and, after the vision that lasted five hours, Ermine is left "on her knees in front of her window, without getting up, without her shoes, in her hair shirt with another shirt on top and a little kerchief on her head, just as she had left her bed at the beginning of the vision" (161). This touching description has all the hallmarks of the *effet de réel* that brings us closer to this strange woman. The next day Ermine hears eight masses, and during four of them she sees both the child and the suffering Christ in great detail (bloody scourges, Christ nailed to the cross with a heavily bleeding wound, wearing the crown of thorns), while the other four masses feature the Host in its plain shape of bread. Thus after Mary's visit Ermine's desire for seeing the child in the Host or the suffering Christ is as strong as ever, and that desire is satisfied on August 15. But, as Jean tells us, "from mid-August on she saw the Host in the priest's hands only in its common form" (161). It seems that Mary's lesson brought forth one last burst of eucharistic visions, followed only by another celestial vision of stars and sweet melodies, just a day before her final and fatal malady grips her (*le mal de la mort la print*; 163).

Ermine's Ascetic Practices

Ascetic practices of different types and of different degrees of severity were part and parcel of medieval religious life. What one could call "the ascetic model" comprised "along with fasting, the prohibition of sexual pleasure, deprivation of sleep, restriction of speech, poverty, mortification of the flesh, self-mutilation, and compulsive weeping."[61] Some of these practices, such as fasting or the wearing of a hair shirt, could be constants in a penitent's life, while others, such as scourging or other self-tortures, were often reserved for special occasions, often as the atonement for sins considered especially heinous.[62] Giles Constable lists the "three most prominent motives" of penitential practices as "the expiation of sin, the expression of devotion, and the avoidance of sin."[63] This kind of self-harm showed some gender differences, not so much in the form the torments took as in their function. For married women, in particular, Katrien Heene argues, self-mutilation could be a form of empowerment, something that was denied them in the patriarchal power structures of medieval society.[64] The feminist critic Laurie Finke suggests that "mystics took disciplines designed to regulate and subject the body and turned them into what Michel Foucault has called 'technologies of the self,' methods of consolidating their spiritual power and authority, perhaps the only ones available to women. . . . For women mystics, excess—the repression of the body, the mortification of the flesh—paradoxically becomes revaluation of the self in relation to spiritual power."[65] In this context the body is not rejected but rather becomes a valued instrument that allows women to express their piety and strive for the imitation of Christ's suffering. Yet authoritative clerics often frowned upon extreme forms of ascetic penance, and not only those practiced by women. Not a few Churchmen tried to rein in those men and women who practiced almost continuous extreme physical penance. Even some of the extreme penitents themselves, while not abandoning their own practices, were careful not to recommend them to others.

Arnulf, a thirteenth-century lay brother from Villers in Belgium; Henry Suso and Elsbeth of Oye (hailing from fourteenth-century Germany and Switzerland, respectively); and Dorothea of Montau, Ermine's almost exact contemporary whom we have encountered before, can serve as examples here and as a backdrop for our examination of Ermine's practices and Jean le Graveur's efforts to instill the ideal of moderation in his penitent.

Arnulf of Villers used rods and stems of trees in order to beat himself, rolled in nettles, and embedded a rope in his flesh until it began to fuse with his body and produced worms as well as a horrible stench. But his most dreadful invention was a vest of hedgehog pelts that he fabricated from as many as eleven skins and tied tightly around his body with ropes so that they would not get loose and thus be less painful. Goswin of Bossut, Arnulf's biographer, comments on the reactions of the four abbots who were Arnulf's superiors during his life at Villers: "Some may be puzzled and think that the abbots concerned were very indiscreet, to say the least, in allowing this man to apply to his body these hedgehog pelts, so horrible to look at and to touch, and indiscreet in the first place to let him so afflict himself beyond measure with any of these instruments. . . . These abbots gave him leave to apply the bodily torments, but they also at times forbade him, fearing he might collapse under a martyrdom so multiple and extensive. He, though, . . . strove to twist out of them any permissions they had withdrawn."[66] A number of key terms appear here: the notion of being "indiscreet" in the sense of lacking *discretio,* that is, the discernment to know what is permissible and what is not; the idea of "measure," denoting behavior within the norms of reason; and finally, the concept of martyrdom: when actual martyrdom was no longer possible, self-inflicted tortures replaced those meted out by evil pagan persecutors in the early centuries of the Christian religion.

Wearing spiky garments was also the habit of Henry Suso who was one of the most inventive self-tormenters. Hair shirts and iron chains were apparently not sufficiently painful for him, so he devised a "tight-fitting hair undergarment for the upper part of his body, with a hundred and fifty nails embedded in straps in this garment, with the points directed inward, and he slept in this device."[67] This passage comes from his autobiography, *The Life of the Servant,* which depicts these kinds of excessive self-castigations as necessary steps on the road to perfection. But Suso did not encourage his female readers to imitate these practices. On the contrary, he explicitly ordered Elsbeth Stagel, the Dominican nun, for whom he ostensibly wrote, to "abstain from any such forms of behavior, on the grounds that women are too frail for such harsh practices."[68] He believed that moderation should govern all penitential acts. Werner Williams-Krapp speculates that Suso may have known the story of Elsbeth of Oye, a Dominican nun from Oetenbach near Zurich. In her " 'diary designed for circulation, Elsbeth tells of horrendous attacks of anxiety and describes gruesome self-destructive practices: she drives a nail-studded crucifix into her flesh and ties it to her body with a belt, she sits endlessly in her rotting habit and does nothing to ward off the maggots and worms gnawing at her flesh, she flagellates herself with a nail-studded whip etc." Christ, Mary, and Saint John the Evangelist "encourage her to continue with her practices, even though the pain and suffering have become almost unbearable."[69] The presence of these three holy personages confirms that Elsbeth achieved the mystical experience she had sought through this kind of self-torture.

Often, the wounds produced by this kind of self-harm were likened to those of Christ. Dorothea of Montau, for example, "would place nutshells and other sharp objects in the mysterious wounds that spontaneously erupted all over her body." She also wore a rough hair shirt or submerged her wounds in brine in order to keep them open. Her biographer Johannes of Marienwerder related these wounds to Christ's suffering in complex ways and even "assimilated them explicitly with the stigmata of Christ." Unlike some other confessors, however, he did try to rein her in but praised her "manful heart" lodged in a weak woman's body.[70]

These few examples, admittedly at the extreme end of the spectrum, show that medieval penitents were capable of the most shocking brutality when it came to self-inflicted suffering. They also show that the idea of moderation, usually voiced by figures of authority and sometimes by the penitents themselves, frequently, though not always, hovered in the background. Their position was that although extreme bodily penance was one important element of sanctity, admiring these practices in others should not incite every Christian to imitate them.

How, then, do Ermine and Jean fit into this complex of ideas? A long passage that Jean situates between the end of his prologue and the first part of Ermine's *Visions* (which begin with a specific date, the Eve of All Saints' Day, October 31, 1395) is filled with some biographical information concerning Ermine and her husband and announces some of the major themes of the text to come. The intercalated passage recounts how Ermine and her elderly spouse arrived in Reims, how she became a widow, and how Ermine came to Jean le Graveur for advice and ended up living off the courtyard of his institution.[71] Immediately after reproducing her promise that she would obey him as "does a monk his superior" (51), Jean begins to list and analyze her ascetic practices, such as prayers that last all night; but the most extreme is Ermine wearing an extremely tight rope-belt that begins to fuse with her flesh.[72] No scene better crystallizes the issues of devotion manifested in corporal penance than this one, and it does so very vividly and dramatically. In a very effective technique that he adopts throughout *Visions*, Jean inserts bits of revealing dialogue into this key scene.

Knotted ropes and tight horsehair belts were a staple of medieval ascetics. Arnulf of Villers was an extreme example we looked at above. Women ascetics also used hair shirts and tightly knotted ropes to torment themselves; they also beat themselves with chains, nails, thorns, or nettles and cut and burned themselves.[73] Many penitents seemed to use these tortures to assert mastery over their bodies. Jacques of Vitry, for example, writes of Marie of Oignies: "And because she clearly did not have power over her own body, she secretly wore a very rough cord under her clothing that she bound with great force." He then adds, "I do not say these things to commend the excess but so that I might show her fervour. In these and in many other things wherein the privilege of grace operated, let the discreet reader pay attention that what is a privilege for a few does not make a common law."[74]

Jean le Graveur shares Jacques of Vitry's sentiments but expresses them quite differently. We can see the great stylistic difference between Jacques of Vitry and Jean le Graveur. While Jacques simply states that Marie wore this cord and then adds his commentary advocating moderation for less holy individuals, Jean constructs a little drama that illustrates perfectly what it meant to be a confessor who had to rein in an overeager penitent.

Jean le Graveur strongly objects to Ermine's wearing the double belt that by then had embedded itself into Ermine's flesh. It is in fact Ermine herself who alerts her confessor to the pain she feels because of it. When Jean commands her to take the belt off, she confesses that she cannot do so because her own flesh has grown over it. Jean is horrified and stunned—and modern readers as well undoubtedly cringe at the image of the flesh-covered belt. Jean cannot suggest a method for the removal of the belt, but Ermine ingeniously finds one: she attaches one end of the belt to a strong nail in her wall and moves away quickly, which solves the problem of the belt but leaves her partly flayed. The text then skips forward to the moment after Ermine's death when a woman who put Ermine into her shroud notices marks and scars of extreme beating; Jean then inserts another piece of dialogue in which Ermine asks him how she can ever do sufficient penance in this world. It is here that Jean offers an important lesson on "discretion." That is, love is often more important than extreme penance and should guide our devotion. Ermine tries to concentrate on love and sweetness but also tells Jean forcefully that she "hates" her body and its sins that she must expiate. Other details follow: Ermine throws herself on the floor in front of the crucifix in the friars' church or lays herself out in her room, calling herself a *charogne* (a word that means *carrion* but also has sexual connotations) and asking for punishment (53).

At this point Jean mentions the *aventures* inflicted by demons that Ermine has to endure, indicating October 31, 1395, as the date of their onset; that date then reappears at the beginning of part I. We now understand why Jean asks Ermine to report all her adventures to him every day: he needs help! "I am a simple man," he tells Ermine, "and you and I equally need some advice from higher up, that is, the prior of Saint-Denis" (54).

It becomes clear that Jean felt overwhelmed by the task confronting him: not only to guide Ermine's devotions and ascetic practices but also to protect her from the *aventures* and at the same time to ensure the orthodoxy of all the unsettling things happening around him. The compression of all these issues into a drama taking up about three folios preceding Ermine's *Visions* proper establishes an important framework centered on the question, what are the "proper boundaries of healthy devotion" and asceticism, a question often considered by Jean Gerson who was particularly sensitive to "devotional excess" in women.[75] (He, as we recall, was the final arbiter on Ermine's experiences.) In the course of the *Visions*, Ermine's practices are rather mainstream and avoid the excesses of the belt adventure. Nonetheless, there are moments of more extreme penitential practices that call forth her confessor's commentary, insisting on moderation. Jean does not endorse her practices wholeheartedly, nor does he propose Ermine as a model for others to follow, just as Jacques of Vitry would not encourage ordinary mortals to imitate Marie of Oignies's extreme behavior—although their admiration would of course be welcomed. Jean here tries to tread the middle ground between admiration and caution and sometimes even reaches a point of interdiction.

Compared with the hundreds of instances of demonic attacks, the moments of intense physical asceticism are rare in *Visions*. They mostly belong to the category that Giles Constable identified as "to show devotion." These are ongoing practices, like wearing a hair shirt or fasting, that are not extreme. Throughout the text Jean tries to prevent Ermine from fasting too often, generally citing her fragile health. On Christmas Eve 1395, for example, Ermine wants to fast on bread and water, but Jean "did want to allow it because she was ill and slept little or not at all." Ermine obeys and takes a little pitcher with wine with her to her room—which is promptly thrown to the floor by a mysterious hand. Instead of being upset, Ermine exclaims, "Thanks be to the Lord, now I am no longer tempted [to drink the wine]" (66). This brief scene reveals much about Ermine's asceticism and Jean's attitude toward it. Ermine wants to obey Jean's exhortation to moderation, but when the wine "disappears" not of her own volition, she is gratified that she can fast in the way she had originally desired.

This ongoing moderate asceticism, then, illustrates Constable's second category. Jean dealt with Constable's first category, the expiation of sin, in the preliminary passage we just analyzed: Ermine saw herself as a terrible sinner, and in a sense all her actions were aimed at expiation of these unspecified sins. For Constable's third category, "to ward off temptation," we can look to one striking scene that takes place about six weeks before her death and that Jean highlights as outside of Ermine's routine. She beats herself savagely to combat what are most likely sexual feelings. We saw in Chapter 2 that Ermine frequently suffered from what she called "ugly dreams," meaning dreams of a sexual nature. Having been a married woman, she naturally remembers what sexual activity had been like. Usually, she berates herself violently for having these dreams. But in the scene on July 3, 1396, a "bodily temptation," "horrible and strong" assails her in her waking hours. In this instance Ermine uses corporal penance to ward off temptation. She beats herself viciously until the blood spurts from her body, all the time sobbing ferociously. She then ties her hair shirt over her wounds and is unable to sleep—but is apparently freed from temptations (144).

No explicit commentary accompanies this scene, although it is followed the next day by Ermine's vision of a five-foot-tall Christ in the Host during elevation at mass. Christ himself relates the brutal scourging he experiences here by telling Ermine, "If you beat yourself yesterday for love of me, this is nothing compared with the beating I am undergoing for love of you." But Jean couches this pronouncement in grammatical ambiguities: *et sembloit qu'il peust bien dire a la femme* (and it seemed that this is what he could have said to the woman; 145); the word *sembler* (to seem) followed by the subjunctive of the word *pouvoir* (can) reveals some extra caution that Jean applies to Ermine's report of this particular vision.

This scene, which takes us to within six weeks of Ermine's death, condenses many aspects of her ascetic practices and Jean's attitude toward them. We see her severe beating as on the one hand a response to sexual temptations that assail her and on the other as an attempt to imitate Christ's suffering. Jean's attitude ranges from "no comment" to a cautious acceptance of her vision of Christ speaking directly to Ermine. The will to believe everything Ermine reported was strong, but the possibility of demonic deception was ever-present as well. Demons did not only attack and deceive, however; they often openly challenged Christian dogma as well as the very devotional and penitential practices we just explored.

Demonic Challenges to Ermine's Beliefs and Practices

These practices obviously did not please demons, as the following examples show. First, let us return to Arnulf of Villers, the designer of the hedgehog vest. Goswin of Bossut tells us: "Another day, Arnulf was alone in his cell and was, as usual, wearing himself thin with a scourge. Then there appeared to him a demon, seemingly human in form, but diminutive. This demon, to show how the penitential discipline saddened and irked him, now took one impetuous swipe and knocked the scourge out of Arnulf's hand." Arnulf then wrestles the demon to the ground and beats him up. Finally, the demon escapes "all gloomy and ashamed."[76] Demons clearly do not like it when Christians show devotion, either through physical torments or devotional acts of various sorts. Demons mocked Christina of Stommeln's efforts at asceticism by telling her that her suffering was meaningless and that it "is sinful to live in celibacy."[77] And Dorothea of Montau struggled against a demon who tried

> to turn her mind away from worthwhile activity and prevent her contemplation of heavenly bliss. This he initiated through malicious suggestions like this: "Turn away from God, for it is useless to perform good deeds. You will not reach God anyway." When she was at her prayers he spoke thus: "Why do you want to pray and exert yourself, interrupt your sleep and suffer cold, when none of it is of use to you?" Whenever she gazed longingly towards heaven, he said, "Why do you look to heaven. You will never enter it anyway." . . . Whenever she wanted to attend church, give alms, endure distasteful things patiently, or perform other good works, he practiced his thousand wiles on her, in hopes of turning her from her good intentions. . . . But with the help of God's mercy, she did not give in to his evil suggestions but cleaved to God with still greater diligence.

Johannes of Marienwerder adds that Dorothea would have preferred large wounds on her body to the demon's "vicious suggestions."[78]

Demons also insinuate that Christians do not need the help of the Church in their devotions, a truly heretical temptation. Margery Kempe, for example, was told by a devil "that she didn't need to confess but to do penance by herself alone."[79] Thus demons try to derail Christians' pious ways of life by preventing their adherence to dogma and the practices it requires.

These demonic challenges have, I believe, a paradoxical function: Jean le Graveur uses the demons that haunt and vex Ermine to challenge the tenets he considers orthodox;[80] this means that he can *reaffirm* orthodoxy because any deviations are suggested by demons in moments of intense "temptation." Demons also have the function of testing the faith of believers, and they therefore dangle in front of such believers possibilities of a less arduous life, a life without asceticism, and without painful time-consuming devotional practices. Demons, as Christine Ruhrberg argues, "distill in themselves everything that exists outside of religious norms, everything that should be excluded and finally threatens these norms."[81] The demons' temptations, if resisted, in the end reaffirm and strengthen a pious person's beliefs.

These temptations can be divided into two large groups: those that challenge Christian dogma and those that denigrate penitential and devotional practices. Both kinds appear at times as auditions and at other times as apparitions. The former occurs in the form of a "voice" that yells at (*hucher*) Ermine; the latter arrives in Ermine's bedroom in the shape of humanoid demons, counterfeit saints, and animals.[82]

Ermine's faith is constantly being tested, and Jean shows us a number of doctrines that are being challenged by demons: Christ's sacrifice as manifested in the Eucharist, his crucifixion, the Resurrection, and the afterlife. These are of course some of the central tenets of the Creed.

One of the most crucial questions concerns the function of Christ's sacrifice. Does baptism mean automatic salvation? This is what a demonic voice suggests to Ermine in late January 1396. We need neither penance nor good works, it claims, for Christ has already saved all sinners. This fact, the demon insists, is not made public because then no one would want to do good deeds.[83] It is the demons who will end up in the abyss after the Last Judgment, but no baptized Christians need fear hell (75). This claim seems to undermine the entire edifice of Christian dogma and practice and must therefore emanate from a demon. True to his technique, Jean le Graveur articulates the doubts and anxieties plaguing many Christians and nullifies them by putting them into the mouths of demons. As we saw earlier, the Eucharist also created anxieties: how could bread become flesh simply by being elevated in the priests' hands?

On February 6, 1396, after confession and communion, a demon approaches Ermine and whispers into her ear that what she just consumed was not the body of Christ but just a piece of bread, for if she had eaten the body of Christ, she would now be filled with contentment—which she is not, given that he, the demon, is plaguing her at this very moment. The voice suggests that if Christ had been truly divine he would not have let himself be killed so shamefully. Ermine retorts that she has indeed swallowed Christ and that she has received the one "who was born from the Virgin Mary on Christmas and who died for sinners on Holy Friday." Jean comments, "And the voice told her these things in order to make her abandon her faith. But God's mercy comforted her so greatly that she remained steadfast" (84). A similar challenge arrives on Maundy Thursday, March 25, 1396, when demons threaten to crucify her. They lay her out on the floor in a

cruciform shape, pull so hard on her arms that they almost come out of their
sockets, and taunt her: she should ask her God for help—but how could he
help her when he himself had been so shamefully crucified? Ermine replies
that she will gladly be crucified for her sins if it pleases Christ, for tomorrow
is Good Friday when he himself died for love of all believers (101–102).

On February 13, 1396, another doctrine, that of the afterlife, is questioned
by yet another demon who establishes his credentials by reminding Ermine
that he saved her from injury earlier that day when she was lifted from her
window and dumped in the churchyard. Ermine curses him, but he persists
in giving her ideas: after death, he claims, all humans will be nothing but
"*bestes mues* (dumb beasts), there is no hell and no paradise." "Dirty demon,"
Ermine retorts, "you thought you could make me abandon my faith, but I
will not believe you." She spits in his direction and taunts him: "*O corne
assez, o corne bien,*" which means more or less "just go on with your nonsense,
see if I care" (89–90).[84]

About four months later Ermine is distressed at mass when she feels
deprived of the Eucharist (she sees the priest's hands empty at elevation) and
goes to weep in her room. A demonic voice tells her not to be afraid of
damnation because after death humans will be just like dogs. There is no
such thing as a soul and there is no resurrection. If there were, God would
already have returned to Earth some of the people who died for the faith.
But this has not happened because people rot after death and could therefore
not return to Earth under any circumstances (141). In a single verbal attack
the demon denies the existence of the soul, possible resurrection, and the
afterlife.

The scenario Jean constructs around these demonic challenges to the
faith is similar every time, although the circumstances range from the trauma
after a physical attack to anxiety about the Eucharist. Each time the demons
deny one of the essential elements of the Creed, and each time Ermine states
the articles' essence and professes her adherence to it. Given Jean's trouble
(explored earlier in the chapter) in instilling the full text of the Creed in
Ermine, we can certainly read these passages as a kind of dramatization of
the fruits his labors have borne: she not only remembers the Creed, but she
lives it.

In conjunction with the challenges to Christian dogma we find plentiful
attacks on the devotional and penitential practices that make Ermine's life
that of an exemplary Christian aspiring to perfection. The demons target

Ermine's attempts to do penance, including her desire to be poor, her habits of fasting and wearing a hair shirt, her church going, her desire to become a recluse (which they counter by urging her to go out and beg), and especially her desire to take frequent communion.

In late November 1395 a concerted demonic attack takes aim at precisely the elements that we considered above as crucial to Ermine's devotion. A young demonic couple begins to have sex on the floor of Ermine's bedroom (more about that in Chapter 4) and taunt her: You are quite evil. You are killing yourself with fasting and not sleeping, with wearing a hair shirt, tying a rope around yourself, and lying on a narrow bed of straw. You think you can escape from us? No way, you will rather end up in two hells. It would be much better for you to be comfortable and do your body's bidding because you cannot help but be damned (58–59).

And a bit later a counterfeit Saint Andrew advises her to take off her hair shirt and amuse herself. "Do not kill yourself" (*ne soyes mie omicide de toy mesmes*; 59), he adds, thus in fact articulating the message of caution that many Churchmen transmitted to extreme ascetics.

Throughout Ermine's *Visions* we hear demonic voices insinuate that penance is unnecessary. Again and again demons tell Ermine that what she considers a sin is in fact permissible. Dancing and pretty clothes, for example, are hardly reasons for damnation (99). However, in a seemingly contrary move, the demons also urge Ermine to leave her comfortable life, go to church less often, and go out and earn some money (140). One lengthy exchange Ermine has with a demon highlights the choices Ermine has to make and sets her behavior into the context of late medieval models of piety: one demon urges her "that she should go out into the countryside and beg for pardons for God's love and that her life was too comfortable" (74).[85] Another one suggests, "You could very well go and see good people and without sinning ask for pardons in the churches below the town, and you would be much happier" (99).[86] What the demons suggest here is in fact a kind of life choice: that of wandering around as an itinerant penitent, collecting indulgences at various churches in the region and perhaps asking for alms as well. This way of life would correspond to that of the kind of beguines who did not live in communities but "roamed about the country in penitential bands, begging for their livelihood."[87] Such a choice would be endangering Ermine's salvation and is therefore represented as a demonic temptation by Jean, who does his best to dissuade Ermine from choosing such a life.

In the thought of many Churchmen of the period, these "women on the loose" were considered a "breeding-ground for doctrinal error and moral aberration."[88] That begging in public was a contentious issue becomes clear in stories told in a number of *Lives* of holy women. Thomas of Cantimpré's *Life* of Margaret of Ypres (1216–1237), for example, highlights the conflicts that could be caused by a woman's desire to go begging. Margaret was, in Barbara Newman's estimation, a "troubled and rebellious teen" trying to assert herself in a strong matriarchal family structure.[89] We already encountered her in Chapter 2 in the context of her intense relationship with Friar Zeger of Brabant. In addition to starving herself almost to death, Margaret repeatedly tried to go out and beg in the streets, but each time Friar Zeger ordered her back home. She got around this interdiction—in the mulish and slightly devious way that seemed to characterize much of her behavior—by claiming to beg "for the lepers" to whom she could otherwise give nothing. The parish priest countervenes Friar Zeger's explicit order by giving Margaret a small coin. "In this way he satisfied both the beggars and his conscience," her biographer astutely observes.

But Ermine is not tempted by mendicancy. Her socioeconomic class differed dramatically from that of the bourgeois Margaret of Ypres, and she had been too close to becoming an actual beggar when she was widowed for her to embrace this lifestyle by choice. So when Ermine rejects the idea of going begging, the demon suggests that she could become a recluse and that he, the demon, would take care of everything she needs. Ermine does not like this solution either, so the demon, like some indefatigable career counselor, suggests that she go out and work since she is healthy and strong and should not accept alms from those around her who are weaker (74–75). This advice alludes to the controversy in which the mendicant orders were embroiled, that of the *mendiant valide*, or the healthy beggar. Healthy strong men—and women for that matter—their critics said, have no business going around begging.[90]

This exchange with demonic tempters thus lays out the whole range of choices a woman like Ermine might have had: to live as a public penitent and/or beggar; as a recluse (while being ministered to by demons); or as a working woman. The first and last of these suggested ways of life are in fact exactly what the beguines tried to practice, although manual labor was acceptable while begging was not.[91]

But as we saw, Ermine's actual way of life did not correspond to any of these choices. The demonic suggestions for another way of life thus point to the anomaly of her situation: basically penniless, she lives under the protection of an Augustinian friar, tries to adopt a semimonastic schedule, and strives to learn some of the basic tenets of the Catholic faith.

The Eucharist, as we saw earlier, was the absolute central element of Ermine's faith. We explored eucharistic visions and miracles and saw that demons interfered frequently with the celebration of this sacrament. In the context of demonic challenges to devotional practices we will take a brief look at Ermine's desire for frequent communion. We noted that after the Fourth Lateran Council communion was an important but rare occurrence, usually limited to once a year.

Yet pious people, women in particular, ardently desired frequent, even daily, communion. Some confessors tried to accommodate the wishes of the women they were in charge of. Johannes of Marienwerder, for example, gave in to Dorothea of Montau's "overwhelming hunger and need" for the Eucharist, which she expressed with "weeping, wailing, sighing, and screaming." For the twenty weeks before her death her confessor served her the Eucharist every night, but he was careful not to let other people see what he was doing, although he had his bishop's permission. Every night he locked the Host into a reliquary that he deposited in a pew within reach of Dorothea's cell. Christ was thus always available to her and spoke to her reassuringly directly from the pew, or so it seemed to Dorothea. This one example of one of Ermine's contemporaries must suffice here to show what kinds of anxiety surrounded a woman's wish for frequent communion. Yes, her confessor placates Dorothea's yearning, but he does so in secret so as not to give ideas to other, perhaps less blessed, individuals.

For Ermine communion is situated at the nexus of a range of contentious issues. First, there seems to be a conflict between Ermine's parish priest and her confessor that is highlighted by yet another *corneur* demon: "You are a bad woman," he says, "to take the risk of taking communion from the subprior (i.e., Jean) without getting permission from your parish priest. And you know well that your *curé* would not give this permission. I, however, am willing to come to your room and give you communion secretly and as often as you like" (83–84). Ermine chases away the demon and confesses herself (to Jean, not the parish priest), but the demon returns and tells her that the Eucharist is nothing but a piece of bread and that Jean and the other religious lie to her if they claim it is Christ's body. The same scenario—offers of limitless communion, doubts concerning the nature of the Host—is replayed many times throughout the text. The crucial elements here are the frequency

of communion as well as its secrecy offered by the demon. We can infer, then,
that for Jean le Graveur, Ermine's extreme desire for communion (sometimes
several times a day and in her own room) was deeply troubling and needed
to be moved into the realm of the demonic in order to be extirpated.

A Heavenly Vision

It would be sad if Ermine's piety and devotion were never rewarded with a
heavenly vision. Luckily, Ermine is privy to some true visions that, however,
we need to disentangle from the multiplicity of demonic apparitions and
other disturbing experiences. This close intertwining of the demonic and the
divine makes Ermine's *Visions* quite different from many other stories about
holy men and women. Of course, not everyone is granted a heavenly vision,
but when it occurs, the biographers most often set them apart in special
sections or chapters.[92] Returning once more to Goswin of Bossut and Arnulf,
the lay brother of Villers, we see a strict separation between the account of
demonic vexations and what Goswin calls "loftier visions."[93] First, Arnulf,
"drenched in a copious dew of heavenly grace" sees Jesus gazing upon him;
Jesus then points to the heavens and says, "Look upwards and contemplate
what wonders I show you." Arnulf then lifts up his eyes "and saw the heavens
open wide." This phrase recalls many biblical passages, such as the opening
of the book of the prophet Ezekiel or the Acts of the Apostles (7:55) and
provides the backdrop for the rest of the vision: "In such measure as mortals
are allowed it" Arnulf gazes upon the choirs of saints and angels as well as
upon the Virgin Mary. When Christ asks him whether he is now satisfied,
Arnulf indicates that he wants things that are even more sublime. Eventually
he is "plunged into an unsearchable abyss of divine light" and is granted a
vision of the Trinity. After Christ disappears Arnulf "wound his way back
from this height, like one awaking from a heavy sleep." Goswin tells of an
almost identical vision in his biography of Abundus, monk of Villers; indeed
it is so similar that the pious twentieth-century translator, brother Martinus
Crawley, felt compelled to speculate that "one might suppose [these visions]
to be a literary creation of Goswin's."[94] But what matters is that Goswin
wove a wonderfully evocative tapestry of marvelous imagery, feelings of joy
and privilege, shot through with plenty of biblical references to ensure the
orthodoxy of these special moments in his holy subjects' lives.

Jean le Graveur, in the mode of the diary he constructs of Ermine's experiences, never separates the holy from the demonic but shows how one intertwines with the other throughout each day and night of Ermine's life. Thus, on the evening of May 31, 1396, the eve of the Feast of Corpus Christi, Ermine is being vexed by three green lizards and three black ravens who try to pick at her face, when she hears a sweet melody outside her window, opens it, and sees the heavens open. Unlike Goswin of Bossut, Jean le Graveur offers no biblical references for this phenomenon. In the opened space Ermine sees a blinding light (*clarté*; 128) that contains crowds of people, but she cannot discern who they are because her eyes hurt too much. She continues to kneel at her window, and while she is enjoying this consoling vision, three large snakes wind themselves in and out of her dress—but she hardly notices and remains by her window. The fact that Ermine cannot quite make out the individuals in the heavenly crowd suggests that the vision remains somewhat obscure, that she still "sees through a glass, darkly."

On July 7, 1396, Ermine receives the confirmation that this vision was truly divine. The hermit Paul the Simple who appears as both a counterfeit and real saint in her room comes to assure her that God had sent heavenly visions, including the one on May 31, to her.[95] He takes her by the hand, but she cannot see him (147). A few days later she receives proof that he is the real saint for he transforms himself "into a small shape of about a foot across, very shiny" (*en une petite forme de environ un pié de grant . . . tres reluisant*; 152), and looking out her window, Ermine sees the "glowing shape" ascend to heaven, which opens for it, swallows it up, and quickly recloses. This saintly ball shape and its "roll" up into the heavens are very peculiar: in fact, I know of no other instance of this particular form of ascension.

Just ten days before her death Ermine is again on her knees, praying by the open window. She sees three great rays of light that move from the earth all the way to heaven. Then she falls asleep but leaves her window open. Suddenly she is awakened by a bright light, loud music, and a sweet odor. She jumps out of bed, and in a touching bit of realism that removes our text from the totally generic, we learn just how she was dressed: her hair shirt with a nightshirt on top, without shoes and a little scarf on her head. Wonderful stars emit lights that resemble those of huge torches. Here Jean weaves in a personal observation that helps inscribe this vision into the liturgical calendar. Writing about the stars, he muses that Ermine's seeing stars is fitting because the Virgin Mary is often called *estoille de la mer* (star of the sea; 159) and therefore the stars fêted the Virgin on the eve of the Feast of her Assumption (August 15).

Ermine now receives the grandest visions of all: the heavens open and Mary, with a golden crown and accompanied by two angels, begins to speak to her. This time no demonic apparitions interfere with the vision's beauty. Mary's major function here seems to be the validation of Ermine's eucharistic visions and affirmation that Paul the Simple was a true saint sent down to comfort her. Ermine has her doubts: she is not worthy, she claims (160). But Mary reassures her that she is indeed worthy, for Christ can give grace to whomever he pleases. Mary then adds some crucial remarks: "He gave you the confessor you need; do not leave him and believe in him all your life. I expect that he will survive you." Again, through Mary's endorsement the relationship between Ermine and her confessor becomes central. Ermine is worthy of heavenly grace because she is under the authority of her confessor, an authority that is linked directly to the problem of the discernment of true and false visions we will explore in the last chapter. Here the validation of the vision is bound up with that of the bond between a woman and her confessor, and it is offered by the mother of God herself.

After conferring this wonderful twofold approbation Mary ascends back to the heavens, which close after her, but the music and perfume remain for another five hours. The next day Ermine attends no fewer than eight masses. Interestingly, after the August 14 vision of the Virgin no more human figures, not the suffering Christ, not the little Christ child, appear in the Host during communion despite Ermine's ardent desire to see once more "something that relates to the Passion or the child" (161). Complete orthodoxy has reasserted itself. Ermine still sees some heavenly stars a few days later and also hears some sweet melodies, but it seems that the overwhelming vision of August 14 signals the winding down of Ermine's experiences of demons and saints. What remains to be told is her holy death: on August 25, 1396, the feast day of Saint Louis, Ermine dies of the plague, an illness she contracted while caring for one of her neighbors. She appears posthumously to a little girl, Isabelle, whom she takes with her to heaven.

In her *Visions* Ermine emerges as a simple but deeply devout woman who struggles to master Christian dogma and to follow Christian precepts in the face of ceaseless demonic onslaughts. Jean shows us how Ermine is challenged again and again to renounce some of the most important tenets of the Catholic faith: the existence of the soul, the Resurrection, the truth of

Christ's sacrifice, the need for penance and good works. That these challenges were whispered to her by demonic voices does not make them any less real: doubts and heretical beliefs abounded in medieval society, and demons were believed to be everywhere. Keeping the faith was an unending struggle, and Jean le Graveur's aim was to show that a simple woman like Ermine could indeed win the battle if her faith was strong enough. The final heavenly visions validate not only her way of life but also Jean's role in it. It was her extraordinary faith and her submission to her confessor's guidance that allowed her to become a champion battler of demons and an expert discerner of spirits, the topics of our next two chapters.

CHAPTER 4

Ermine and Her Demons

On January 28, 1396, the prior of Saint Denis in Reims ordered Ermine to do penance at Saint-Maur, a chapel at a certain distance from her home. As she hurried along the busy streets of Reims on this cold wintry day, she was suddenly accosted by a man she did not know. Or was it a demon in the shape of a man? Jean le Graveur is not quite sure. Ermine, not surprisingly, was consternated as he grabbed her rudely by the chest and said, "Where are you going, you whore? Are you going whoring?" Terribly scared, she answered sweetly, "Not at all, sir, on the contrary, I'm on my way to Saint-Maur." "By God's blood, you are lying," he said. "You are going whoring, you only live from whoring, you dirty evil whore. By God's death, I may just kill you." He held her by the chest for quite a long time while telling her all this. She was very ashamed, for bystanders heard his insults that were given without any reason. Then he let her go without beating her.[1]

This demonic attack, taking place as it does in public, in full view of passersby "who heard the villainous words he said to her," brings Ermine's trials and tribulations out into the open. The vicious assaults she experiences every day and night in her bedroom have now pursued her into the street. But Ermine is not easily deterred from her penitent errand. She does manage to get to Saint-Maur, but while she is praying, a voice, that of *le corneur*, or the deceiver, teasingly enters her ear and complains that she trusts her confessor more than him. Indeed, this demonic voice claims that it protected her from further harm in the street when she was being threatened and defamed by the humanoid demon. Why mingle with such people, the voice wants to know, when they will only do you harm (80–81)?

FIGURE 6. An angel and a demon imitate the gestures of a man and woman conversing on a road outside a medieval city. From Bartholomeus Anglicus's chapter on angels in his thirteenth-century encyclopedia *De proprietatibus rerum* (On the properties of things). London, British Library, Royal MS 15 E II, fol. 38; 1482. Reproduced by permission of the British Library.

Most of Ermine's demonic encounters take place in her room, but this
one exposes her to the gaze of all who pass along the street. Jean le Graveur, in
his account of Ermine's troubling encounter, does not present the humanoid
demon as a vision but rather tells in an astonishingly matter-of-fact way that
Ermine met a demon in the street. He makes no effort to probe deeper into
this apparition or into the question of whether this demon was "real" or a
delusion on Ermine's part. Indeed, the danger of "sensory delusion" and the
"focus on the central issue of distinguishing reality from non-reality" that
became one of the dominant problems of early modern theoretical texts on
demons and witches does not come to the fore in Ermine's *Visions*.[2]

Jean maintains this sober, neutral tone throughout the text. Ermine is
haunted continuously by horrible demons and dangerous, often disgusting,
animals, but all of this happens in her ordinary surroundings.[3] What will
the townspeople of Reims think of this disturbing confrontation between a
supposedly pious woman and a man who throws the most outrageous sexual
insults at her? Could people think her deranged? Demon possessed? Her
reasonable stance toward the demon would probably reassure people, but
nonetheless some suspicions may come to the surface. Could this demonic
encounter expose Ermine to accusations of being a witch? Had people in the
1390s already established the link between demons and sexual license that
became so prevalent in the late fifteenth-century treatises on witchcraft, like
The Hammer of Witches?

Let us look at one case in Paris that is about contemporary with Ermine's
experiences in Reims. In 1390–91 the provost of Paris conducted a trial
against four accused *sorcières* in which he linked the accusation of prostitution
(*ribaudie*) to that of sorcery.[4] These women were reputed to have used magic
to intervene in various amorous plots. Through their overt remarks and
actions in sexual matters they had acquired a bad reputation. And, as the
French historian Claude Gauvard stresses, "An inquiry into someone's reputation is essential in order to create suspicion."[5] So could the public incident
I described above incite the bystanders or even the authorities to consider
Ermine a sorceress or a witch? And did the word *witch*, or *sorcière*, already
have the connotations it acquired in later centuries when the great witch
crazes swept through Europe?

Right at the beginning of the *Visions*, Jean le Graveur had referred to
Ermine as a "woman of good reputation" (50) and had revealed her fear of
gossip. When Jean urged her to tell him every morning what had happened
to her at night, she agreed but insisted that Jean should tell no one in the

town about it, clearly fearing for her reputation (54). She was aware that bringing her demons out into the open could be dangerous. People might think her a magician or witch, a *sorcière*. And indeed we find this very word within Ermine's *Visions*: in one striking passage one of the major demonic impersonators of saints, the ancient hermit Paul the Simple, warns Ermine that she could be accused of being a *sorcière* (153), for "news is going around town that you had some trouble with the devil and that he spoke to you several times." He adds that she might be imprisoned and tortured in order to confess her contacts with the "enemy" and that it would be better for her to leave town and go to a country "where no one knows you." Ermine parries this threat with her usual aplomb by telling the demonic Saint Paul the Simple "Get out of here, stinking satan."

But with the use of the word *sorcière* this demon—and Jean le Graveur by reporting it—has raised some thorny issues. While in later centuries we would have no doubt that *sorcière* is a reference to a witch who has dealings with demons for sexual or maleficent purposes, in Ermine's time people would be more likely to think of "traditional" magic, that is, using magical formulas to summon demons and to enlist them for various, mostly nefarious, services. This is in fact the meaning Jean Gerson gives the word *sorcière* in a sermon dating from 1391, the first one in which he inveighed against contemporary superstitions; and in a later tract against superstitions relating to misguided beliefs in auspicious or inauspicious days, Gerson again singles out "old women sorcerers" whom he attacks bilingually as *vetuale sortilegae, gallice* (that is, in French) *vieilles sorcières*.[6]

The University of Paris, spearheaded by its chancellor Jean Gerson, went out of its way to indict this type of magic and in 1398 published a document of official condemnation of these practices. And just two years after Ermine's death an accused sorcerer, a physician named Jean de Bar, was tried for sorcery and executed in Paris. He was accused of using magical formulas and getting demons to do his bidding. Interestingly, his detailed confession appears in one of the manuscripts, dating from the late fifteenth century, that also contains Ermine's *Visions*.[7] Perhaps the person who put together this manuscript wanted to create an implicit contrast between the traditional practices of sorcery and Ermine's strange experiences, which in the third quarter of the fifteenth century could increasingly be interpreted as manifestations of witchcraft. Certainly, the warning that the demonic saint Paul the Simple utters—possible imprisonment and torture—reflects exactly what happened to Jean de Bar. This threat of judicial persecution as a consequence of interactions with demonic forces places Ermine at the crossroads of the "traditional" indictment of sorcery, as it was defined in the condemnation of 1398, and newer kinds of accusations related to the codification of witchcraft that begins to take shape in the late fourteenth century.[8] Yet Jean's narrative does not raise these issues explicitly.

Nonetheless, the belief in evil magic and the nefarious powers of demons could create a dangerous atmopshere for someone like Ermine. How can Ermine's confessor and scribe, Jean le Graveur, avoid letting his pious charge get caught up in the whirlpool of accusation and persecution that swirled around the old concept of the sorcerer and the newly evolving concept of the witch? In the period in which Ermine is haunted continuously by demons, the first contours of the later witch crazes become visible. In the older kind of magic, which relied on book learning and intricate magical formulas, men were dominant, and they were prosecuted as magicians or witches, often for political reasons. Even today we speak of "political witch hunts." But as the fifteenth century progressed, women were believed to be more prone to demonic possession and witchcraft because they were intellectually and physically inferior and could therefore be more easily corrupted. They were also believed to be more porous, more open to external forces than men.[9] These forces could be demonic or divine. As historian Tamar Herzig argues, "The very qualities that render women more susceptible to the devil's machinations also turn them into privileged conduits for divine revelations that confirm the tenets of Christianity."[10] Jean le Graveur's project of creating a holy woman in the shape of Ermine must therefore ensure that her role in the midst of demonic onslaughts will not be that of a witch receptive to demonic seduction nor that of a sorcerer conjuring up demons for nefarious purposes; he must not create the appearance of Ermine's active participation in any demonic practices in order to skirt the danger of both sorcery and witchcraft accusations. This is why the lone mention of the word *sorcière* comes out of the mouth of a demonic personage: the term is thus nullified at the very moment it is uttered. But the fact of the unceasing demonic assaults remains, and therefore Jean labors hard at fitting Ermine into another paradigm: that of the established patterns of ancient and medieval hagiography where the endurance of demonic assaults is a sign of saintliness.

For Jean, Ermine's tribulations fit into the venerable tradition of monastic spiritual combat where sexual temptations are incarnated by demonic apparitions in both human and animal form. Drawing on the lives of the early desert saints, hagiographers throughout the centuries reported gruesome attacks and seductive temptations delivered by a variety of demons in myriad shapes in order to buttress their subjects' claims to holiness. The ubiquity of demons was a given in medieval culture. Reading through the rich collection of miracle tales by Caesarius of Heisterbach (written between 1220 and 1235), for example, we can see that medieval monks as well as laypeople were constantly aware of being surrounded by demons. Frequently demons played the role of seducers, such as the well-dressed dandy who either woos or rapes young women in some of Caesarius's tales.[11] Demons could take on the shape of beautiful women if necessary or appear as black men, as they do indeed in Ermine's bedroom.[12]

Often the demons' activities belong in the realm of vexations, as was the case for the abbot Richalm von Schöntal (active from 1216 to 1219) whose story bears some resemblance to Ermine's.[13] His ceaseless visions of demons were recorded by a redactor who, just like Jean le Graveur, felt compelled to write down every day what Richalm told him. Richalm himself then became involved in the redaction of his visions and corrected and completed them, something that the illiterate Ermine would of course not have been capable of. The demons plaguing Richalm interfere with his activities in every sphere of his life: they attack priests during mass in his monastery and also himself, so that he loses his place in the liturgy and his peace of mind. Each monk seems to have his own companion demon (*Begleitteufel*) who has a title corresponding to his victim's job: for example, there is an abbot demon, a porter demon, a prior demon, and so forth. Sometimes when some of them are idle because "their" monks are unoccupied, they band together for a collective attack on Richalm. Colds, coughing fits, hiccups, nervous tics—everything is the work of demons. In this compulsive attribution of each and every small annoyance to the interference of demons, Richalm seems to be unique.[14] But nonetheless his case testifies to the belief that demons are omnipresent and that no living being is too insignificant for demonic attention. Indeed, Richalm proclaimed his feelings of inadequacy and doubts about his ability to live up to his role of abbot. Demonic vexations can help explain his many missteps and failures and thus seem to have a psychological function.

For Ermine both vexations and attempts at demonic seduction abound. It was Jean's task to report these demonic encounters in a way that would protect Ermine from the different dangerous currents converging at that time, be they related to sorcery or witchcraft. Reading through the *Visions* in its entirety is a curious experience: the drumbeat of demonic apparitions is relentless, the repetitive structure of the text is almost numbing. At the same time, readers cannot but feel great empathy for the victim of these continuous assaults. As Ermine tries to construct a life of holy piety for herself, as we saw in the last chapter, demons impede her efforts at every turn. We can discern three major currents in the demonic assaults: those that have some sexual aspects often linked to extreme violence; a whole series of vexations, including demonic kidnappings; and finally attacks by vicious animals that also sometimes have sexual overtones. Although all of these occur often concurrently and in no particular pattern for the sake of analysis, we have to divide them up and treat each in its own separate section, although there will necessarily be some overlap.

Demons and Sex

Speaking of demons that haunt ancient desert monks, David Brakke contends that encounters with demons are "simultaneously attractive and frightening in [their] condensed visual representation of the self's erotic desire."[15] The great historian of the early modern witch craze Norman Cohn has shown that as the Middle Ages progress, demons are no longer mere bringers of evil fortune but have "penetrated into the souls of individual Christians. . . . Demons have come to represent desires which individual Christians have, but which they dare not acknowledge as belonging to themselves."[16] And as the notion of the witch develops, the sexual aspects of demonic encounters take center stage. Indeed, as Walter Stephens affirms, as we move into the fifteenth century, "tremendous energy was expended . . . to have demonic copulation recognized as the foundation of witchcraft."[17] By far the largest part of the *Visions* is taken up with Ermine's nocturnal tribulations caused by the apparition of hideous animals and disturbing demons. While not all of these encounters have sexual connotations, many of them do. Jean's depiction of these encounters and Ermine's role in them is a crucial component of his overall project of Ermine's sanctification.

Although the frequency of her demonic encounters makes Ermine stand out in her suffering, she was by no means unique. The thirteenth-century German holy woman Christina of Stommeln, whom we encountered in previous chapters, was victimized by demons and often involved in violent and disgusting supernatural experiences quite similar to Ermine's; her French sister's nocturnal tribulations thus fit into well-established patterns. Is it possible to define precisely who inflicted these tribulations? Christine Ruhrberg notes that the distinction between the Devil, devils, and demons is not systematic or meaningful in most saints' lives.[18] The most striking constant in demonic apparitions is paradoxically the ability of demons to change their shape: they can appear in any form, be it human, animal, angel, or saint. It is therefore impossible to know what the demons "really" look like. The animals impersonated by demons can be rabid lions, bears, and serpents as well as more innocuous creatures like cats and flies. As for the human shapes assumed by demons, they can be handsome and seductive strangers; they can even be your nearest and dearest, neighbors, or friends. This belief persisted and interestingly became an obstacle in many of the much later witchcraft persecutions. In his vast study of early modern demonology Stuart Clark describes a trial in seventeenth-century England where the judges felt they could believe none of the witnesses because "if friends and neighbours might be devils without any detectable difference," where can any certainty be found?[19]

Of course, demons can also appear as the stereotype of the devil as he is depicted in medieval illustrations (see Fig. 7). Even Jean le Graveur is conscious of a certain tradition in the depiction of demons. On Christmas Eve 1395 he reflects—in a most interesting aside to his audience—on the shape of demons. He admits that when he says "they had an ugly shape" (laide forme; 66), he was thinking of demons in hell. But of course, he says, we do not know what demons look like in hell, and even if we knew, it would be impossible for us to bear to look at them. The demons Ermine sees, he muses, are just like demons as they are represented in the theater: with mouths like ovens, foot-long tongues, and eyes like burning torches. Sometimes they are small, sometimes they reach the ceiling, sometimes they speak, sometimes they are silent (67). And it is indeed this stereotype, issuing from a distinct pictorial tradition, that Ermine encounters very early on in her visionary career. Might Ermine have attended a performance of a liturgical play featuring the devil in the streets of Reims?

In late November 1395, in two of the earliest entries in Jean's account of Ermine's tribulations, we find two striking apparitions of demons illustrating their shape-shifting abilities. One of them is a man blacker than coal,[20]

> horribly hideous and reaching up to the ceiling, with a huge mouth
> full of flames just like the opening of an oven, and a tongue, redder
> than fire, hanging out of his mouth, and his extended arms blacker
> than coal, and his eyes throwing fiery rays that made the woman

FIGURE 7. Devils or demons could take on many shapes, as Jean le Graveur acknowledges. From the *Livre de la Vigne de Nostre Seigneur* (The book of our Lord's vineyard), France, c. 1450–1470. Bodleian Library, Manuscript Douce 134, fol. 99r. Reproduced by permission of the Bodleian Library.

think that these rays would burn out her own eyes. He had won-
drously big horns and ears, and he was blacker than anything on
earth and hairy all over, and he tried to kiss the woman. And there
is no one on earth who could comprehend this hideousness. And
she affirmed to me, the subprior, by oath that she would rather
suffer any torment on Earth than this one. And she would have lost
her mind if God had not protected her by His grace. (56)

How does Ermine combat this demon? She pulls out her tablet with images
of the *arma Christi*, the trusty weapon we analyzed in Chapter 3, brandishes
it in the direction of the demon, and falls over backward; and although the
demon seems to vanish, she feels so "filled with the devil" that she avoids
even her trusted confessor for a while. This feeling of having the demon
inside herself approximates the idea of possession, although Jean does not
explicitly make this connection nor does he propose any kind of exorcism.
But the fact that Ermine does not want to see her confessor points to the
tug-of-war between the demons and Jean that is evident throughout the
Visions and that we analyzed in Chapter 2. Each party seems to fight for the
"possession" of Ermine's soul and body.

The very next evening we see that a demon can also assume the form of
a dear family member: a demonic voice wakes her, claiming to be that of her
late husband. But Ermine instantly recognizes a demon and spits at him, and
he vanishes. The next night a demon sits on the roof in front of her window:
holy water dispatches him quickly. But immediately another humanoid
demon appears, saying that he is a friend from the countryside and urging
her to return to her hometown. Then, still during the same night, three
demons take her by the ears and shake her, empty out her basket of kindling,
smash her lamp, and throw her pillows across the room (57): there seems to
be no end to her tribulations.

On January 1, 1396, a bearlike creature with a flaming mouth enters
Ermine's room, followed by a pig whose skins seems to be on fire. Rays
emanating from its eyes almost blind her (68). These demonic animals
threaten her and then pee on the floor in front of her bed, but Ermine does
not notice this disgusting detail until she steps in it the next morning. Here
we should pause a moment to see what kind of proof Jean le Graveur adduces
for this disturbing desecration of Ermine's bedroom. He assures his readers
that Ermine had no tumbler full of wine or water near her that anyone could
have overturned, although, he adds, she did have a pitcher with water near

her, but it was safely behind her bed and still full the next morning. In its
quotidian quality this explanation resembles one that Thomas of Cantimpré
offered in his thirteenth-century *On Bees* (De apibus), a work that Dyan
Elliott calls "a primer on the sheer range of demonic virtuosity" of masquerading as humans and causing vexation. "Thomas was awakened by what he
took to be his confrère urinating at the foot of his bed one night. Disgusted,
Thomas was about to upbraid him when he realized it was a demon because
he heard his companion snoring beside him."[21]

While urinating can certainly have sexual connotations, the two examples we just looked at do not explicitly allude to that possibility. In other
instances, such as one in November 1395 when a hideous demon tries to kiss
Ermine or a demon in the shape of her late husband insinuates himself into
her bedroom, sexual undertones emerge, and Jean suggests that these are
demonic attempts at corrupting his pious charge (56). Demonic attempts at
seducing humans have a long, venerable history. In the context of Christian
spirituality these attempts are tests meant to confirm a monk's or other holy
person's virtue and steadfastness. Resisting these attempts thus testifies to a
person's holiness. Let us accompany for a moment Arnulf of Villers, the
thirteenth-century lay brother associated with a Cistercian abbey, whom we
already encountered in Chapter 3 as an example of extreme lay piety and
ascetic practices. His job was to transport grain to the monastery's mills and
then return with bread for the workers at the granges. A harmless enough
occupation, one would think. One day, one of many that finds him engaged
in these errands between the abbey and its granges, he has an unsettling
encounter:

> He had let his domestic go along ahead of him with the cart, while
> he followed along quite a way behind and all alone. Suddenly, at a
> spot where the road emerged from a wooded area, out from the
> woods stepped three women, all heading toward him and blocking
> the road where he was to pass. They gradually approached until he
> came to a halt: at this, one of them spoke up, while the others
> remained silent. She said to him: "Come on brother; come along
> now! Choose among the three of us the most pleasing in your eyes
> and involve yourself with her as your fancy takes!" Upon hearing
> this, and thanks to the Holy Spirit, Arnulf recognized under the
> appearance of these three women three demons that were trying to
> seduce him. So he had recourse to the well-known bodyguard, the

FIGURE 8. A woman frightened by a demon appearing in her bedroom on the left and, on the right, consulting with a bearded man who may be her confessor. The miracle is entitled "About a woman who was tormented carnally (*charnellement*) by a demon and was delivered by invoking the Virgin Mary." From the Miracles of the Virgin Mary by Jean Miélot (1456), illustrated by Lieven van Lathem. Bibliothèque nationale de France, MS fr. 9199, 6v; 1460–65. Courtesy Bibliothèque nationale de France.

sign of the cross, and put his trust in the Lord. . . . He swung back to the woods and skirted around the three, leaving the roadway to them, and himself hurrying after the domestic and the cart.[22]

This rather amusing episode shows us that a spiritual battle against demonic seduction can sometimes be won by a simple brandishing of the cross, a method that Ermine also frequently employs. The demons here take a shape that they believe will appeal to Arnulf, a man after all. But he can walk away from the temptresses, while Ermine is most often captive in her bedroom when the demonic assaults occur. And, interestingly, the sexy demons that appear to Ermine are both male and female, an intriguing variation on both the older hagiographic stereotypes and the more modern one of the witch crazes.

How does Ermine behave in her encounters with demons, and what do these encounters signify? We have to remember here that Jean le Graveur repeatedly states that he only chose to recount the most marvelous of Ermine's experiences. So we have to assume that he omitted many more demonic assaults. As he does throughout the *Visions,* Jean shapes what we can know about Ermine's comportment, and therefore the episodes he recounts must have a special significance. Before examining Ermine's experiences in light of Brakke and Cohn's above-cited contentions regarding the double-edged quality of sexy demons (they are frightening *and* seductive) and their links to human desires, let us see what "actually" happens in these episodes.

We remember that Ermine first came into Jean le Graveur's orbit as a forty-six-year-old woman, soon to be the widow of her seventy-two-year-old peasant husband, whom Jean describes as frail and elderly. Although forty-six is not the prime of life for a woman in the fourteenth century,[23] the accounts of the physical work she does just before moving into the room off Jean's institution suggest that she was robust and in relatively good health, still a sexual being, as we will see when she is wooed by demons. As we saw earlier, Ermine began her career as Jean's chosen holy woman with episodes of extreme penance, tying a rope around her waist that then embedded itself in her flesh. She clearly stated the reason for this severe castigation of her body : "I hate my body for the sins it committed" (*Je hay mon corps pour les pechez que il a fait*; 53). The past tense indicates that she is thinking of her married life and her past sexual activities. Hatred of her sexual past is the premise, then, that defines Ermine's relationship to her own body. Ermine's sexually tinged experiences with demons in human shape are excruciatingly repetitive but can nonetheless be grouped in some clusters of which I will consider a few in detail.

After the initial demonic experiences we looked at earlier (the horned devil, the demonic husband, and the "friend" from the countryside), things come to a head on Sunday, November 28, 1395: her cushion is violently snatched from her bed as is her rosary from her hands. Both are found the next day in the churchyard. She goes back to bed and sees a piece of paper ripped from the wall, followed by a pot of holy water thrown in her direction, which is then shattered on the planks of her bed.[24] After a violent fight with a demon who tries to take away her tablet with the *arma Christi,* the two sexy demons we already met in Chapter 3 appear: "Suddenly she saw in the middle of her bedchamber a young and handsome man and a young and beautiful woman; they began to embrace and kiss each other and then lay down on the floor and committed a sin together. And the devil did all this in front of her because he wanted her to take evil pleasure in fleshly sin (58)."[25] Once the young couple is done, the man stands before Ermine's bed and taunts her: you kill yourself by fasting, he sneers, and practice all sorts of penance (hair shirt, cords, bed of straw, staying awake all night, etc.), but it is all for naught! You'll go to hell anyway and would be better off enjoying your body (58–59). After haranguing her some more, the couple leaves.

Interestingly, Jean adds no comment to this rather lengthy narrative. The "temptation" is framed as a voyeuristic experience: Ermine is witnessing an episode that could occur in a *fabliau* or in one of the more sexually explicit romances. But what is important is that this scene of sexual intercourse is performed exclusively for her. This is not a demonic attack or an incubus trying to seduce Ermine, nor the calling forth of demons associated with traditional magic. It is a sexual object lesson that demonstrates sensual pleasure and encourages her to abandon the castigation of her body—because she is damned anyway and no amount of physical penance will change that fact. This questioning of the value of penitential practices fits into the challenges to orthodox beliefs we explored in Chapter 3. The human and seductively beautiful form of the couple resembles some of the tempters familiar from older saints' lives, all the way from the women who tempt the desert father Saint Anthony to brother Arnulf's three enchanting ladies who waylay him on his daily errand. What makes this scene remarkable, though, is that we witness the sexual act of a couple. Usually, male saints are tempted by female demons, and female saints are attacked by male demons. Here, a young demonic couple tries to corrupt Ermine by example and not by violent attacks or active seduction. And when they focus on Ermine's body, they tie together sex and the uselessness of physical forms of penance. What "hidden desire" could be revealed here? Ermine was not a nun but a widow who had undoubtedly led an active sexual life when married. This young couple's function, then, may be to recall to Ermine actions that she now considers a sin, to relive what had been but to reject it in her new life of penance and saintly aspirations.

About ten days after the embarrassing scene in the streets of Reims that opened this chapter, Ermine is lifted up and kissed by a demon in her room. He then stretches out next to her in bed but does not molest her: he begins to snore and vanishes only in the morning, leaving behind him a feeling of intense cold.[26] A mere three nights later, on February 11, 1396, Ermine has a very "ugly" dream (*un songe moult lait*; 88), a term that denotes a sexual dream. Angered by this dream Ermine wakes up and finds herself in the company of three male demons, dressed in black hoods and tights, with little mantles attached just below their buttocks and extremely pointy shoes.[27] They want to tempt her into evil carnal pleasures and expose themselves to her (*lui monstroient leurs ordures*; 88). Since she has some lights in her room, she hides her face in the bed in order not to have to see the demons' genitals. They then threaten her with taking her straight to hell; one of them grabs her by the feet and slings her over his back as if she were a cow. They hang her by the feet from the ceiling—her dress is reversed and falls over her head—and then drop her. Miraculously, she is not hurt, only horrified. Before leaving they taunt her by promising to come back when she is less well armed (89), implying that at present her piety protects her from the ultimate outrage.

The motif of the reversed dress seems to be a realistic touch, but it takes on a deeper significance when we look at the *Life* of the saintly Cistercian nun Lukardis of Oberweimar (1274–1309). Lukardis suffered from a large number of illnesses and often had what appear to have been seizures while lying in bed. She would arch her back and elevate her stomach with head and feet seemingly nailed to the bed. Her hagiographer underlines one feature he considers miraculous: when Lukardis stood on her head with her feet in the air (which she seemed to do for a long time [*longo tempore*]) her dress seemed to be glued to her calves, so much so that "one would think it was firmly sewn together."[28] Lukardis was thus spared the immodesty of having her body exposed during her trancelike stance. Ermine is not so fortunate. In an incident dated November 11, 1395, demons drag poor Ermine by her feet around her room so violently that "she found herself on her stomach with her hair shirt and nightshirt so hiked up that she lay with her naked stomach on the floor" (59). This incident occurs just two days after the sexual exhibitionism of the young demonic couple, which, as we recall, also took place on the floor. Although these two events are not explicitly linked, Ermine's lying almost naked on the floor with her shirts upside down seems to be a strong sexual image. We saw in Chapter 2 how tricky it may have been for Jean le Graveur to describe such a scene without indicating any kind of voyeurism on his part.

A similarly sexually charged incident occurs some time later. On April 30, 1396, Ermine is propositioned (*requist . . . de villenie*; 113) by a squire (*un écuyer*), and later the same day she has another "ugly" dream. Again she wakes up and finds three male demons, as black as people from overseas g3Ir

(*d'oultre la mer*, 113) in her room. They do not utter a word but expose their
genitals. As if this were not enough, now three sexy female demons appear,
dressed in fashionable black gowns with necklines so low that they show parts
of their breasts.[29] All the demons approach her bed "as if they were wanting
to commit a sin" (*comme se ilz voulissent faire pechié*; 113). Ermine quickly
hides her face in the bed, and when the demons are done, they sound a
trumpet! They then disappear, leaving behind a great stench.

May 14, 1396, is another very bad day for Ermine. A huge viper almost
strangles her,[30] and a demon tangles her up in her cloak, in fact imprisons
her in it until matins. At the same time, another viper slithers up her body,
and when she finally gets loose and listens to the matins service from her
window, a demon kisses her and holds her in a tight embrace till daylight
appears. "Thus," Jean comments, "she spent the night in this battle without
sleeping" (120). A mere two nights later

> a demon grabbed her from behind, threw her on the ground and lay
> down alongside her. He had the face of a man but made of black
> leather, and he was so heavy that the woman could not get up, and
> he was as cold as an icicle. And he breathed two or three times on
> her and throughout her bedchamber with a breath more stinking
> than that of a dead body. The woman was so filled with stink that
> she thought she would die [*crever*]. And he held her like that under-
> neath him from the first bell of matins until daybreak. No one said
> anything, neither the one nor the other, but while she was in this
> trouble, a voice came near the woman and said twice "Do not be
> frightened, woman, they will let you go soon." (120)

A couple of weeks later Ermine has another "ugly" dream. Angered by the
sexual feelings this dream conjures up, she leaves her bed and gets dressed.
Looking to the side, she sees a fully dressed demon lying near her. He vanishes when she throws holy water on him.

What are we to make of these kinds of episodes? We know that Ermine
steadfastly resisted the many temptations the demons put in her path. Toward
the end of her life the hermit Paul the Simple, this time in his incarnation as
a true saint, testifies that Ermine had "many strong temptations especially of
her body" (*moult de fortes temptacions et par especial de son corps*; 144) and
that she was twice asked to marry (presumably by demons), but that she told

Jean many times that she would rather be burned alive. When tempted, Ermine addresses herself as "dirty, stinking carrion" (*orde charongne puant*, 144) and flagellates herself until the blood runs down her body. This kind of extreme mortification is quite common in the lives of medieval saintly women. But how common were the sexual torments inflicted on Ermine?

Exhibitionist demons were not as common as demons inflicting pain and vexations. Having sex in front of visionary women is an activity located at the extreme end of demonic intervention in human life. Two examples come to mind, each associated with a woman whose travails with demons were extraordinarily complex and dramatic. Christina of Stommeln, for six weeks in a row, suffered the nightly apparitions of a demon who brought a woman and a child with him, claiming, "There is no joy greater than the joining of a man to a woman and that which a woman has with a child." He then proceeded to have sex with the woman in front of Christina. While watching this scene, her biographer says, she was "greatly tempted." Christina also confessed to imagining a seduction by a man of "ill repute" who threatened to rape her at knife point. She then imagined how she grabbed his knife and stabbed herself in the thigh.[31] Christina thus resorted to bloody self-punishment (in this case in her imagination only) equal to that employed by Ermine to resist sexual temptation.

Francesca Romana (1384–1440), the noble married saint from Rome whose discernment abilities will come to the fore in Chapter 5, had similar experiences, even though she was not alone in bed: "Sexual demons appeared to her nightly as naked men, women, and children engaging in sodomitic orgies, all the while as she was lying in bed beside her husband."[32] Even worse than Ermine's episode with the demon who almost kills her with his bad breath is a horrible incident where the devil brought a decaying male corpse to Francesca and pressed her down on it. Although no one else could see the corpse, everyone could smell it: her family recognized "the horrid odor that pervaded the room and stuck to her clothes for days despite all their sanitary efforts." From then on Francesca associated this smell with any male body.[33]

Margery Kempe, Francesca's contemporary (Margery was born around 1373 and wrote her book in the 1430s), can also provide some points of comparison. In chapter 59 of her book she describes how certain doubts about the word of God resulted in a punishment that for twelve days made her fall into "many hours of foul thoughts and foul recollections of lechery and all uncleanness, as though she would have prostituted herself with all manner of people." She was subjected to the "horrible and abominable" view of male genitals belonging to priests and other men of all religions. The devil ordered her to choose which one of these men she would like to have first but added that eventually she would have to prostitute herself to all of them.[34] Linked by the idea of a holy woman being likened to—or even condemned to be—a prostitute, the two texts differ in their use of the exhibitionist motif. While Ermine witnesses male demons exposing themselves as a prelude to their having sex with female demons, Margery is urged to choose her own sexual partners, a scenario that is closer to that of many later stories involving incubi and succubi, as well as those that feature the temptation of male saints like brother Arnulf of Villers.

What distinguishes Ermine's experiences is the frequency of demonic sexual temptations and their very personal nature. The dramatization of the demons' appearances in Ermine's chamber is so detailed and so lively that we seem to be witnesses to some obscene playacting. The minute descriptions of the demons' black outfits and of their words and actions, the blowing of the post-intercourse trumpet, the snoring demon stretched out next to her in bed—all these features individualize Ermine's story and give a specific cast to her sexual temptations. The demons do not assault her sexually, although they do treat her roughly. Ermine is forced to witness sexual scenes and to suffer the proximity of demons who have kissed her. But would she ever have been truly tempted by these demons, as "witches" were believed to be in so many tales of demonic sexual contacts?

The idea of women's voluntary copulation with demons is prominent in such late medieval treatises as the *Hammer of Witches,* authored in 1486–87 by the Dominican inquisitors Krämer and Sprenger.[35] Walter Stephens has shown that Krämer located the divide between women being pestered by demons against their will and women searching out demons for copulation around the year 1400. Krämer also tried to demonstrate that the later kind of devil worship often involved sexual submission to demons. Thus Ermine's steadfast refusal of the demons' advances can be seen on the one hand as an imitation of the ancient desert fathers but on the other as a conscious rejection of what was quickly becoming a determining feature of the "witch."[36] Indeed, Ermine fits very well into the older paradigm of the heroic struggle against demons initiated by figures like Saint Anthony. However much the demons accuse Ermine of being a whore, in Jean's text there is no indication that she would ever give in to, let alone pursue, the black, leathery creatures appearing in her bedroom. Still, Ermine, as we saw, hated her body. In the modern age of psychoanalysis we cannot help but speculate that the demons

and their multifarious sexual activities are linked in some way to what David
Brakke called "the self's erotic desire."[37] Jerome Kroll and Bernard Bachrach
go even further. They suggest that as we analyze the strange behavior of some
saints, we "seem to shrink from drawing some obvious conclusions." That is,
we refuse "to acknowledge mental disorder of some sort when it is obviously
present."[38] Before speculating on Ermine's mental state let us segue from
demons in human form to those in animal shape and see whether sexual
connotations dominate here.

Animal Trouble

During the last ten months of her life Ermine is haunted by a veritable
demonic and unruly zoo. Animals sometimes played a role in the activities of
sorcerers and later on would be part of rituals related to witchcraft, such as
the Witches' Sabbath, where people were believed to adore (and worse) goats
or cats. To avoid any kind of association with witchcraft or demonic possession, Jean strives to present the kind of "animal trouble" Ermine experiences
as part of a venerable hagiographic tradition. The ancient desert saints play a
prominent role in this domain.[39] Mostly they were tamers and friends of wild
animals, but some, like Saint Anthony, were subjected to horrible torments
and temptations in the shape of animals. In *The Golden Legend*, the popular
thirteenth-century collection of saints' lives by Jacobus de Voragine, we read
that once, after a savage attack by demons, Anthony was left for dead. But
then "lying prostrated by the pain of his wounds, in the strength of his spirit
he challenged the demons to renew the combat. They appeared in the forms
of various wild beasts and tore at his flesh cruelly with their teeth, horns, and
claws. Then of a sudden a wonderful light shone in the place and drove all
the demons away."[40] Saint Anthony provided the prototype or model for this
kind of animal trouble. His iconography is replete with the most horrific
creatures, reflecting the boundless medieval imagination of evil. These creatures are part of "demonic bestiary, . . . a frightening zoo of . . . evil creatures
whose task it was to attack and terrify the saints."[41] As Christine Ruhrberg
observes, "In the high and late Middle Ages demons appear primarily as
dangerous, horrifying, or disgusting animals. There are hagiographic models
for just about every kind of animal in the role of persecutor, except the
friendliest of domestic animals, such as sheep, cows or calves." It is the task
of these demons to physically tempt and torment humans: they belong to the

ugly and transient part of the world and can thus represent humans' lowest instincts and desires.[42]

Christina of Stommeln is one of the extreme cases of a would-be saint who had plenty of animal trouble: "Eight days before the Purification, when I was praying . . . before my bed, I heard the sound of a toad, and I felt the presence of a demon. At first I was scared by its voice, but, regaining my courage, I [continued] . . . my prayer. I heard it coming closer to me, then I felt it enter my clothes. After that I sensed it slowly climbing over my members, until finally it placed itself over my chest. Its nails pressed my flesh so hard that it left deep wounds after it. Thus, wherever I went, it remained there for eight days. . . . This was no small hardship for me." Aviad Kleinberg, who cites this passage, adds "But what does this episode mean? Clearly Peter [of Dacia, her 'hagiographer'] did not know." John, the schoolmaster who writes her *Life*, repeats again and again an account of demonic assaults of this type (e.g., a "snake . . . crawled over her, entered her body, and stayed there for eight days"), but neither he nor Peter provides an explanation. As Kleinberg puts it, "Rather than attempting to understand Christina's own spirituality—a spirituality laying great emphasis on violent, repulsive, negative images, laden with sexual suggestions—Peter preferred to emphasize in his reconstruction of Christina his own spirituality."[43] Did Jean le Graveur also strive to shape Ermine's image in light of his own spirituality? How does he deal with the strong sexual imagery of many of the episodes involving animals?

For a modern audience the kind of scenes "of penetration, . . . defilement and contamination" we find in Ermine's *Visions* and many saints' lives have strong sexual connotations. Elizabeth Alvilda Petroff speculates that for a medieval audience serpents in female saints' lives were "symbolic of the threat of sexuality."[44] Umiliana de' Cerchi's experiences with a serpent (she tied her feet together to prevent it from entering her body) and Benvenuta Bojani's nightly encounter with a demonic snake that pressed itself against her naked body suggest that "sex is demonic" and that perhaps sexual fantasies surfaced in the form of demonic attacks.[45] In Dyan Elliott's formulation, "demonic possession is essentially a hostile takeover."[46] There certainly is a nightmare quality to many of these incidents, reflecting what William Short calls "the inner wilderness" associated with the apparitions of animals.[47] But these tense moments with snakes can also be occasions for self-recognition and growth, as Petroff argues for Saint Verdiana of Castelfiorentino, who, although at first terribly frightened, eventually domesticates her snakes. She apparently

consciously modeled herself on Saint Anthony.[48] Another striking example
is Saint Colette de Corbie (1381–1447), the great reformer of the Franciscan
order we encountered in the previous chapter. Her biographer Pierre de
Vaux equals Jean le Graveur in the lengthy and minute description of the
vexations and anguish caused by demonic animals in the saint's life. The
list of animals haunting Colette bears a close resemblance to Ermine's
demonic zoo: horrible toads, vipers, spiders, thousands of ants, snails, and
lots of insects, especially flies. The historian Pierre Boglioni speculates that
this list may reflect a personal phobia of Colette's, although the almost
identical cast of animal characters in Ermine's *Visions* would not support
this point. But he also suggests that the urban and bourgeois milieu where
Colette spent her life may have determined which animals could cause
particular anguish to the saint. As for Ermine the continuous animal invasion creates a constant psychic horror.[49]

Ermine fits into these patterns in diverse ways. Here is a sample of the
large variety of creatures appearing to her: one night a strange being snuggles
up to her in bed; she thinks it may be her cat, but no, "it brayed loudly with
the voice of a pig" (67)! A couple of nights later three huge animals resem-
bling bears appear (even though her window was closed), with flaming snouts
and long hair, followed by a pig with its skin on fire.[50] One night Ermine
sees a gigantic dog with red eyes sitting on her windowsill (55), followed by a
huge serpent, a black crow, and a bear. On January 31, 1396, a big cat curls
up on her chest; she mistakes it for her own but then with fear and trembling
realizes that it is a demon. After she chases it away with a stick, another
rolled-up cat with red eyes like fire appears on her bed; this time she is afraid
to beat it and it eventually disappears (82). Some time after that she lies down
in her bed and is tormented by flies, which get under her dress and crawl up
her body. This battle lasts several days; she finally escapes and is comforted
by her confessor, but as soon as she gets home, it all starts again (97). On
Easter 1396 a "voice" encourages her to doubt the Eucharist, and that same
evening seven bats fly in front of her face; she uses the flyswatter Jean le
Graveur had given her, but they will not leave. They finally do so at daybreak
but leave behind a terrible stink (102).

It is difficult to choose one animal out of this whole zoo for closer analysis. For me, the incidents involving toads and serpents are particularly significant. Let us first look at toads. In her lengthy analysis of the toad episode
in the *Life* of Christina of Stommeln, Ruhrberg traces this animal's sexual
connotations, in particular the relationship to the female genitals and desire.[51]

Nonetheless, she warns against an overly simplistic equation between traditional iconographic representations and symbolic values and a "psychological" (or psychoanalytical) analysis of her protagonist. The toad, then, more than most of the other animals that haunt Ermine—an exception would be the snakes—is closely linked to sexuality in the medieval imagination, but it also has so many other connotations and functions that we can linger a bit over this not terribly attractive creature.[52]

The association between the toad and *luxure* (excessive sexuality) as well as desire for riches and pride is of long standing in medieval culture. In a sculpture from about 1130 at Moissac a voluptuous woman is attacked by a toad lodged between her legs, while snakes suck on her breasts. Another sculpture at Charlieu shows a woman being penetrated by snakes while a toad latches on to her breast.[53] In his *Scala coeli* (ca. 1327–1330) Jean Gobi tells of a woman who does not confess to the sin of adultery with a relative, dies, and then appears in a frightening vision to two friars: she is being tormented by snakes, toads, lizards, and dogs. The toads, the woman in the vision explains, are latched onto her eyes to punish her for her "luxurious glances."[54] In other instances toads represent the female genitalia. In a positive sense we find numerous votive offerings in the shape of toads related to good outcomes in childbirth.[55] In a more ribald vein we can look at a German *fabliau* where the woman's sex separates itself from her and is mistaken for a toad as it roams the streets. Eventually the two are reunited.[56]

A striking example of the association of toads with sexuality can be found in the *Life* of Ida of Nivelles (1199–1231). When a young woman disregards Ida's advice to stay away from a priest but rather engages in sexual relations with him, Ida has a vision of two toads: "By the Lord's revelation she *saw, and, behold* (Apoc. 4.1) two great toads appeared, a male and a female, with the male visibly mounting the female. By this she understood that that sinful fellow and this sin-laden lass had reached the stage of fornication. A short delay and the male toad went totally crazy, veered away, and off he went; but the female with an unwavering gait, made her way to Ida, who tucked her about with her cloak."[57] The girl, abandoned by her lover, returns to Ida's convent of La Ramée, does penance and never strays again. This vision confirms that toads could represent human sexual activity in a medieval context. Ida's protective attitude toward Madame toad is very touching here and a far cry from what happens to those who are attacked by these same animals.

Christina of Stommeln has frequent encounters with toads. One of the most dramatic attacks, briefly mentioned above, occurs when Christina is lying in her bed praying and a toad enters her dress, ascends to her chest, digs in, and remains there for eight days. Finally it dawns on Christina that this is a demon and that all she has to do is admonish him and throw him to the ground. The demon admits that he is vanquished and promises not to reappear.[58] While Kleinberg argues that the meaning of this episode remains obscure to the hagiographer and thus to us, I would propose with Ruhrberg that the toad demon is sent as a test to Christina: she conquers him through her faith and he becomes powerless.[59] This incident fits into the pattern of hostile attacks by animals that are quite common in hagiography: although not sought after, these attacks serve to exemplify a person's holiness. William Short identifies a three-part structure for these demonic animal assaults: the apparition of the animal-demon; recognition by the holy person; and command to depart in Christ's name.[60]

This brief toad survey shows that apparitions of toads can have all kinds of different modalities and meanings.[61] They can have symbolic and allegorical value or they can be stand-ins for demons that test a person's sanctity. In many contexts, both iconographic and textual, there is a sexual element that comes to the fore. Let us now see how Ermine's experiences fit into these patterns.

Several episodes that all happen in a two-day span (April 15–17, 1396) show the profound significance toads have for Ermine, as described by Jean. On the evening of April 15, 1396, Ermine falls asleep but is soon awakened by the croaking of three toads as large as ducks. As they try to get into Ermine's bed, she chases them with a stick, recognizing them as demons. While she is proud of the fact that she can beat *des ennemis* (demons; 109), she nonetheless has to take refuge on her table for the remainder of the night. Then they vanish, but Ermine searches through her bedclothes just to make sure they are not in her bed. The next night Ermine dreams that she is in the throes of death and that devils and angels are arguing about her soul. Then she sees people with toads attached to their faces who stick their heads into these people's mouths. She wakes up and finds herself in exactly this situation: a fat toad is attached to her face! She manages to pull off the toad and throw it on the ground, where it makes a soft splash and says *oing* (110). Getting out of bed, Ermine slips on some more toads that for all their disgusting slipperiness have beautiful eyes, "as toads commonly have" (*comme ont les crapaux communellement*; 110).[62] Ermine sprinkles them with holy water and they vanish. But she is so overcome with nausea that she has to rinse her mouth with vinegar several times. Finally, in a kind of crescendo, on

Monday, April 17, she finds three huge toads moving around between her legs. Again, they vanish with the application of holy water. One further incident on May 28, 1396, rounds out the picture. As she is praying in her room, she suddenly feels three large toads beneath her. They disappear, and right after this Ermine falls asleep and has one of her many "very ugly dreams" (*songe[s] moult lait*; 124), that is, a dream of a sexual nature. She wakes up and finds stretched out next to her in bed a demon, fully dressed. When sprinkled with holy water, he vanishes.

There are plenty of other toad incidents that fall into similar patterns. Often the toads are part of a whole host of animals, that is, they appear in the company of ravens, flies, snakes, lizards, owls, bats, and other creatures. Looking at the major episodes just presented, we can see several levels of meaning. First, the toads come closer and closer to Ermine's sexual self: from her room (she fears they have entered her bed), to her face, to her sexual organs. Second, Ermine recognizes that they are demons; thus her discernment as well as her ability to vanquish them with holy water are highlighted. Finally, they also appear in a dream that is then transported into reality. The people tormented by toads evoke the damned on their way to hell, as they are shown in countless medieval images and sculptures. Ermine's freeing herself from this toad thus announces her salvation and ultimate victory over demons. By showing both "real" toads in Ermine's room and recounting her dream, where toads are the figurative representation of damnation, Jean achieves the multiple goals of revealing Ermine's gumption, strength, and ability of discernment, all of which then lead to our recognition of her saintliness and election.

More than the toad, serpents have strong biblical connections: from the Book of Genesis where the serpent's corruption of Eve leads to the expulsion from paradise to the Book of Revelation (12:9) where the "ancient serpent" is the equivalent of the "Devil and Satan," the Bible has nothing good to say about serpents. And although there are some kindly, wise, and useful serpents in the hagiographic tradition, for the most part they are associated with the "threat of sexuality."[63]

Ermine suffers from close to a dozen encounters with serpents in various contexts. The first instance, on December 5, 1395, is a dream in which Ermine finds herself in a ditch filled with serpents and dragons where she can find no rest (62). This is all Jean le Graveur says about this horrific dream, although a couple of sentences further he mentions that the devil "brought Ermine ideas against the faith." The association thus seems to be a biblical one: Eve's serpent that was at the root of original sin and the serpent of the Apocalypse come to mind, especially through the conjunction of the serpent and the dragon. The next serpent is no longer a dream but one that enters her bedroom as a physical presence (65). It is ugly and horrible, with a huge tail and its gigantic tongue sticking out "as large dogs do in summer when they are thirsty and hot." The stink coming from its mouth makes Ermine think that all the garbage of the entire world resides in this serpent. The monster approaches and shows its fangs as if to strangle Ermine. But she has the presence of mind to make the sign of the cross, and the serpent vanishes. But the stink remains so strong that Ermine vomits right in front of her bed and cannot eat anything even the next day. To help her Jean gives her a little lavender sachet to put under her nose. This last detail moves this almost archetypal encounter with the hideous serpent into the everyday context of Ermine's life. The scene also shows Jean's solicitousness toward his charge. Who would have thought that an Augustinian friar would come equipped with a lavender sachet?

Some time goes by. Demonic bats, owls, even a monkey penetrate into her bedroom. Then, on the evening of May 3, 1396, as Ermine confesses herself to Jean le Graveur in the Augustinians' chapter house she says, "Pray for me, for it seems to me that my hair is standing on end and my whole body is bristling with fear; I really think that something will happen tonight" (114). And indeed it does. After going into her room, she prays and keeps the light on because of her great fear, a justified fear, for two huge serpents as thick as her arm are curled up near her wall. At first they lie still; then one of them suddenly rises up and hits her with its pointy snout right on her nose. "I myself saw the imprint on her face the next day," Jean adds here (114). Then the other serpent attacks from behind, coils itself around her neck, and tries to stick its snout into Ermine's nose and mouth. She begins to bleed and suffocate. In the nick of time two demonic angels appear, both dressed in white but one with wings and the other without. One of them takes a kind of magic wand and touches the serpent, whereupon it falls to the ground. In return for this kindly act the angel-demons want Ermine's pledge of fidelity. When she refuses and states that only Jesus Christ will have her fidelity, the serpent reattaches itself to her neck and torments her till dawn. Ermine spends part of the next day vomiting.

Events come to a sort of crescendo about ten days later, just after the episode with the icicle-like demon we encountered earlier. Red beasts the size of calves invade her room. They have horns just like dragons, but they do not attack her; they just frighten her. Then another serpent coils itself around

Ermine's neck, and the red beasts come back and attack her. The next day, as she collects dried laundry in the garden, she has an encounter with a demonic impostor claiming to be Saint Mary Magdalene.[64] Over the next few days Ermine is attacked by gigantic toads biting her thigh; by another serpent slithering along her belly and into the neckline of her cloak; by several lizards; by three huge lions (a lady in white, another fake Saint Magdalene, defends her); by three bats that Ermine chases away with the flyswatter Jean had given her earlier as a defense against flies; and more toads. These kinds of attacks continue until Ermine's death in August 1396.

There is no attempt on Jean le Graveur's part to interpret any of this. He draws no moral lessons and does not try to associate any of these animals with traditions coming from bestiaries or allegorical treatises on animals.[65] In medieval culture each animal brings with itself a long tradition of meaning. Even the seemingly innocuous fly, for example, has strong connections to the devil. It was believed that swallowing a fly equaled swallowing the devil. Saint Dominic exorcised flies, as is reported in *The Golden Legend*, and the late fifteenth-century inquisitor Heinrich Krämer reminded his readers that the biblical name Beelzebub meant "Man of Flies."[66] But for Ermine and Jean all animals are equally demonic, and the means to combat them are astonishing: either some demonic angel or counterfeit saint appears and offers to rescue Ermine (sometimes they do, sometimes they do not), or they take the form of the lavender sachet and or the flyswatter that Jean gives to Ermine to sustain her in her nightly battles. The demonic animals are part of Ermine's heroic virtue, one of the elements necessary for sainthood, although Jean does not spell this out explicitly. Further, there is no explicit reference to any of the sexual aspects of the demonic animal assaults nor any attempt to interpret, say, the image of a snake slithering up Ermine's nightgown.

In his later assessment of Ermine's experiences, the famous theologian Jean Gerson, acknowledges her "austerity and affliction." He believes that God has chosen this poor, old woman, illiterate and without any resources, to show that the weakest can confound the strongest. But he does not mention any of the hundreds of animal attacks and even suggests that maybe not everything happened the way Ermine described it but that nonetheless one should have faith in her.[67]

Aerial Journeys

Every child knows that magicians and witches can ride around on broomsticks. For many inquisitors it was a given that in certain heretical sects a person was able to fly through the air.[68] But ordinary human beings experienced flight as well, not as self-propelled aviators as did some magicians, but with some assistance, such as the demons who acted as "invisible helicopters" in so many miracle stories.[69]

In the twelfth century Guibert of Nogent recalled a visionary experience he had as a boy: two devils kidnapped him from a church dedicated to the Virgin Mary and deposited him on its roof. Later he found himself safely within the church walls.[70] Taking people on aerial journeys seems to be a time-honored demonic activity. In later centuries, of course, these journeys became a hallmark of the witch, who was believed to use this demonic means of transportation to attend the witches' Sabbath.[71] Often goats provided aerial transportation. In a seventeenth-century German witch trial a woman testified that a goat would show up like a taxicab at her doorstep and bleat to signal that it was time to fly to a witches' Sabbath dance.[72] Eventually, the demons or demonic animals carrying the supposed witches were supplemented or replaced by forks or broomsticks.[73] Ermine's experiences take place in a period of transition: in an age of belief in demons and magic and just around the beginning of systematic formulations of witchcraft. There is a great danger, then, that the demonic kidnappings she has to suffer could expose her to accusations of witchcraft: we saw earlier that at one point she is warned that her many encounters with demons could place her under suspicion of being a *sorcière* and even land her in jail (153). Again, Jean has to take care not to represent these aerial journeys as witchlike activities but rather make them fit into the pattern of vexations reminiscent of an older tradition of saints suffering demonic onslaughts. Let us remember that Jean le Graveur does not represent Ermine's experiences as visions but as things that happened to her in a waking state. This also holds true for her aerial adventures. Some of them are rather mild. On February 2, 1396, for example, "someone embraced her with two arms and lifted her up in the air; and she did not know where he was carrying her, and she didn't see anything, and no one said anything to her. And he carried her back to her bed and put her down and the one who had carried her lay down behind her and began to snore loudly. And the woman remained like this, with the demon behind her, until morning, and she could not move or get up and yet he did not hold her down. She felt very cold and when it was day she did not know what had become of him and she got up" (85).

Things get worse the following week when she is again lifted up, but this time she is carried high above the courtyard and dumped in front of the

church. She screams but is not hurt. The proof of this misadventure is supplied by her scattered shoes, which Jean orders a friar to collect from the
courtyard (89)! On April 17, 1396, Ermine is reciting her Ave Maria when
three black-clad, black-skinned leathery demons appear, talking among
themselves in an unknown language. Finally they shout at her, "What Ave
Maria? What Ave Maria? We'll forbid you to say your Ave Maria!" (110).
Then

> they grabbed her and carried her away to the ridge of the high slate
> roof of our church, right next to the stone cross, that is, the church
> of the Val-des-Ecoliers in Reims. And while carrying her out the
> window they hit her head badly on the frame, the signs of which
> one could still see days later. And when she was on the ridge of the
> roof, the demons gathered around her and spoke to her in horrible
> voices, but she did not know what they were saying. When she was
> sitting on the roof, she leaned as best as she could against the wall,
> and when she was two feet from the ridge, she clung as best she
> could to the stone cross which is on the gable of the church. And
> she hung on, by God's grace, as best she could.

While the original demons vanish, three new ones appear and taunt her.
They offer to help her down from the roof if only she agrees to leave Jean le
Graveur whom they call a cheat and a liar. They lift her up in the air for a
moment and threaten to drop her. Of course, she refuses to leave Jean and
commends her soul to God, whereupon the demons throw her with great
force from the roof. While she lies unconscious in the courtyard, a man in
white appears and identifies himself as the saintly hermit, Paul the Simple,
who had helped her get back from another kidnapping, which we will discuss
in a moment. He supports her so that she can make it back to her bed where
she stays for a while, still frightened out of her wits. Jean then adds proofs of
this horrific incident: Ermine was wearing a head scarf and carried a rosary
when she was kidnapped. Jean found the scarf the next day in a garden that
lies between the Augustinians' house and Ermine's room, while a servant
found the rosary she had dropped while being transported by demons "in
our churchyard" (112).

Realistic details abound in this episode. Jean's matter-of-fact reporting
on "our church in Reims," the garden, the servant, the scarf, and the rosary
has the effect of making this demonic story true, almost domesticating it. We

are never allowed to doubt Ermine's horrific experiences but only to witness
them and, Jean undoubtedly hopes, to empathize with her and admire her
heroic virtue.

By far the most dramatic event involving an aerial kidnapping is a trip
to the woods of Nanteuil, where the outlaw former papal official Jean de
Varennes holds court.[74] Backtracking to February 23, 1396, we watch Ermine
leave her house and be accosted on the street by three men dressed in black,
riding black horses. Without a word one of them grabs her and throws her
on the back of his horse "as if she were a suitcase" (*comme se se feust une male*;
93), and before she knows it she finds herself in the woods in the midst of an
enormous crowd of demons dressed in black. A huge sack of money is meant
to tempt her, but of course she refuses it and complains that she has been
brought to these woods by air and against her will. This is a crucial point
since it differentiates Ermine's aerial adventures from those of witches who
were believed to attend Sabbaths willingly. Then trumpets begin to sound as
if a huge army were assembling, and the demons begin to talk about "ugly
things," although Ermine does not really understand what they are saying.
The setting of this demonic assembly resembles that of later supposed
witches' Sabbaths, but here again the witch scenario does not come to pass:
the demons vanish and Ermine sees nothing but trees around her. Eventually
a white-haired man (we later learn that this is Paul the Simple) appears and
tells her that she in the woods of Nanteuil. Is this far from Reims? Ermine
wants to know.[75] Yes, she is told, but you can use the steeple of Saint Lié as
a landmark to get safely home. Saint Lié is the place where Jean de Varennes
celebrates his controversial masses. Ermine, as it happens, arrives just in time
for such a mass and is seen by several people who know her well (94). She
then returns to Reims, again aided by the old man.

In this episode the demonic intersects with the political. Jean de Varennes, soon to be arrested by royal officials and probably executed, had retired
to the woods of Nanteuil, where his masses attracted crowds and shored up
opposition to Pope Benedict XIII in Avignon, his former employer. As we
saw repeatedly, Ermine was keenly interested in Jean de Varennes and his
fate. We can assume then that she made the risky trip to Nanteuil in order
to hear him preach. Thus the key to this episode can be found in the commentary Jean le Graveur adds: some people might think that Ermine went to
Nanteuil by herself and then invented the story of the kidnapping, he says.
But no, Jean maintains (in an incredibly convoluted explanation): she was
seen to leave the house at a certain hour and then was seen at Saint Lié

shortly afterward. Ergo, Ermine must have been transported by air (95). A skeptical reader might see a different scenario: a number of people noticed that Ermine was present at the mass Jean de Varennes celebrated that morning. Given Jean de Varennes's reputation as an enemy of the current pope, it seems likely that Jean le Graveur wanted to explain away Ermine's attendance by attributing it to a demonic kidnapping. Thus Jean uses a motif known from saints' lives as well as from magical practices and gives it a very individualized spin. The fact that he insists on the truth of these events and does not try to explain them as diabolical illusions is also important: Jean places Ermine's nocturnal journey not into the developing paradigm of the witches' flight but, as he does with all her demon-inflicted tribulations, into the traditional framework of saintly suffering, exemplified by such figures as Saint Anthony of the Desert.[76] The phenomena in Ermine's *Visions* exist at the intersection of magic, witchcraft, and saintly suffering, and it is the latter aspect that Jean highlights. For him, her experiences are thus manifestations of the painful trials she has to endure on the path to possible sainthood.

What to Believe?

Jean reports all of Ermine's demonic encounters as if they had really happened. Gerson's and other scholars' skepticism as to the reality of these events seems very foreign to him.[77] He does not present Ermine's experiences as hallucinations or even as demonic possession that would require the intervention of an exorcist. The omnipresence of demons is simply taken for granted in this period, and their functions are multiple. In the *Visions* we observe that they have a psychological function: they urge Ermine to leave her confessor and seem thus intent on breaking the close bond that unites these two people. They have an ideological function in that they confirm the reality of the divine: God's enemies can only act in a world controlled by the divine will.[78] If we do not believe this, we would adhere to a dualistic heresy that sees the universe divided into two equally powerful sides that eternally battle each other. The demons also have a political function, and this last category differentiates Ermine's *Visions* from most other texts about visionary women. The frequent comments on the hermit Jean de Varennes and the use of Jean le Graveur's opinion on this controversial personage as a tool to alienate Ermine from Jean show how the political crisis of the Great Schism seeps into human and demonic interactions alike. The appearance of these contemporary political problems also adds to the realism and authenticity of this text. That is, despite the horrific demonic assaults and the demons' malicious attacks on all that Ermine believes in, we are are still in fourteenth-century Reims, in the kingdom of France that has to deal with two popes vying for supremacy, and in the presence of a scholarly community that tries to sort out which kinds of experiences are sent by God and which by the devil. The process these scholars elaborated was that of the discernment of spirits, the topic of our fifth and final chapter.

CHAPTER 5

Ermine and the Discernment of Spirits

Imagine the following scenario: as you are about to go to sleep in your modest dwelling in medieval Reims, you hear the sound of a little bell. The door opens and two small angels enter, followed by a priest dressed in gold. He declares, "I am Saint Augustine," and offers to celebrate a mass right there in your bedroom. You can even stay in bed, and he will minister to you. Would you be pleased or slightly suspicious? Or even very suspicious? This is the kind of case that falls into the purview of the discernment of spirits, an ecclesiastical investigative procedure that had at its heart the possible confusion between demons and angels, a danger succinctly stated by Saint Paul in his second letter to the Corinthians: "For even Satan disguises himself as an angel of light" (2 Cor. 11:14).

The Discernment of Spirits

The discernment of spirits covers a number of different problematic distinctions: how can one decide whether a vision has been sent by God or by the devil? How can one distinguish a truly saintly human being from an impostor? How do we know, when a saint appears to us, whether he or she is the real thing or a demonic impersonator? The answers to these questions, although always present in theological discourse, began to be codified in a systematic way in the late fourteenth century.[1] All three questions will be addressed in this chapter, but prominence will be given to the last one, the answers to which makes Ermine's *Visions* one of the most striking texts of the late Middle Ages. For while demons appear to medieval people in all

Como lo maligno spirito
delegare essa bla dicc

FIGURE 9. Saint Francesca Romana and the Counterfeit Saint Onofrio. Fifteenth-century fresco, Rome, Tor de' Specchi. Reproduced with permission of the Madre Presidente, Tor de' Specchi.

kinds of guises, occasionally even as saints, the massive and variegated invasion of counterfeit saints (many of them bearing the attributes a medieval audience would recognize from images, statues, or stained-glass windows) Ermine experiences in her bedroom has no counterpart in other saintly biographies.[2]

Anxiety about the origins of visions was a constant in Christian thought from the very beginning but came to the fore in a period that saw a growing interest in the "regulation of sanctity" and that perceived "female spirituality progressively as a substantial threat."[3] Discernment procedures were discussed in theoretical treatises but also in prefaces to saints' lives or to revelations. For the theoretical approach a good example is Jean Gerson (1363–1429), the famous chancellor of the University of Paris, who authored multiple texts dealing with the distinction between true and false visions between 1402 and 1423. These texts, while having a theoretical bent, also include numerous illustrative anecdotes. The second category includes the preface to the *Revelations* of Constance of Rabastens. Around 1386 Raimond of Sabanac, the confessor of this pious laywoman from southern France, wrote down her very controversial revelations.[4] He prefaced the text with a treatise on the discernment of spirits that spelled out the criteria he deemed crucial for this process. The person examined must be "spiritual" as opposed to "secular"; he or she must be morally pure and state whether the vision occurred when he or she was awake or asleep. Thus the qualities of both the visionary and the visions need to be examined. Raimond adds the important point that not only could false things be taken for true but that the obverse may also occur: without perfect discernment a visionary may reject true things as false. We will see that this latter possibility caused much anguish to Ermine.

Rosalynn Voaden gives a succinct definition of the procedure of the discernment of spirits as it applies to visions, based on the writings of Alfonso of Pecha (1329/30–1389), the bishop of Jaén and the confessor of Saint Birgitta of Sweden (1303–1373). He treated discernment in a systematic way in his *Epistola solitarii ad reges* (The solitary's letter to kings):

> There are seven signs whereby one may tell a true visionary. The
> first and most definite sign is whether the person lives a virtuous life
> under the rule of a spiritual director. . . . The second sign is that, as
> a result of the vision, the soul feels inflamed by God's love and
> charity, and her faith, obedience and reverence to Holy Mother

Church are strengthened. Third, that the visionary feels a deep
inward knowledge of the truth of the revelation. Fourth, that the
revelations are always and only of true things, and accord with Scripture and accepted teachings. Fifth, a true vision is known by the
fruit it bears. Sixth, true visionaries will have the day and the hour
of their death revealed to them. And finally, seventh, posthumous
miracles will establish the status of the visionary beyond all
question.[5]

These tenets resemble very much those found in other treatises, such as Gerson's *On Distinguishing True from False Revelations* (1401–1402),[6] although
that text is more personal and anecdotal, filled with colorful examples of
problematic visionary women.

One important gauge in the discernment of spirits is the emotion caused
by a vision or an apparition. Fear can be a red flag indicating that demons
are attempting to deceive a visionary—Ermine will illustrate this point
below—while joy can signal the opposite, that is, a divinely sent vision. A
prime example of the latter can be found in the *Life* of Dorothea of Montau.
Her confessor asked her "how she could determine that she had been enrap-
tured and her visions during her ecstasy were neither dreams nor delusions."
She replies that her raptures always leave her filled with ardent love for God
and a clearer consciousness of her sins that "are disgusting" to her. Her body
feels heavy but her spirit feels strengthened. After Dorothea's explanation
Johannes of Marienwerder adds in his own voice that

> Dorothea was granted yet another sign to prove that she had not
> fallen victim to deception, for she was assured of the genuine nature
> of her illuminations by being so filled with joy and passion during
> ecstasy and even afterwards that her soul was softened to the point
> of melting. Such illumination, joy, exultation, and delicious taste of
> divine sweetness in a state of such abject humility and negation of
> her very being she could not have attained from the deceitful spirit.
> Furthermore, the Lord assured her that he himself would keep her
> safe from that evil.[7]

The author here weaves the major components of the discernment of spirits
not into a theoretical treatise but into a narrative about and by Dorothea. As
far as Johannes is concerned, the emotions she experiences as a result of her

raptures can by definition not be caused by deceptive demons. Even so, Johannes feels compelled to add another explicit disclaimer, citing the Lord's promise to protect Dorothea from deception. In one page Johannes employs two different literary means to illustrate Dorothea's discernment abilities and to guarantee the authenticity of her raptures: a dialogue between confessor and penitent in which Dorothea speaks of her experiences in her own voice and an authoritative commentary informed by his own theological knowledge.

Discernment is thus essentially a discourse that has to be mastered not only by the clerics charged with examining visionaries and writing about them but by the visionaries themselves; this discourse "provided both a vocabulary to articulate visionary experience and a set of criteria to evaluate the vision and the visionary."[8] Mastery of this discourse was especially important for women visionaries since they were considered to be an easier prey for demonic deception due to their innate frailty and gullibility. Voaden shows how throughout the centuries visionaries like the twelfth-century Hildegard of Bingen and the fifteenth-century Margery Kempe tried—with very different success rates—to internalize the discourse of discernment in both their actions and writings. Precise mastery of the discourse of discernment could make or break a visionary.

Much anxiety thus surrounded visionary experiences and their written records, something that Dyan Elliott dubbed "the trauma of textuality."[9] The striking example of Francesca Romana (1384–1440) cited by Elliott illustrates this trauma and brings together two aspects of the discernment process: to see whether a vision is divinely sent and whether the messenger is a true person or saint or a disguised demon. When in November 1430 Francesca is "immersed in prayer, her confessor Giovanni Mattiotti, seemingly enters her oratory, equipped with pen and parchment" and wants to proceed to write down her visions in order to turn them into a "great book." Francesca immediately senses a trap in this offer of a potential best-seller and unmasks the figure as a demon, whereupon the would-be ghost writer transforms himself into a dragon and tries to throw her off a balcony. Francesca recognizes this "aggressive" process of redaction as "spiritually lethal," as a dangerous appeal to her vanity.[10] Here, Francesca's humility was key to her discernment: she unmasked the demonic scribe almost instantly and thus identified the origin of the vision as diabolical. But some demons are harder to discern, as we will see shortly.

In Francesca's case discernment was needed in order to distinguish a demon from a human being and to identify the origin of the vision. Another purpose of the discernment procedure was to distinguish true living saints from impostors. In his very entertaining study *Heilige oder Hexen?* (Saints or witches?), Peter Dinzelbacher tells the story of many people (mostly women) who tried to pass themselves off as holy by imitating saintly models of various kinds: for example, a thirteenth-century woman named Sybil, from the area around Metz in northern France, constructed a whole scenario of saintliness that ranged from extreme ascetic practices to demonic persecution. She also told of visions of heaven, the angels, and so forth. When the bishop of Metz finally wants to examine her tribulations at the hands of demons (who had been seen by others as well), she agrees but insists that her door needs to remain closed. The demonic combat escalates: Sybil is heard arguing with her demonic oppressors who assault her with deep voices—but when a witness peeks through a hole in the door, all he sees is Sybil calmly making her bed while "arguing" with herself in different voices. Finally, a hairy demon suit is found as well, which she had donned in order to impersonate her demonic persecutors![11] Here all that was necessary for discernment was a close look through a keyhole. But these kinds of deceptions often had severe consequences: Sybil was incarcerated, as were numerous other pretenders over the centuries.[12]

Many more examples of fraudulent aspiring saints could be cited; some involve feigned fasting and other ascetic practices; others feature fabricated counterfeit stigmata that could be removed with soap and water, as was the case for a sixteenth-century Spanish saint.[13] The many cases of attempted fraud underlined for medieval clerics the importance and necessity of the discernment procedure. It had to be formalized in order to forestall frauds of many different kinds, but the formalization principally followed three lines: distinctions between true and false visionary experiences, between truly saintly human beings and impostors, and between real and counterfeit saints in visions or apparitions were the goals of this process.

These kinds of distinctions were never made in an ideological vacuum. As Nancy Caciola points out, "The discernment of spirits was not a neutral decision. . . . [It] was an ideological act, inflected by local mentalities, the observers' self-interest, and the exigencies of power."[14] Ermine's case can certainly be located within this nexus: Jean le Graveur may have formed the idea of writing down Ermine's experiences and thus making a holy woman of her in order to raise his institution's profile among the many religious orders present in medieval Reims. This motivation would fit into the categories of "local mentalities" and "the observers' self-interest"; the crisis of the Great

Schism provides a backdrop for Ermine's interest in political power, as it is played out through the activities and eventual persecution of Jean de Varennes.

So far Ermine's case has always been associated in scholarship with Jean Gerson, to whom the written record of her experiences was submitted for vetting. In fact, it may have been Ermine's *Visions* that prompted Gerson to write his first extended treatise on the discernment of spirits.[15] But in this chapter we will focus not so much on the theoretical aspects of the discernment of spirits as on the dramatic ones, in particular, on demons masquerading as saints and Ermine's almost uncanny ability to unmask these impostors. For Ermine, discernment seemed to be a performance that she was forced to deliver every night in the last ten agonizing months of her life. One of the central characters will be the ancient hermit Paul the Simple who appears in the *Visions* in both a saintly and a satanic shape, a two-fold role that puts him at the center of the discernment debate.

As André Vauchez has observed, Ermine's superior ability to distinguish between apparitions sent by God and those sent by the devil makes her "a living example of the discernment of spirits."[16] Unlike Raimond of Sabanac, for example, who, as we saw, prefaced the *Revelations* of Constance of Rabastens with a mini-treatise on the discernment of spirits, Jean le Graveur does not lay out the theoretical principles behind discernment as such but dramatizes Ermine's discernment exploits by narrating them in an apparently straightforward manner: she acts out discernment. Here discernment is more than a discourse: it is a performance. Ermine's simplicity and almost total lack of education (we saw in Chapter 3 that she barely masters the Pater Noster and the Creed, and to her confessor's dismay, mixes up the word *seraphim* with the word *Saracen*) would in fact preclude discernment if it is "skill based," as Voaden proposes: "It is important to note that eventually it was also perceived as a skill which could be acquired, with, of course, the assistance of grace, through reading and reflection, diligent study of the Scriptures and the Church Fathers, and familiarity with mystical theology and the lives of ascetics."[17] While this may work for someone like Jean Gerson or even the simpler Jean le Graveur, it certainly would not work for Ermine. Her methods of discernment are dramatic in the true sense of the term: in her discernment performances she does not theorize but acts out the hunt for demons.

Demons were of course everywhere in medieval culture. In popular collections of miracles like that of the thirteenth-century writer Caesaerius of

Heisterbach, demonic apparitions outnumber angelic ones eighteen to one, and Thomas of Cantimpré's *De apibus* (On bees), a kind of "primer of demonic virtuosity" in deception, features three times more demons than angels.[18] In the latter text demons masqueraded as priests and nuns and even as the Virgin Mary, although that demon is quickly unmasked when a Dominican friar is supposed to worship her. A counterfeit Virgin Mary also appeared much later to Saint Catherine of Bologna (d. 1463), who authored a spiritual treatise entitled *Sette armi spirituali* (Seven spiritual weapons), meant as a defense against the devil's wiles. The question of discernment comes to the fore in the last chapter where Catherine states that demons can appear in the shape of Christ or Mary and of angels or saints. She cites the example of Gabriel's Annunciation to the Virgin Mary: her question *qualis esta illa salutatio* (what is this greeting) shows that you have to question every apparition to ascertain whether it is a good or bad spirit. But it was Catherine herself who had been taken in for years by a counterfeit demonic Virgin Mary until God finally revealed the truth to her.[19] Demonic deception is particularly insidious when it takes on the form of the most revered personages in the Christian faith.

Dozens of demons in many different shapes haunted Ermine without interruption during the last ten months of her life. As we saw in Chapter 4, many of them appeared as animals, a veritable perverted menagerie. Others came in the shape of hideous men or seductive women; two of them even had sex right in front of her bed. All of these events occur nightly, or sometimes during the day, and usually all categories of demonic apparitions are mixed together in a single night. But while it is relatively easy to recognize demons in hideous animals or lascivious "people" (especially if they have leathery skin and are dressed in black), it is a lot harder to discern them if they appear "as angels of light." The true test of discernment thus centers on the demonic impersonation of saints, the most perverse counterfeit one can imagine.

Although the modern editor entitled Jean le Graveur's text *Les Visions d'Ermine de Reims*, Ermine's experiences are for the most part not visions but occur in a waking state in her normal surroundings; the demons and holy characters have therefore to be classified as apparitions.[20] In fact, Jean does not use the standard vocabulary for presenting visions (such as "it seemed to her" or "she saw")[21] but employs straightforward verbs, such as "she heard" (a voice) or (something or someone) "came into her room."

Beginning in late 1395 it was Jean le Graveur himself who set Ermine on the path of discernment: the very first auditory experience Jean reports for the eve of All Saint's Day 1395 is that of a voice that sounded exactly like his own; and it is he himself who explains to Ermine that this voice is a demonic one. Plumbing the psychological depths of this scene is not easy, as I suggested in Chapter 2. Does Ermine have doubts about what her confessor conveys to her, doubts about her new way of life? Does Jean want to forestall these doubts by acknowledging that a demon can succeed in impersonating him? In any case, the fact that the voice counterfeiting Jean's appears at the very beginning of the text allows Jean to create a kind of template, a standard scenario for discernment that will be applicable throughout *Visions*. He explains that Ermine heard a voice; said "who is there?"; heard "I am such and such person (*un tel*)"; and then immediately countered with "you are lying, you are a demon, go away!" (55). Following this script she soon is able to unmask even the most skillful demonic apparitions. From the wealth of these kinds of incidents I will choose just a few in order to analyze the techniques Jean uses to make the point of Ermine's superior abilities.

Counterfeit Saints

The first counterfeit saint Ermine encounters seems to have good credentials: he calls her by her name and reveals "I am Saint Léger"; but, he says, he came "without light" (*sans clarté*) because he did not want to frighten her. He then adds a persuasive detail: "You were baptized in my very church," he says, "and belonged to my confraternity." This intimate knowledge of her past life should convince Ermine, but she counters that she is an unworthy sinner and therefore does not merit a divinely sent vision. This display of humility is a standard element of the discernment of spirits. Saint Léger seems to vanish at that point, but Ermine's hair stands on end, a sign of intense fear (58).

This rather brief scene recalls similar scenes in older saints' *Lives*, such as that of Saint Martin by Sulpicius Severus (fifth century c.e.), included in Jacobus of Voragine's immensely popular thirteenth-century *Golden Legend*, where Martin's ability for discernment is highlighted.[22] He sometimes sees demons as pagan gods (such as Jove or Minerva), but at other times the disguise is more subtle: when a man clad in royal robes appears to Martin and repeatedly insists, "I am Christ," Martin is inspired by the Holy Spirit to see right through him: Christ would never dress this gaudily, says the discerning saint, and in addition he would be marked with the stigmata . . . whereupon the demon vanishes, leaving behind a horrible stench.[23]

For Saint Martin the recognition of the demon was triggered by the incorrect appearance of the counterfeit Christ figure. For Ermine the fear she feels signals that Saint Léger is a demonic impostor. Indeed, at a somewhat later point Jean le Graveur identifies the amount of fear Ermine feels as a gauge for discernment. In a crucial passage he addresses his readers directly: "And may it please you to learn that for the events that happened to this little woman and which I have recounted or will still recount when some good spirits came to her, her fear was not as great as it was toward the bad spirits; for toward the good spirits her fear was less and got smaller and smaller, but toward the bad spirits her fear was large and grew ever larger. Nonetheless, no matter what they told her, she could not truly believe that good spirits came to her for fear of being deceived and because of her great humility" (80).[24] This is the only passage in this very long text that deals explicitly with the discernment of spirits as it applies to Ermine. It lays out the criterion of fear as a key to her discerning abilities and at the same time highlights her humility: because she deems herself unworthy of true saintly apparitions, she suspects even true saints of being demons.

Returning to the passage on Saint Martin in *The Golden Legend*, we can see that some sort of script for discernment scenes was available to Jean le Graveur, but most of these scenes were rather brief. By contrast, in the *Visions* the demonic apparitions of counterfeit saints are so complex and elaborately staged that one could almost consider them miniature plays. We will explore in detail a satanic mass celebrated by a counterfeit Saint Augustine,[25] apparitions of Saint Nicolas and Saint Mary Magdalene, and a two-act play centering on Saint Peter.

On a particularly trying Easter Sunday when, after mass, Ermine is assaulted by seven bats and countless lice (attacks by demonic animals happen daily), she lies down for a bit, only to hear a little bell announcing the arrival of several demons dressed as angels (102). Jean tells us these were *sathenas* (demons), but Ermine is not forewarned the way we as readers are. The angels come with incense, dressed in white albs, and carrying chalices. A priest dressed in gold follows them, carrying a communion vessel—but it lacks the customary cross, Jean informs us. The priest addresses Ermine as *belle fille* (beautiful daughter) and adds, "I am Saint Augustine" (*Je suis saint Augustin*; 103). It is certainly ironic that the most elaborate scene starring a demonic counterfeit saint should feature Saint Augustine, the patron saint of the very order that Ermine's confessor belongs to. The demonic Saint Augustine explicitly targets this member of "his" order when he accuses Jean le Graveur of offering her false doctrine and of giving her only bread, not the true Host, at that day's mass. He sits down on her bed and offers her a "real" mass with the "real Host." Ermine is suspicious: why celebrate mass in bed when she is perfectly healthy? Undeterred, the demon pretending to be Saint Augustine proceeds to celebrate the mass, and when it is time for the Host, Ermine sees a little baby that promptly begins to howl to show that it is *chose vive* (a living thing). Even this miraculous event—so much desired in late medieval culture, as we saw in Chapter 3—leaves her cold. "You are the devil," Ermine shouts. But the two little angels retort that the priest is "my lord Saint Augustine, the flower of the doctors of the Christina faith" (*monseigneur saint Augustin, la fleur des docteurs de la foy chretienne*; 104). But Ermine knows better and identifies him as a demon, and after a while the whole show vanishes.

Here the battle for Ermine's soul revolves around questions of doctrine, centered on communion and the Host. The fact that Ermine is granted—by a demon!—exactly the kind of vision (the "child in the Host") that was one of the hallmarks of late medieval piety emphasizes the urgent need for discernment. The demons stage an elaborate "liturgical play" for Ermine, but her steadfast faith permits her to see through the deception and send Saint Augustine and his little angel—or rather demon—helpers packing. It may be this heroic feat of discernment that earns Ermine a true vision of the Christ child in the Host some time later, appropriately on the day of Corpus Christi (June 1). As Ermine solemnly walks in the procession, she is almost toppled by a demon, but two women catch her at the last moment. She then sees the Eucharist carried by the priest in a crystal monstrance: first she sees it looking like bread and then as a living small child and then again as bread. While she sees the Host as a child, she falls into rapture and forgets her surroundings (128–29). Thus Jean shows us two occurrences of the child in the Host theme: one a demonic counterfeit and one a truly divine vision. In each case Ermine's reaction confirms her discernment abilities.

A scene with Saint Nicolas offers a slightly different scenario. On May 29, 1396, he appears in her room, iconographically correct in a bishop's attire, complete with miter and crozier, and chases away three troublesome demons. To make doubly sure that he is recognized, he is accompanied by elements from his legend come alive: three young women in white and three young clerics in white. Nicolas explains that these are the young girls he protected from being turned into prostitutes by their impoverished father by offering him some gold pieces, and the three young men he resuscitated. For good measure he adds, *"Je suis saint Nicolas"* (124). And yet Ermine immediately accuses him of being a fake by stating flatly that he is not Saint Nicolas but a demon (125), although for us readers there is no discordant element in his appearance. He vanishes, but the very next day he returns. Ermine had been attacked by demons and tied up, just as calves and lambs are tied up when they are taken to the market, Jean specifies (127). Saint Nicolas (one of his specialties is the liberation of prisoners) this time appears accompanied by a group of prisoners who, when Ermine again accuses Nicolas of being a demon, testify to his deeds: "For sure, my beautiful daughter, this is our lord Saint Nicolas, who has delivered us from the same trouble that you are in right now" (*Certainement, belle fille, c'est monseigneur saint Nicolas qui nous a delivrez de tel mechief que tu es*; 128–29).

Although Ermine still does not believe them, Nicolas miraculously unties her, and then when she persists in her disbelief, ties her up again, whereupon he and his entourage vanish. Finally a prayer to Christ results in her liberation. But she is so bent over that she can hardly stand up, and even the next morning witnesses see the welts the ropes had made in her arms and legs. Here we have an extremely elaborate scenario: Saint Nicolas appears with his correct iconography and even brings along witnesses: the people he had saved and who star in the legends surrounding the saint. They are even given speaking parts, testifying to the saint's miraculous powers. And yet Ermine again sees right through him and his supporting cast. Rather than relying on the so-called saint (who *does* in fact loosen her demonic bonds), Ermine turns to Christ for her liberation. Here it seems to be her refusal to accept saintly intercession that leads to perfect discernment.

Let us pause for a moment and consider whether the appearance of counterfeit saints was a common occurrence in medieval culture. While the appearance of demons and angels was extremely common, that of clearly marked counterfeit saints was not. For a comparison we can look at Francesca Romana whom we encountered at the beginning of this chapter. The dramatic fresco in the Roman monastery Francesca founded, the Tor de' Specchi (Fig. 9), brings to life Francesca's encounter with a demon pretending to be Saint Onofrio, the hermit saint who lived in fourth-century Egypt. Francesca was born in 1384 in Rome into the noble family of the Bussas and was married at age thirteen to a member of the equally noble Ponziani family.[26] She abhorred sexual relations with her husband but submitted to them (all the while inventing horrible self-tortures) and had several children. Her wealth allowed her eventually to purchase the Tor de' Specchi buildings, which to this day house nuns devoted to the saint who died on March 9, 1440, and was canonized in 1608. Francesca's *Life* was written by Giovanni Mattiotti, who was her confessor in the last ten years of her life.[27] He carefully separated divine visions from diabolic apparitions, a division that is reflected in the artwork still extant in the Tor de' Specchi monastery, where the church features vividly colored frescoes showing Francesca's life and miracles, while the refectory is decorated with *grisaille* scenes from the demonic attacks she suffered.[28]

Demons appeared to Francesca frequently in the shape of nude men, women, and children, and some of them engaged in sodomitic acts right in front of her.[29] Like Ermine she was sometimes accosted by demons in the shape of men who propositioned her. Once when she was walking down a street in Rome, the "malignant enemy" (*malignus hostis*) in the shape of a richly bearded old man sidled up to her and asked for her help with "a little thing" (*una re petita*) and then uttered a "dishonest petition." Francesca, who abhorred carnal vices more than anything else, immediately recognized this man as an evil spirit and addressing him as "sordid demon" asked, "Did you really think I would not recognize you just because you assumed a human form?" Francesca proceeded to kneel down and in a "manly way" (*viriliter*) sent the demon packing.[30] Mattiotti uses the word *cognoscere* (to recognize) in a matter-of-fact way to dramatize Francesca's discernment: her virtues enable her to simply *know* who is a demon, and no further explanation seems necessary. We saw earlier in this chapter that when the demon took on the shape of her confessor, Francesca's humility sufficed to unmask him.

A scene especially relevant to our inquiry here is the apparition of the counterfeit Saint Onofrio. It is important that this saint had earlier appeared to Francesca as the real thing. In vision LXXXIV he had come to her to discourse on the dangers of worldly love.[31] Francesca was in the midst of horrific demonic attacks (demons stole her books and threatened to throw her into a stinking latrine) when Onofrio appeared to her:

> On a certain night, while God's servant was engrossed in the above-mentioned holy prayers and meditations in her little bed, the old enemy, jealous of her tranquil state of mind, came to her in the shape of a rustic man, carrying in his hand a walking stick, as if he

were a traveler. He told the blessed woman that he was Saint Onofrio. And therefore he had the desire to go to some deserted place,
and he begged her to go with him, for he would choose the most
beautiful place for her.[32] But Christ's servant, seeing his visible but
false brightness and his maliciousness, responded by saying, "Oh,
you miserable being, how vile are you! You thought you could
deceive me with this miserable brightness and persuade me to go
with you. I want to remain where it pleases my Lord and I desire
nothing else but what He desires. You, vilest of beings, step back in
the name of the blessed crucified Jesus Christ and vanish into the
abyss which is your habitat. As soon as the evil enemy heard the
name of holiest Jesus, he immediately began to beat the earth and
dig a hole, and springing forth from this wanted to beat up the
blessed woman; but because God forbade it he did not succeed.[33]

How did this counterfeit saint identify himself? The only attribute he
carries is a rustic stick. The horns and the cloven feet visible in the striking
image from the Tor de' Specchi are not mentioned in the text. In fact, Mattiotti gives us no visual clue as to the apparition's true identity. The "temptation" represented by this counterfeit saint is purely psychological.[34] Thus it
is Francesca herself who discerns what her biographer calls *fictam lucem*, or
fake light or brightness, simply through her saintly virtue, not through any
telltale outward signs.

But let us return to Ermine and the parade of counterfeit saints she
receives in her bedroom. Mary Magdalene makes several appearances. On
Christmas Eve 1395 a snow-white woman with a golden crown walks into
Ermine's room (a *sathenas*, as Jean alerts us), returning two rosaries to her
that someone had taken from Ermine. "*Je suis la Magdalene*" (66), she
informs her. When Ermine accuses her of being a stinking demon, the lady
immediately transforms herself into one: her beautiful crown turns into two
gigantic horns. About a month later Mary Magdalene reappears. Ermine
again takes her for a demon: I remember you, she exclaims (78). But this
time she is the real thing, as becomes clear to Ermine in a very long scene in
which Ermine weeps for her sins. The Magdalene assures her that this is the
first time she has visited her, and therefore she cannot be the demon Ermine
had encountered previously in her shape. She consoles Ermine but also predicts further tribulations that Ermine will have to bear for the love of Christ.
The Magdalene then announces that she and her angels are leaving and will

not be back. Before departing she stresses that Ermine should believe everything her confessor tells her (79).

How does Ermine's discernment function here? First, the woman in white recommends that she should trust her confessor, Jean le Graveur. This is a sure sign in Ermine's *Visions* that a true saint is speaking. Second, Ermine feels little fear. This is the moment when Jean addresses his audience directly (in the passage cited above) and presents Ermine's degree of fear as a gauge: the "good" saints cause less fear in her than the "bad" ones (80). Discernment is thus linked to Ermine's emotional state that both she and her confessor can read correctly. But alas, just when we thought that Mary Magdalene could now be trusted, here she is again, carrying her box with ointment (she explains that she carries her box so that Ermine will recognize her; 122) and urging her to leave her confessor. Two weeks later there is a replay: this time the Magdalene is accompanied by an unnamed woman with a lily who vouches for the Magdalene's saintliness, as did the prisoners that accompanied Saint Nicolas. At that moment Ermine is being tormented in an otherworldly, wild demonic dance but nonetheless has the presence of mind to shout at the impostor—who, it is significant to note, again urges Ermine to leave her confessor—that she trusts the Magdalene in heaven and not her demonic counterfeit on earth (131). The two women leave, and the demons toss Ermine around the room and almost throw her out the window.

What can we make of scenes like this? Do the many sightings of counterfeit saints in this text represent a warning against the very idea of saintly intercession? Let us look at one more two-act drama, this one starring Saint Peter. On January 8, 1396, a demon arrives, calls Ermine by name, and states "*Je suis Saint Pierre*" (70), adding that he has come to comfort her and specifying that he has the keys to paradise and will admit her after her death. When Ermine declares herself unworthy of saintly visits and accuses Saint Peter of being a demon, he begins to beat her, blackening one of her eyes and almost knocking out her teeth. He then lifts up her dress and kicks her in the chest, whereupon he vanishes (71). The traces of this brutal assault remain visible for days. Act 2 in the drama of Saint Peter: on January 21, 1396, Ermine hears a sweet melody, and four angels in white robes arrive to take her hands in their little hands, announcing that they are bringing her great joy (76). Ermine, not surprisingly, is doubtful when a priest arrives, tonsured and holding a book, announcing "*Je suis Saint Pierre*." "*Tu es*," says Ermine, "*saint Pierre d'enfer*" (You are Saint Peter from hell; 77), and you beat me up just a short time ago. But Saint Peter insists that this is the first

time he has seen her, and the angels chime in by declaring that they are not
demons. They then proceed to comfort Ermine some more by playing beautiful music. She has a feeling of peace and joy. After they leave a sweet perfume
remains in her room. This scene is clearly a replay of January 8 but with a
revised script: here Jean does not identify the visitors right away as demons,
as he does so frequently when counterfeit saints are in the offing. Here
Ermine's doubts are overridden by divine manifestations that aid her in the
process of discernment. Her actions illustrate another version of true discernment, the one I mentioned earlier in the context of Raimond of Sabanac's
treatise, namely, where he says that "a hasty, indiscreet, and thoughtless person . . . given to fantasies . . . would receive false things as true and"—this is
the important point—"reject true things as false."[35] This "fear of illusion,"
treated at length by Ernst Benz in his extensive study of visions,[36] has been
internalized by Ermine, which is why it takes her a long time to finally believe
that on this occasion it is the true Saint Peter paying her a visit. This two-act
drama of Saint Peter thus illustrates the trajectory of Ermine's path to perfect
discernment by ringing the changes on Saint Peter: in the first act he is a
demon, in the second a saint; and in the end Ermine is able to discern which
one is which.

Saint Paul the Simple, as mentioned earlier, plays a central role in this
drama of discernment. Saint Paul first appears to Ermine in February 1396
after a demonic aerial kidnapping that had stranded her at a mass, celebrated
in the woods outside of Reims by Jean de Varennes, the outlaw former papal
official we already encountered many times.[37] Paul guides her swiftly back to
Reims and thus prevents people from pursuing the unpleasant questions her
absence had provoked. Paul also aids Ermine in the process of discernment,
helping her many times in unmasking demonic impersonators.

Paul the Simple is one of the most complicated characters in Ermine's
Visions; he is a strange, shape-changing saint. Paul is a kind of guardian angel
for Ermine: in addition to guiding her back to Reims after the demonic aerial
journey to the forest of Nanteuil (93), he once saved her from a serious fall
when she was being tossed around by demons (111); he repeatedly defended
her against demons and even lions. In other instances he played the role of
spiritual guide and discerner of spirits. But five times throughout the text he
is actually being impersonated by a demon. In fact, at one point the "real"
Saint Paul tells Ermine that demons appeared to her many times in his shape
(*les sathenas sont venuz a toy en mon nom*; 146). It is only toward the end of
the *Visions* that the Virgin Mary—in a grand final vision of the opened

heavens—authenticates Paul the Simple as a saintly hermit sent by Christ to protect Ermine in her tribulations. Before Ermine's eyes he ascends to heaven in the shape of a small but intense ball of fire (152).[38] How can Ermine tell when Paul the Simple is not himself but a demon?

Paul first appears as a satanic impersonator about six weeks after their initial encounter on the road from Nanteuil. Jean le Graveur leaves no doubt about the saint's impersonation here: "A demon came up to her, dressed and speaking just like the hermit who had accompanied her back from the woods of Nanteuil and taken her down from the church roof " (*Vint ung sathenas deu costé elle, en habit en parole et en forme de l'ermite qui l'avoit ravoyee es bois de Nantuel et rapportee de dessus du moustier*; 117), thus evoking another incident where demons had placed Ermine on top of the church roof. His aiding Ermine seems to be his identifying characteristic, but here he is a *sathenas*, a demon, despite the fact that he says explicitly *"Je suis saint Pol le Simple"* (117). So how do we know he is a demon (in addition to Jean's assurance)? He urges Ermine to leave her confessor! This in fact becomes the touchstone for discernment in *Visions*: each time someone tries to persuade Ermine to leave Jean in order to go back to her friends in the countryside, this someone is unmasked as a demon. Thus in his demonic shape Paul suggests that she should get married again (after all, it is one of the Seven Sacraments, he assures her [145]), and he makes her doubt the truth of the Eucharist (148). Even after Ermine witnesses his ascent to heaven in the shape of a little fireball (152), in his satanic manifestation he remains on earth to goad Ermine further: he contradicts the pronouncements of the real Saint Paul the Simple concerning Ermine's special elect status and the goodness of her confessor by urging her to reject her confessor and leave him (142). Thus Ermine, by sticking to Jean le Graveur, performs the first tenet of discernment as we defined it at the beginning of this chapter: "to live virtuously under the guidance of a spiritual director."

The central function of the counterfeit saints in Ermine's *Visions*, then, is that of a gauge or yardstick for an evaluation of Ermine's discernment capabilities and consequently as a gauge for Ermine's holiness. In addition to the heroic virtue she shows in the face of threatening animals and brutal demons in human shape, she has acquired the kind of sixth sense, the charisma, that is only given to the truly humble and virtuous, as Gerson claims: the true discerner of spirits does not proudly advertise his or her abilities but rather "performs" discernment by confronting demonic impersonators head-on, saying, "you are a fake and I know it!"

Jean Gerson's Judgment

We saw that the key element in Ermine's encounter with demons in various guises was her faithfulness to her confessor. This personal element, centered on the relationship between (would-be) holy woman and confessor, was not mentioned by Jean Gerson when he penned his judgment of Ermine's case as requested by Jean le Graveur's superior, Jean Morel, a canon and subsequently prior of Saint-Denis in Reims. The letter Gerson sent to Morel is in fact Ermine's major claim to fame.[39] Most scholars who mention Ermine do so exclusively in the context of Gerson's later treatises on the discernment of spirits. It seems plausible that Gerson's first treatise on this topic, *De distinctione verarum revelationum a falsis* (On Distinguishing True from False Revelations; 1401–1402) was written in reaction to Ermine's case. His letter to Jean Morel, approving Jean le Graveur's *Visions*, also has often been cited, but generally without any reference to the actual contents of the *Visions*.[40]

Morel solicited Gerson's judgment on two major points: the orthodoxy of Ermine's experiences and the question on whether Ermine's *Visions* should be widely circulated. Dyan Elliott characterizes Gerson's reaction as follows: "A model of scholarly method, Gerson's analysis is shaped into three conclusions, . . . all of which are devoted to limitation, containment, and damage control."[41] Gerson concludes that the content of the *Visions* does not contradict Scripture and could even be inspirational. Ermine's faith, simplicity, and humility endorse the text's truth. And yet Gerson insists that the book should not be widely circulated and should only be made accessible to "those who are stable in their way of life and concerned with their own salvation."[42] Nonetheless, a number of manuscript copies were made: first at Jean le Graveur's home institution, the Val-des-Ecoliers in Reims, and then in Gerson's clerical circles in Paris, if we can believe the testimony of a seventeenth-century historian.[43] Thus, even though one of Gerson's aims seems to have been the containment of Ermine's story, he nonetheless contributed to a wider circulation of the text, albeit confined to a clerical milieu.

Gerson's prudent but positive reaction was reversed about twenty years later when in *De examinatione doctrinarum* (On the examination of doctrines; 1423) Gerson spoke of his "near-seduction" by "a certain Ermine de Reims." Gerson congratulated himself on his prudence back then: God protected him from completely falling for this strange woman, and now he sees things differently.[44] Let us dig a little deeper into the letter to Jean Morel and the 1423 treatise that mentions Ermine.

It certainly makes sense to speak of Ermine's case as part of the debate on the discernment of spirits. The procedure of the discernment of spirits began to be codified just around the time of Ermine's visions. It did not change substantially over the next few centuries.[45] Moshe Sluhovsky sees three major types of discernment: discernment effected by the visionary himself or herself; "community discernment" by the visionaries' neighbors or followers; and "official discernment by church authorities."[46] What is missing from this list are some of the discernment mechanisms that are quite common in Ermine's *Visions*, that is, a saintly apparition aiding Ermine in distinguishing real saints from demons and the red flag that goes up every time a counterfeit saint urges her to leave her confessor. Ermine's fidelity to her confessor as one of the important gauges of orthodoxy is Jean le Graveur's strongest and most original contribution to the discernment debate. In some ways Jean le Graveur undoubtedly intended his book as a guide to the discernment of spirits, a script to the drama of his heroine's superhuman abilities. This may be the reason for the text's excesses—the very excesses that probably led to Gerson's cautious stance.[47]

What is missing in the many analyses of Gerson's letter is a consideration of the second point he makes. Scholars often cite the "first conclusion," where Gerson states that examples of demonic assaults can be found in the *Lives* of many of the ancient desert saints and that therefore we can believe Ermine's accounts; this is in fact a rather noncontroversial argument. The third conclusion states that the book should not be circulated among "ignorant people" (lest they get ideas about imitating Ermine) and goes on to praise Ermine as a woman "poor in spirit but rich in faith" whose defeat of demons—Gerson pictures them in his mind as "furious, roaring, and gnashing their teeth" (173)—is admirable and praiseworthy. He lists her virtues as humility, a firm faith, and a "prudent and ignorant simplicity," a list he takes up again and amplifies in his 1401–1402 treatise on discernment.

The "second conclusion," in my view a masterpiece of bureaucratic double-speak, has not been commented on very much. I believe that a closer look at this lengthy paragraph in conjunction with the actual text of the *Visions* will reveal the major reason for Gerson's changing attitude toward the strange case of Ermine de Reims.

Around 1400 Gerson had many personal connections to the city of Reims. We saw in Chapter 3 that Gerson's treatise *Le doctrinal aux simples gens* (Teachings for simple people) was widely circulated by the archbishop of Reims, Guy de Roye, in 1387. One of Jean Gerson's brothers, also named

Jean, was a monk at Saint-Denis in Reims starting in 1394. The request to examine Ermine's *Visions* thus did not come from strangers but from a milieu to which Gerson had multiple links. This personal aspect in my view explains much of his positive yet ultracautious judgment.

The structure of the "second conclusion" is tripartite: the middle part, which I consider crucial and which has never been placed into the context of Gerson's and others' ideas, seems especially significant to me. It deals with the question of oaths and perjury and is framed by two mini-treatises on the believability of "miracles."

Under which circumstances, Gerson asks, should we believe in the "miracles" recounted by Jean le Graveur? It is striking that an appeal to social conventions and "civility" precedes any mention of the "faith" one should have in miracles. Gerson states that it would be "uncivil" to cast doubt "with stubborn ill will" on the "facts recounted in this book." These are not the words of a theologian but of a man of the world who is concerned about keeping the social fabric intact. This social fabric is defined in part by the faith one needs to have in people's oaths (*serments*). What would happen, Gerson asks, if we refused to believe what others present as the truth? He states that in this context natural law is confirmed by divine law: that we should treat others as we would want to be treated ourselves. Therefore, anyone living with "civility" needs to lend credence to what others say unless there is clear evidence of "falsehood."

I would like to place these statements into a two-fold framework: first, given the crisis in France caused by the madness of King Charles VI, the Great Schism, and the continuing conflict between England and France, the topic of people swearing oaths and perjuring themselves was a major one in the political writings of the time and also surfaced in Gerson's sermons. Second, these remarks are clearly a response to Jean le Graveur's concerted efforts to establish the truth of Ermine's "adventures" and thus of his narrative.

The issue of the trustworthiness of someone's oath or word (*parole*) was one of the fundamental ones in didactic writings in the tradition of the mirror for princes. The flattery—and the concomitant untruthfulness—of wily counselors presented a major danger to the stability of the kingdom according to numerous political writers of the time. Christine de Pizan, Gerson's contemporary and ally in the *Debate on the Romance of the Rose*,[48] made the keeping of one's word and perjury into one of the most important themes of her political treatises.[49] Gerson himself addressed this problem in his famous sermon "Vivat rex," preached before the royal court on November 7, 1405, whose main subject was the king's obligation to preserve the health and unity of the body politic. Here he argues that *fainctez paroles* (untrue statements) could induce even the angels in paradise to fight each other. For him the kingdom is endangered by honey-tongued flatterers whose destructiveness should not be underestimated. A flatterer is a skillful liar, an *envelopeur de parollez*, that is, someone who covers or envelops his statements in false-hoods.[50] Thus, if one cannot trust people's word, the very structure of society crumbles. The fact that Gerson personally knew and felt he needed to trust the main actors in Ermine's drama determined his attitude toward Ermine's *Visions* just as much, if not more so, than any theoretical ideas about the discernment of spirits.

It is important to remember that Jean le Graveur himself had erected an impregnable defense against any doubts that readers of his text might have harbored in regard to the veracity of Ermine's experiences and Jean's tran-scription of them. We saw in Chapter 2 how Jean constructs the opening and the ending of his text by using dramatic scenes of his own interaction with Ermine, enlivened by dialogues between the two whose purpose it is to ensure the truth of what Ermine is telling her confessor. Ermine swears holy oaths, reliable witnesses are present, and so forth. In May 1396, for example, Jean adds an explanation to some events that assure us of Ermine's discernment capabilities: because of her strong faith in God she was able to see through the hermit Paul the Simple's disguise and unmask him as a demon (117). He also insists again and again on his own role in getting the truth out of Ermine. As we saw in Chapter 3, during one of Ermine's eucharistic visions Jean makes Ermine get up from the floor, where she lies face down in an ecstatic faint, so that she can tell him the truth about what she saw (137). Finally, the scene of her death features multiple layers of truth-telling.[51] Jean questions her again about the truthfulness of the things she told him, and then asks her to repeat her claims to truth before six people, three religious men and three honest women (164). Ermine now says that even though she did not report everything she saw verbatim (*propres paroles*), she certainly relayed the true substance of what she heard and saw. In addition, in her final confession to the priest who gives her the last unction, she reaffirms once more the truth of her accounts. Who is Gerson, then, to doubt the veracity of Ermine's tales?

Finally, let us consider Gerson's musings on miracles and their possible "natural" explanations. Does Jean le Graveur in fact claim that Ermine either experienced miraculous events or performed miracles herself? A careful read-ing of the text reveals that during Ermine's lifetime the *only* event that Jean le Graveur explicitly designates as a *bel miracle* in the *Visions* is the moment when Ermine gets stuck in her cloak and is "miraculously" liberated. Alas, a "good woman" who lived in a room next to Ermine and heard her complaints "saw nothing" (*et n'avoit la femme riens vu*; 90) and can therefore not be used as a witness to this "miracle." Furthermore, Ermine gets stuck twice more (in her cloak and her head scarf) and gets out without a miracle, although not without developing a sweat caused by anxiety (*et suoit moult fort de mechief*; 153). However, in the passage between Ermine's last confession and her death Jean le Graveur inserts some reflections on Ermine's life as a whole.[52] Here he reminds his readers that Ermine was a working woman who was able to provide for herself before being struck with the strange adventures we have just read about. And then he refers to her ability to defend herself, with God's help, against demons as a "true miracle."

It was most likely this passage that induced Gerson to dwell on the plausibility of miracles. The only event explicitly labeled as "miraculous" in the actual *Visions* was as trivial as it was ridiculous and was probably not something either Churchman wanted to highlight. But Jean le Graveur's global claim on Ermine's abilities as miraculous provoked Gerson to speak seriously about natural explanations of miracles, finally concluding that when in doubt we should believe an event to be miraculous rather than merely natural. Gerson thus endorsed the conclusion his *confrère* from Reims had reached.

In 1415, at the Council of Constance that finally resolved the Great Schism, Gerson wrote another treatise on the discernment of spirits, *De probatione spirituum* (On the proving of spirits) where he "advises discerners of spirits to consider three possibilities: the content of visions are divine, diabolical, or merely human. He does not, however, provide specific guidelines for distinguishing between them."[53] Here he alludes to the visions of Saint Birgitta of Sweden and Saint Catherine of Siena as having contributed to the Great Schism through their visions that urged Pope Gregory XI to return the papacy from Avignon to Rome and thus set in motion the events that led to the double papal election.[54] But he does not mention Ermine. We have to wait another eight years for him to take a second look at the discernment of spirits and the peculiar events that took place in Reims in 1395 and 1396. In 1423 Gerson is in exile in Lyon, and although he still is nominally chancellor of the University of Paris, he cannot return to Paris after the English invasion of France in 1415 and the taking of Paris in 1418. Further, he is in disgrace with the Duke of Burgundy, an ally of the English invaders, whose murder of his cousin Louis of Orléans in 1407 he never condoned, as did a number of other Churchmen at the time. Thus Gerson now has some leisure to look back on the strange case of Ermine de Reims.[55]

In his *De examinatione doctrinarum* (On the examination of doctrines) Gerson gives us a very personal account of what happened around 1400.[56] Toward the end of his treatise Gerson alerts his readers to "women and laymen" who want to "usurp" sanctity and holy teaching. Many people speak about these topics without rational sense, he states, but "based on fantasies coming from their disturbed minds."[57] These people do not necessarily want to deceive; indeed Gerson divides them up into several groups: those who have been deceived but do not know it and do not want to deceive others, and those who do not believe that they have been deceived; finally there are those who want to deceive and invent marvels (*fingendo mirabilia*) that they know to be false—and of those there is an infinite number. He adds that he has been often consulted as an expert and that had he written down all the things he was told, he could have done so to great effect. It is at this point that he evokes his "near-seduction" by the case of Ermine de Reims. He confesses (*fateor*) that what he had heard from "certain people of great reputation" had almost "seduced" him at the time. But God wished him to temper his response, and he did so, thus sparing him "the mockery and contempt" that some might have directed at him. Not only that, but he then wrote his treatise on the distinction of true and false revelations.[58] One can almost hear Gerson exhaling here, recalling his narrow escape.

Gerson does not fully repudiate Ermine, however. One gets the impression that he would classify her as one of those who do not want to deceive but believe that what they experienced was true. A stark contrast appears in a story most likely added some time after Gerson's death at the end of his 1423 treatise.[59] It tells of a woman in Bourg-en-Bresse in Savoy who exemplified the kind of person Gerson described as a willful deceiver. She feigned miracles by claiming that she was charged by God with redeeming sinners (three per day: the first two were easy, the third required great effort—or so she said);[60] burning coals at her feet signaled when these sinners were about to be swallowed up by hell, and she could thus intervene. She could also discern the maliciousness of demons and fell into ecstasies and prophesied; in other words, she fit the profile of many other holy women we encountered in these pages. But this unfortunate woman did not have a confessor to shore up notions of her sanctity; she lacked the crucial support system that would have saved her from the torture eventually inflicted upon her by the rector of a church in her hometown. Not surprisingly, she confessed that she had perpetrated this fraud in order to be given alms so that she could live and alleviate her poverty. This rather modest desire is termed "cupidity" here. She finally was not condemned as a heretic but as a sick woman suffering from seizures who should do penance. Whether anyone eventually came to the aid of this impoverished, desperate woman—which is exactly what Jean le Graveur did for Ermine—is left open. In any case, with the diagnosis of what may have been epilepsy, this text looks toward later medical explanations of these kinds of phenomena that culminated in the modern-day views and practices we briefly surveyed in the Prologue to this book.

Returning in conclusion to Gerson's 1401 letter to Jean Morel, one is struck by a rather convoluted sentence where Gerson seems to say that the true miracle in this story of Ermine de Reims was that this uneducated (*idiota*) woman could express what she saw and heard, whether invented or not; that is, Gerson seems surprised by her articulateness. Finally, another crucial element in the letter is the mention of the "people of great reputation" who urged him to believe in Ermine. This personal element, as I suggested earlier, came to the fore in the letter's "second conclusion," where Gerson appeals to civility and the obligation of members of a civilized society to believe each others' oaths and affirmations. For if Churchmen begin to doubt each other, all hope for a society based on trust is surely lost. Thus the strange case of Ermine de Reims became a touchstone for Gerson: he *had* to put his trust in Jean le Graveur and thus Ermine, or else the bases of his beliefs would have begun to crumble. By 1423 France itself was crumbling, and all the men in Reims for whom Gerson had felt such loyalty were dead. He was done with Ermine, but others were not, as we shall see in the Epilogue.

EPILOGUE

In 1648 Jacques de Foigny, who had been the last subprior of the Val-des-Ecoliers in Reims before its move to Soissons in 1617, wrote a work entitled *Les merveilles de la vie, des combats et victoires d'Ermine, citoyenne de Reims* (The marvelous events of the life, the combats, and victories of Ermine, citizen of Reims).[1] Like Gerson he refers to Ermine as *"une femmelette, pauvre, ignorante, plus forte que celui que se vante de renverser tout le monde"* (a poor and ignorant little woman, stronger than the one who boasts that he can vanquish everyone). He reminisces about how he obtained his sources, one manuscript of the Latin translation of Ermine's *Visions* coming from the famous abbey of Saint-Victor in Paris and from which a kind, venerable monk sent him the material missing from his own copy, which was in French. He informs us that his manuscript was written on parchment "in the language which people spoke 250 years ago" and filled with abbreviations; that it had been manhandled (*tracassé*) over the last few centuries in Reims and much damaged and that, worst of all, some of the pictures had been cut out of it. These pictures depicted *fort bien* (precisely) Ermine's visions and apparitions. Alas, this manuscript and the images we would have loved to see have disappeared, as have a number of other manuscripts of the *Visions*.

Some time before De Foigny wrote his *Merveilles* a certain Jean Rogier, who died in 1637, wrote a history of Reims in which he alluded to Ermine by saying that he heard that her grave was in the church of the Val-des-Ecoliers and that he in fact had read a Latin version of her *"visions estranges"*; he also mentioned Gerson's letter and his opinion that the "book should not be given to the public."[2] Rogier's and De Foigny's activities show that interest in Ermine's story continued into the seventeenth century and that she was linked on the one hand to the city of Reims and on the other to Gerson. Indeed, Ermine and Gerson were destined to make their way through the centuries together.

A number of scholars in the Renaissance and the seventeenth century showed great interest in medieval visionary women. The prime example is Jacques Lefèvre d'Etaples, one of the greatest of French humanists, who in the 1520s published the visions of Hildegard of Bingen and Elisabeth of Schönau, two extraordinarily learned and productive women.[3] Ermine, though less learned and accomplished, also captured the interest of later scholars—and not just in Reims—who helped diffuse the manuscripts of her *Visions* beyond her hometown and Paris. One example that has been studied by the German scholar Paul Gerhard Schmidt is the rector of the University of Freiburg, Johannes Sutter, who died in 1539.[4] In the 1490s he taught in Paris and was then called to Freiburg in 1502 to replace colleagues who had died of the plague. While in Paris, he had translated the French works of Jean Gerson for one volume of the edition that Jakob Wimpfeling published in the early years of the sixteenth century. Was Sutter's interest in Ermine spurred by what he read about her in Gerson's works? It appears most likely, for he traveled from Paris to Reims where he purchased a Latin version of the *Visions* directly from the friars of the Val-des-Ecoliers. Right away he crossed out the former owners' names and replaced them with his own, and also indicated how much he paid for the text (as any good book collector does). He then added many marginal notes and some stylistic corrections; that is, he worked his way through the text like a true scholar.[5]

The example of Sutter, who was undoubtedly alerted to Ermine through the works of Gerson, shows how despite Gerson's efforts to dissociate himself from this peculiar visionary, the two seem inextricably linked. As I have indicated throughout this book, this linkage reappears in most modern scholarship, especially in the area of the discernment of spirits. But it is also true for the early and later fifteenth century where various Gersonian texts cohabit with Ermine's *Visions* between a number of book covers. To close out this book I will therefore take a quick look at the manuscripts that survived and see what they and the way they were put together can tell us about Ermine and her early reception.

What the Manuscripts Can Reveal[6]

Five manuscripts of Ermine's *Visions* have survived, two in the original French and three of the Latin translation made by Jean de Balay, a subprior at Saint-Denis de Reims, a short time after Gerson rendered his first cautiously positive judgment of Ermine in 1401–1402.[7] The most interesting of these manuscripts is Bibliothèque nationale de France (BnF) fr. 25213, the manuscript Arnaud-Gillet used for her edition. Containing only Ermine's *Visions*, this was the manuscript submitted to Jean Gerson by Jean Morel, the prior of the abbey of Saint-Denis de Reims. With seventy-nine folios this rather slim volume was portable and could be easily conveyed to Jean le Graveur's superiors and then to Gerson. At the end we find Gerson's cautious approbation of Ermine's visions in Latin (fols. 78v–79v), which we analyzed in Chapter 5. The letter is in a section entitled *L'approbacion de ce livre*, (The approbation of this book) which also details how and why Jean le Graveur went about submitting the text to Gerson.[8] The fact that the text was written in French indicates that this document had a preliminary nature: it is a redacted transcription of Ermine's reports on her strange, multifarious experiences and was not meant as an official entry in a planned canonization proceeding. The almost simultaneous translation into Latin, however, suggests that Jean le Graveur and his colleagues may have had further plans for the text.

Of special importance is also manuscript BnF fr. 25552, where Ermine's *Visions* appear among French works by Jean Gerson.[9] It is by far the longest text (fols. 152r–303v) among the twenty-odd in the manuscript. Gerson's approving letter, which can be found at the end of BnF fr. 25213 is missing, however, and although there is an announcement of this text, the following folio remains empty, a strange waste of precious writing space. The manuscript was rearranged in the third quarter of the fifteenth century when folios 313r to 315v were removed from another Gerson manuscript (BnF fr. 24841; Calvot and Ouy no. 26) and bound into this one. These folios contain the "confession" of the sorcerer Jean de Bar, who was burned at the stake in 1398, just two years after Ermine's death.[10] De Bar was a native of Champagne, the same region that sheltered Ermine, and a *mestre fizicien* (physician) to the French king Charles VI. Supposedly he indulged in his magic incantations and rites in the forests near Brie. The practices he is accused of closely resemble the ones mentioned in the articles of the 1398 condemnation of *ars magica* pronounced by the Faculty of Theology at the University of Paris, whose chancellor was of course Jean Gerson.[11] These practices include the use of magical words and charms; the invocation of demons; the use of magic mirrors to "ban" demons into them and thus make them subservient; and the use of hair and fingernails for magic purposes. This list is typical for late fourteenth-century magical practices.

FIGURE 10. This drawing of Ermine's tomb on the *page de garde* of the manuscript (Paris, Bibliothèque nationale de France, lat. 13782) was added in the seventeenth century. The writing around the image and below it states that Ermine experienced many marvelous things (*merveilles*) and that she died on the feast day of Saint Louis in 1395 (an error for 1396). It also states that she was buried in the left lateral nave of the Church of Saint Paul du Val-des-Ecoliers. Courtesy Bibliothèque nationale de France.

One wonders why, a generation after Gerson's death, this confession was moved from a codex featuring only texts by Gerson into a manuscript that also contains Ermine's *Visions*. I can offer nothing more than hypotheses here. Ermine's experiences and Jean de Bar's magic practices both belong to the realm of the supernatural over which Gerson set himself up as an arbiter. The "new" manuscript put together by a *remanieur*, an assembler of manuscripts, highlights the expertise of Gerson's by assembling in the same manuscript two famous cases in which Gerson was involved in various ways: he was instrumental in the redaction of the university's condemnation of magic in 1398, which led to the execution of Jean de Bar, and, as we saw, he repeatedly judged the case of Ermine—first rather positively just a few years after Ermine's death and more than twenty years later very negatively in his *On the Examination of Doctrines* (1423), where he speaks of his near seduction by the case of a "certain Ermine de Reims."[12]

But perhaps the *remanieur* of BnF fr. 25552 also wanted to create an implicit contrast between the traditional practices of sorcery and Ermine's visionary experiences, which in the third quarter of the fifteenth century could increasingly be interpreted as manifestations of witchcraft. Indeed, we saw that within the *Visions* the word *sorcière* is used: in one striking passage one of the major demonic impersonators of saints, Saint Paul the Simple, warns Ermine that she could be accused of being a *sorcière* (153), that she might be imprisoned and tortured in order to confess to her dealings with demons: in other words, exactly what happened to Jean de Bar. This threat of judicial persecution as a consequence of demonic vexations places Ermine at the crossroads of the "traditional" indictment of sorcery, as it was defined in the condemnation of 1398 and of newer kinds of accusations related to the codification of witchcraft that takes shape in the period of the refashioning of BnF fr. 25552. These newer accusations appear in the works of Johannes Nider (d. 1438), author of the *Formicarius* (The ant hill), and of the Dominican inquisitors Heinrich Krämer and Jakob Sprenger whose 1486–87 *Hammer of Witches* became the prosecutorial handbook *par excellence* for the witch hunters of the subsequent centuries.[13] The codicological afterlife of Ermine's *Visions* can thus open a window on the reception of a case like Ermine's and of Gerson's role as a judge of supernatural experiences and activities in the following century.

The Visions of Ermine de Reims

The full text of the Visions occupies about 120 printed pages in Claude Arnaud-Gillet's modern edition, which is followed by a complete translation into modern French. The following translation constitutes about one fifth of the whole text, concentrating on some representative passages and those that are especially important for the analyses offered in this book. Added transitions between passages appear in brackets.

Here begins the prologue of the new story telling of several marvelous things that happened recently in Reims, with God's permission, to a simple and humble creature named Ermine.

To the honor, glory, and praise of the sweet, loving Jesus, lord of heaven and earth, savior and creator of all creatures; and also to the shame and confusion of the enemy,[1] who with God's permission—in order to deceive poor sinners—transforms himself sometimes into a male or female saint, sometimes into an angel, sometimes into human form, that is, a live or dead man or woman, sometimes into the shape of an animal, sometimes into the shape of a bird, sometimes into flies of various forms, sometimes into a voice of a person that God permits him to use, and sometimes into a shape of metal. And in order to uncover his cleverness and deception I, poor and unworthy sinner, subprior of the church of Saint-Paul in Reims, of the Order of the Val-des-Ecoliers,[2] have written here about some marvelous adventures which feature all the shapes I described above, and which I heard from the mouth of a simple little woman of good will, who confessed herself to me for several years and told them to me as the truth, and which in my simplicity I have written down with God's help as best I could, just as she told them to me every day.

And because these things are so marvelous that they are hard to believe, I, her confessor, one day when she wanted to take communion, asked her to stay after her confession and said, "Ermine, you have told me many things that are difficult to believe; are they true?" Whereupon she put her hand in mine and said, "You can be certain, sir, that I have not lied to you with a single word, and there is no oath that I would not be willing to swear, and I'd rather have my head cut off than that I would knowingly perjure myself before God." After that, in the evening she left the church, as she did every day: very fearful and trembling because every night she thought she would die.

[Jean presses Ermine twice more on whether she is telling the truth and each time she says yes.] And however many times I asked her, I believed her because of her simplicity she was incapable to invent the marvelous things that you will read below; and also our prior,[3] I and all the friars in our house, and the people she lodged with, had seen the many injuries around her face that the demons had inflicted on her as well as the black puncture mark. And another woman of good will, named Marie d'Aubenton, who lived near her and visited her often and did many good things for her during her illnesses, swore that she had seen her naked body badly beaten and with blue marks in many places, and she also saw other clear signs that showed that all the facts were true. And these things were so well known that the people who slept in two rooms near hers testified that several times they had heard the noise that the demons made in her room. And again on her deathbed she affirmed under oath that these things were true, and she did so before six notable people, namely, three virtuous priests and three good and honest women. And she said it again that it was the truth when she received extreme unction, before the priest who had given her the unction and the people who were present.

It seems to me that this booklet is very profitable because of many things that are contained therein, some of them hidden and some of them evident. For one can find there a remarkable affirmation of our faith by considering that all the power, the knowledge, force, and cleverness of the infernal enemies were marshaled against this poor, simple, and ignorant woman, but that she by virtue of her faith and through God's help was, after some time, victorious against them. Some of the pains of hell are described in this booklet and also some knowledge of the joys of paradise. There is also a notable and edifying manifestation of the Passion of our Lord in the Holy Sacrament on the altar,[4] and an excellent guide to recognizing the cleverness of the enemy. [Jean now evokes Saint John who in the Apocalypse, or the Book of Revelation, predicted the coming of the Antichrist: just so, God revealed things through Ermine, and Jean's book is therefore a guide on how to protect ourselves against the wiles of the devil.]

And if it happened that some things should be transmitted to us via dreams, visions, or other revelations, we should give no credence to them and should not believe that we are worthy of such things being shown to us.[5] And we have to strive to follow the common doctrine approved by Holy Church and put our trust wholly in God, and never doubt His mercy, no matter what kind of peril or tribulation may come our way, and also without glorifying ourselves for any grace, sweetness, or consolation that we may receive. Let us attribute all bad things to our sins and all good things to the grace of God; we should above all ardently desire that His will be done, as did this simple and humble creature as best she could; she was so steeped in true and profound humility and so confirmed in the ancient and secure doctrine of the blessed saints that she never wanted to do homage to any spirit that was shown to her, nor believe anything that was said to her, nor firmly believe anything was truly good, whether someone tried to convince her through promises or threats. Rather she believed deep down that she was unworthy of seeing or hearing anything good, as we will see below. [Jean closes the prologue by commending himself to God and expressing the hope that his book will profit his readers.]

[This part is not dated]

In the year of Our Lord 1384 a man named Regnault and a woman named Ermine, his wife, came from the Vermandois to live in Reims in a street called rue Neuve, quite near the church of the Val-des-Ecoliers. Regnault and Ermine were simple people of good reputation but with few possessions in this world. The man was old and weak and could do nothing but go to church, and it was the woman who had to provide for them. In the summer she cut grass in the marshes and collected straw in the fields and sold it, and with the money she earned she bought what they needed. And it happened that Regnault passed away; he was seventy-two when he died and Ermine was forty-six. After her husband had died Ermine's friends came to Reims several times in order to take her back to the countryside. They told her that she was all alone and poor and that in Reims she would remain poor because she had no friends there, but that if she went back with them to the country, they would take care of her for the rest of her life. She came to me, the subprior of the Val-des-Ecoliers, for advice because I had been her confessor and also her husband's when he was still alive. I told her not to go back to the country and that she had begun to serve God and that she should persevere for the rest of her life and trust in God who would never fail her. She believed me and sent back her friends without their achieving what they had hoped for.

And I made her live in a little room of about sixteen feet square near our priory whose windows looked out on the courtyard of the church of the Val-des-Ecoliers and from which one can hear our masses day and night. And I commanded Ermine[6] to get up every night to hear the matins[6] we chanted in the church, and she answered that she would do so gladly, and not just that but anything I might advise her to do for her salvation, because she wanted to obey all my commands for the love of God, and she did so until her death, for she always asked my permission as a monk would ask his abbot.

[Ermine begins her new way of life that consists of little sleep and almost constant prayer.] She fasted according to the commandments of the Church, and also on Wednesdays and Saturdays, and she ate what God gave her, and on Fridays she fasted with bread and water. And it happened one Friday night that she put away her table, and her bread and water, and kneeled down to commend herself to God; then she got up and was so preoccupied with God that she forgot to eat her supper and went to bed. And a little before midnight she woke up and tried to remember whether she had eaten; so she ate a little bread and drank a bit of water in order to obey me, for I had forbidden her to spend a day without eating. And she asked me several times for leave to fast every day, but I did not want to grant her this request because she lived too modestly and also because of the mischief that was done to her.[7] She also fasted on the eves of the five feasts of Our Lady, always with bread and water.[8]

As for her bed, she slept on a narrow bed of straw and was always dressed in a hair shirt with a cord or two belts which were made from horse hair, had several knots in it, and was worn on her naked skin. And it happened once that she was bathing and the belt shrank, but she did not take it off, day or night. Once when she was talking with me, she said, "Sir, my belt hurts me more than usual." And I told her, "Then take it off"; and she answered simply, "Sir, I cannot"; "Why not?" I said. She answered, "Because it entered my flesh and the skin has grown over it in several places." And when I heard this I was stunned and told her, "I want you to take it off!" Then she said, "I beg you, for the love of God, that you permit me to keep it on until it rots for then it will fall to pieces, for I don't know how I will get it off now." I responded, "You have to take it off somehow. You managed to tie it around you with great pains and God willing you will be able to untie it with great pains, which will be penance for your sins." She answered, "I will gladly obey, however much it hurts, for I can never suffer enough." She had the habit of saying "I can never suffer enough."[9] And then she left.

The next day when she saw me, she said, "Good news!" "What news?" I said. "I managed to get the belt off." "And how did you do it?" I asked. She answered simply: "I will tell you how I did it. When I undressed last night, I untied the belt in front and started to tug on one end and then on the other, but I could not get it off and it hurt very badly. Then I saw a big nail sticking out from the wall in my room, and I tied one of the ends of the belt to the nail and I moved away quickly and the belt hung on to the nail. But I can tell you that I am flayed all around my body, at the places where the belt had been." And when I heard this, I forbade her to ever tie anything so tightly around her that it entered her flesh. A good woman who had taken care of her during her illness and put her in her shroud told me that when she wrapped her in the shroud, she had marks on her body in many places that looked like recently healed wounds where one could see the scar tissue, and it looked as if she had beaten herself.

Before the adventures[10] began, she confessed herself to me every week, but when the adventures began, she realized the peril she was in and began to get into the habit of confessing herself every day and to take communion once a week, and she continued this until her death. And the first time I heard her confession, she told me, "When I look at my sins and think about them and God's justice, I don't know what to do so that He will have mercy on me. And for that reason I beg you to prescribe such a great penance that it will allow me to appease God and do a part of my penance in this world." I answered, "Penance is a very good thing, but you have to do it with discretion, and doing penance is not sufficient, but you must try to guard against sin, and show great contrition for your sins, and love God with all your heart, for one reads in the gospels that God told the Magdalene 'her sins, which are many, are forgiven, for she loved much.'"[11] [Ermine shows ardent love for God, which pleases Jean very much.] She had such repentance for her sins and so hated her body that she sometimes told me simply: "I hate my entire body for the sins it committed against God and if I could do so without sin I would stick a sturdy knife in my heart."

[The following scene takes place on November 28, 1395, early on in Ermine's visionary "career." It is a night of vexations: she is beaten; someone (the French is the indeterminate *on*, of course suggesting a demon) tosses her pillow and rosary out the window . . . finally she goes back to bed.]

She saw that someone tore a paper image from the wall where it was attached by a nail and threw it on the floor. Then she saw an earthen pot rise up into the air; it had holy water in it, and someone threw it at her. It missed her but shattered on the planks of her bed, and holy water was all over the place. Then someone grabbed the tablet[12] she was holding in order to take it away from her. She pulled in the other direction and screamed, "You will not get this tablet, demon, unless you pull out my arms with it." After a rather long fight he let her go, but with all this she saw no one.

Suddenly she saw in the middle of her bedchamber a young and handsome man and a young and beautiful woman; they began to embrace and kiss each other and then lay down on the floor and committed a sin together. And the devil did all this in front of her because he wanted her to take evil pleasure in fleshly sin. When they were done, the young man went up to her bed and said, "Aren't you miserable, you who kill yourself with fasting, not sleeping, wearing a hair shirt, stringing a cord around your waist, and sleeping on a bed of straw? Do you think you can escape from us? I assure you, you can't; on the contrary, you will have two hells.[13] It would be much better if you lived a pleasant life and that you satisfy the appetites of your body, for you will never be able to avoid eternal damnation." And after they had talked for a while, they left.

[The following is a pretty typical account of a series of "vexations." Notable are the facts that the "voice" disguises itself as Jean le Graveur's voice and that a demon takes on the shape of her late husband. The date is December 5, 1395.]

It happened one Sunday evening, the 5th of December, that after communion she was beaten, and these things happened on the preceding days: someone took away her rosary three nights in a row, and several times when she was kneeling in prayer she was thrown on the floor; and at night she was slapped once or twice. So it happened that one night she was slapped while asleep and another time while she was praying. And when she was in bed, the demon was screaming outside, imitating my voice, and she got up and opened the window, and she was slapped violently and saw nothing. Another time someone called from outside with my voice, and she believed that it was the demon and so she said, "I will not come out, demon." And the demon answered from outside, "Come here, come here." And when he saw that she was not coming, he went to her, and while she was praying, he slapped her so hard that she fell on the floor. And sometimes when she was asleep, she felt as if her room was upside down; and sometimes she felt as if she were falling into a ditch full of serpents and dragons and she could not get any sleep. And sometimes, when she was awake, the demon brought her ideas that were against the faith. Later, during another night, when she was in bed, a demon came who was dressed and spoke like her husband, and he came and lay down on her cloak behind her. She said to him, "Go away, demon, you are not my husband." But he did not leave but remained lying behind her for a long time and breathed like a man who is asleep.

[Demons can also disguise themselves as angels. Note here how Jean describes the process of discernment. The date is December 18, 1395.]

The next Saturday at about ten in the morning, when the woman who was taking care of Ermine went out for a bit, a demon came and wanted to pull her out of her bed in the middle of the room. When the woman came back up the stairs and the demon heard her coming and he could not achieve what he wanted, he kicked Ermine in the chest and left. On that same Saturday, in the evening, with her window closed and her candle burning, she was lying in bed, feeling very weak, when two demons arrived in the shape of angels, that is, white as snow with golden hair and wings, and they were of a beautiful shape and had dimples in their cheeks and chins; and they brought with them such a bright light that it seemed as if the sun was shining indoors and also such a great smell that it seemed the room was filled with spices. And one of them was holding a golden candlestick with golden candles, and he stood at the foot of the bed; the other one had an instrument that is called a *vielle*[14] and stood near her head. "We have been sent by Our Lord in order to comfort you in your tribulations; we are God's angels." Then she said, "I am not worthy of God sending me his angels, for I am a poor sinner who hardly deserves to live for the sins that I have committed against God." Then he began to play the *vielle* so sweetly that it was wonderful to listen to, and the sick woman experienced a great conflict, for she had the vision of the two of them which was so beautiful that it was a marvel to behold; she also had the sweet odor, and she had the bright light and the sweet sound—all this seemed to her to be a little paradise. This is how her body experienced it, but in her spirit she was so terrified that she trembled all over, for she knew very well that these were demons. And later after he had played the music for quite a while, he stretched out his hand toward the sick woman and said, "Beautiful daughter, let me touch your illness and you will be cured." But she held up her hand and said, "Do not touch me, demon. Do you think I'm so stupid that I think you are an angel? I know well, through God's grace, that the two of you are demons." And she spit in their direction and they left.

She remained very pensive, thinking over what she had seen; and she had looked at them so much that she could not close her eyes. Soon after, while she was thinking and not sleeping, a huge, horribly ugly serpent came into her room. It had a rolled-up tail, an enormous head and round mouth, and had a huge tongue coming out of its jaws, just like big dogs do when they are thirsty and hot in summer, and out of this serpent's mouth came such a horrible stink that it seemed that all the garbage of the world was piled up inside it. Then the huge serpent approached her and stretched out its fangs toward her as if it wanted to strangle her. She made the sign of the cross and held her hand in front of her throat, and the serpent drew back and left. But the stink remained and made her so sick that she vomited in front of her bed and lost her appetite. She could not eat anything all the next day, and I gave her a lavender sachet to put under her nose.

[Christmas Eve 1395: Ermine has resisted the temptation to drink her wine with the help of a demon who threw her tumbler on the floor. Now a counterfeit Saint Mary Magdalene appears, and we have another example of Ermine's discernment. Jean's musings on the actual shapes of demons are remarkable.][15]

After she had had her supper, she closed her window and her door and began to pray. A demon in the shape of a beautiful woman arrived; she was white as snow, had a beautiful gold crown on her head, and said, "Dear daughter, I have come to return to you the two rosaries that someone stole from you. You should know that I am the Magdalen of whom one says that she was such a great sinner, and I have come to comfort you. You should take comfort in Our Lord and have hope in God." Then Ermine answered, "You stinking demon, you are filled with deception." And as soon as Ermine had said this, the demon changed into a horrible shape and the crown that had been so beautiful and tall transformed itself into two horns. And shortly afterward two demons appeared and beat her very badly and did great mischief to her all night and then began to dance.

I have said several times earlier, when I was speaking of demons, "they transformed themselves into an ugly shape" and that no living person could tolerate the shape they have in hell. But the most awful shape that Ermine saw them in was what I described above, the Wednesday on the eve of Saint Catherine, when they were so horrible that one cannot even imagine it. Most often she saw them in the shape that we give them in theatrical plays. Sometimes they had mouths like ovens with tongues coming out of them that were a foot long, burning stronger than fire and with eyes like torches, with rays of light coming out of them. Sometimes they had horns, sometimes huge ears; sometimes they were dressed in short garments and sometimes in long ones; sometimes they were small and sometimes they reached the ceiling; they were always blacker than coal and sometimes gave off some kind of light but sometimes not; and sometimes they talked and sometimes they did not.[16] And the little woman affirmed to me, her confessor, with a solemn oath, that she believed and knew with certainty that in all the adventures that are recounted here God has kept her spirit and her body safe, and each time it was a miracle, for she was so fearful that a cat or mouse or any noise she heard scared her to death.

[The second part of *Visions* begins on January 19, 1396. Ermine is visited by a counterfeit angel, snow white with multicolored wings and golden hair, who urges her to repent more. He sounds like a real angel. Jean describes how demons can change their voices.]

And nonetheless, although he spoke in a soft voice and said beautiful phrases, she was very much afraid and for that reason knew that this was a demon. And you should know that every time [the demon] came in an ugly shape, he spoke in a crude and horrible voice; and when he came in the shape and clothes of a man, he had a human voice and spoke very beautifully; and when he came in the shape of a saint, he spoke extremely pleasantly in a soft voice.

[On January 21, 1396, a demon tries to persuade Ermine to leave by mentioning that a man had threatened to kill her. She is convinced that this was the demon himself. He taunts her by suggesting she go to the police (*la justice*) to complain! The vision that follows this scene seems to be ambiguous. Real angels and saint or not?]

It happened on Saturday, the feast day of Saint Vincent, that she prayed quite late in the evening, when she heard a very sweet melody that came closer and closer until it entered her chamber, and four angels arrived, of whom two carried musical instruments made from silver and called *rebecs*;[17] one carried an incense burner, and the fourth carried two silver candelabras with burning candles in them. They came close to the woman and played on their instruments for a long time; the other one perfumed her room with incense. They wore white albs and were small: they looked about seven or eight years old, like the little choir boys one finds in the big churches. They had golden and multicolored wings, golden hair, and extremely beautiful faces, that is, beyond human nature. With the perfume that surpassed all human perfume, the vision of their beauty, the light of the candles, and the melody produced by the instruments, it all seemed like paradise. And after they had played for a while they all approached the woman who was on her knees and took her hands into their little hands and said, "My sister, my friend, my daughter, my companion, Our Lord has sent us to you in order to show a bit of the joy that exists in heaven, so that you will guard against sin, and will love Him, and will do only good, for if you do evil you have seen the ugly and horrible demons with whom you will go, and if you do good you will go with us, and for that reason sweet Jesus, the sweet savior, shows you evil and good to advise you to be good." Then the woman said simply, "I am happy to see you, but I believe that all of you are demons, for I am not worthy to receive such grace from Our Lord as you want me to believe." All of them responded together, "Truly, dear friend, we are not demons, but we are angels sent from God to you."

Then came a priest, dressed as a priest, with a tonsure and a white chasuble sparkling with gold. He was carrying a book and said, "Dear friend, I am Saint Peter, and God sent me to comfort you, for He takes pity on all sinners; no one can sin so much that, if he repents with all his heart, He will not have mercy on him. You can see this by the example of the Magdalen who was such a great sinner, but when she repented, He forgave her all her sins and did such a great honor to her that she was the first one to whom He appeared after His blessed resurrection." "You are," said the woman, "Saint Peter from hell. I remember well that recently you came to my bed and said that you had the keys to paradise, and I did not open my eyes because I knew well that you were a demon, and when you realized this, you hit me three times in the head with your fist and kicked me in the chest with your foot."[18] He said, "I have never hurt you, beautiful daughter; this is the first time I have come to you." "I don't believe you," she said, "I am really astonished that you think me so stupid. I am one of the pitiful sinners in the world, and you want me to believe that God would send me his angels and Saint Peter? All of you are demons, and to make things brief, I will do nothing that you tell me to do unless the subprior advises me to do it, and I will tell him everything as soon as I get up in the morning." "That's fine with us," they said, "do everything he tells you to do, that will be a good thing. But truly, beautiful daughter, we are not demons."

And they began to play even more beautifully compared with before, for two of them played their instruments and two of them sang with their clear voices, and the melody could not have been sweeter for they all made music together. And one of them said to the woman, "Look at us, dear friend, how the four of us make such beautiful music together, imagine what joy there will be when all of us will be together in heaven." And after they had played and sung together for a long time, they came to her and one after the other took her by the hand, saying "Adieu, beautiful friend, make sure you do only good things." And then all five of them left; but a beautiful odor remained in the room until the next morning. This vision lasted from nine in the evening until matins, which we sing around midnight.

[This scene takes place on January 28, 1396. Here we encounter Ermine outside of the confines of her bedroom and can see that even in public she has to put up with the demons.]

The prior of Saint-Denis, who was the confessor of the archbishop of Reims, had confessed this woman several times and believed in the truth of her adventures. Once he assigned as penance to her that she was to walk to Saint-Maur, a chapel located next to Saint-Nicaise of Reims. She went there the Friday after the conversion of Saint Paul and encountered a man, or a demon who had taken on the form of a man, she did not know. He grabbed her rudely by the chest and said, "Where you going, you whore? Are you going whoring?" Terribly scared, she answered sweetly, "Not at all, sir, on the contrary, I'm on my way to Saint-Maur." "By God's blood, you are lying," he said. "You are going whoring, you only live from whoring, you dirty evil whore. By God's death, I may just kill you." He held her by the chest for quite a long time while telling her all this. She was very ashamed, for bystanders heard his insults that were given without any reason. Then he let her go without beating her.

[February 22–23, 1396, the first weekend of Lent: Here Jean tries to tie in Ermine's experiences with certain biblical passages. We read how Ermine was kidnapped and transported to the woods outside of Reims and what happened to her there.]

[Ermine spends an unpleasant night in her room, which stinks as if it is filled with putrefying corpses. Jean then comments, addressing his readers:]

And you should know that some of the adventures that happened to this little woman during Lent have some relationship to the Gospels that we are accustomed to read in holy church on the Sundays of Lent.[19] But she did not know what to think or make of them because she was illiterate and also, they did not happen on the proper Sundays, but some of them happened the week before and others the week after, and only some on the very Sunday when we read the appropriate Gospel text.

On the Wednesday after the Sunday of *brandons* we read in the Gospel:[20] *Ductus est Jhesus Christus in desertum* (Jesus Christ was led into the desert [Mt. 4:1]. A good lady named Marie d'Aubenton lived near our house, and she had visited the woman of whom I speak in her illnesses and she knew about and had seen many of her adventures. And she had asked Ermine to come over and help her with the laundry. And it happened on the above-mentioned Wednesday, a little after matins, that a demon, with the voice of a little girl who lived in Marie's house, called out to the woman from the street, and the woman got up and went to the window that looks out on the street and saw the demon in the dress and with the voice of the little girl. The girl said, "Come on, Ermine, my lady wants you to help her with the laundry." And she responded, "No, it's too early." "And when will you come, then?" "When the morning bell rings." Ermine went back to bed and then got up when the morning bell rang and made the sign of the cross. And when she went down into the street, three men arrived, dressed in black and looking human, on three black horses. And one of them grabbed her and threw her on his horse as if she were a suitcase, and one moment later she found herself in the woods. She looked around and saw no horses but around her so many demons that she could not count them, and they all looked like men and were dressed in black.

She threw herself onto the ground and commended herself to God. They came toward her and said, "There you are, now we've got you, you are in our hands. Give yourself over to us and we will not harm you." The woman responded, "I will give myself over to my sweet Lord Jesus Christ, not to you." Then three demons approached her in the shape of people of her hometown who had loved her very much and done many good things for her. They said, "And why, Ermine, do you not want to commend yourself to us? You remember well all the good things we have done for you; are we not good people?" "You are, all of you, demons," she responded. Then they brought a large sack full of gold florins and put it in front of the woman, saying, "Take some of these florins; you are a poor woman, there are lots, no need to spare them." She answered, "I don't want any." "So what do you want?" they said. "Should we take you back?" "I don't want anything to do with you," she said. "You brought me here into these woods against my will, and when it will be my God's will, He will help me, I trust Him completely." Then the demons spoke with each other in horrible voices, but the woman could not understand what they were saying. And then they blew their trumpets, so loud that all the woods were filled with such noise as if a whole army had arrived. And after they had made this noise for a long time, they were silent.

Then the woman got up and saw nothing; she had been on her knees in their midst for about an hour. She looked around and saw nothing but woods and no path. So she kneeled down on the ground and began to pray to God. After a while a man arrived, dressed in a goat skin and with a long white beard. He said, "What are you doing here, woman, are you asleep?" She answered, "I am praying." "Who brought you here?" he asked. "It is God's will that I should be here." "And do you know where you are?" "No, I don't know where I am, nor what time it is, nor what day." "You are," he said, "in the woods of Nanteuil."[21] "Is that far from Reims?" she asked. "No," he said, "are you from Reims?" "Yes," she said. "Do you want me to show you the way back?" he asked. "Yes, sir, please do." Then he bent down and took the woman by the hand and helped her get up. He led her through the woods where there was no path or road, and when they were out of the woods, he said, "Do you see there the steeple of Saint Lié, dear daughter? Go there without fear and you will be safe." And the woman said, "You did me a great service, sir, may God reward you." And when she had walked a bit, she turned around but did not see her man anymore.

After that, she arrived at Saint Lié and was present at the mass celebrated by Jean de Varennes, and she was seen by several people who knew her well.[22] And when she returned to Reims she came to a little valley between Sainte Geneviève and the "tree of the young people," and there is a little stream and some stones one can use to cross it There she saw a man approach, dressed in a goat skin and with a white beard, who said to her, "Dear daughter, do you recognize me? I am the man who led you out of the woods this morning, and I will also lead you out of here for you will meet with some harm here." And he took her by the hand and led her out of the valley and up a hill and said, "There is Reims; you can now go safely and don't have to worry anymore." Then the woman said, "Good-bye, sir, and may God reward you for the service you have rendered me." She advanced a little and then looked back, but she did not know what had become of her man. And she retuned to Reims safe and glad, for the demons had not beaten her up but only frightened her.

Some people might say or think that she went to the woods of Nanteuil and to Saint Lié and then said that someone had taken her there. But those who know the facts would never say this because the people who live in the same house with her, and who were in bed below and she above, heard her walk in her room before matins over their heads in order to go to the window to the street to speak with the demon who called out to her in the voice of the little girl who worked for Marie d'Aubenton and who said, "My lady wants you to come and help." And they heard her answer, "I certainly won't come now, it's too early." And the demon responded, "And when will you come?" And they heard her say, "When the morning bell rings." And when the morning bell rang, these witnesses assured me that they heard her go down the stairs from her room and pass by their beds, and they said to her, "Ermine, where are you going so early?" "I'm going," she said, "to help Marie d'Aubenton with the laundry." And as soon as she went out the door, someone abducted her to the woods of Nanteuil, which is about three leagues from Reims, and she was taken as quickly as one can turn over one's hand, and she would not have been able to leave Reims on her own at that hour because the gates were not yet open. And also she was seen at Saint Lié so early in the morning that she could not have walked there by herself after the gates were opened. And all this was witnessed by a man named Jacquet de Colmanté who often went there and had gone there that morning on horseback. He brought me the news about her for we did not know what had become of her.

[February 28, 1396]

The Monday after the Gospel reading *Assumpsit Jhesus Petrum et Jacobum et Johanem, fratrem eius* (Jesus led Peter, Jacob, and his brother John up a mountain; Matthew 17:1) at about midnight, when the second bell of matins was sounded in our house, the woman was up and had opened her window in order to hear matins. Three demons came into her room, dressed in goat skins and with long beards like hermits, and one of them looked exactly like the man who had led the woman back from the woods of Nanteuil; and he said to her, "Don't you know me, dear daughter? I am the man who found you in the woods of Nanteuil last Thursday and sent you on your way and protected you from the demons who would have taken you to hell if it were not for me." "I believe firmly," said the woman, "that they would have taken me to hell if God had not protected me, and you would do so now if God were not protecting me out of His goodness, for the three of you are demons." [The demon then recounts how he had met her at the stream and pointed her toward Reims. The three hermitlike demons offer her money just in case Jean le Graveur dies and she is left penniless. Of course, Ermine refuses. The three keep on talking for a long time, trying to convince her that they are not demons.] Then the demon who had talked the most took her by the hand so that she would do his bidding. And when they saw they had not succeeded, they left.[23]

[This scene takes place on Easter Sunday 1396. It illustrates Ermine's trouble with bothersome animals and then segues into one of the dramatic scenes of demonic apparitions, this one focused on the Eucharist and a type of vision that became very popular in the later Middle Ages: the "child in the Host."]

The following Sunday, which was Easter, the woman went to communion in her parish church and then to hear the great mass in our priory. At the moment of Elevation[24] a voice said to the woman: "Do you really think that this is God who is being elevated there? No, it's just a little piece of bread. It's great heresy to believe something like that. I will truly show and give to you your creator whom you will see with your own eyes. You believe things you cannot see—isn't that the utmost stupidity? I will show him to you so clearly that you will not be able to refuse to believe, unless, of course, you take leave of your common sense."

On Easter evening the woman commended herself to God as devoutly as she could, lit her lamp, closed her window, and went to bed. Seven bats arrived that flew in front of her face and bothered her so much that she could

not sleep. She got up and took a flyswatter that I had given her to defend
herself against the flies that I mentioned earlier.[25] She tried to chase the bats
out of her room, but they refused to leave. She therefore went back to bed,
exhausted, and put the flyswatter next to her. The bats came back and tired
her out completely. As soon as the bells for matins were rung, they departed
but left behind such a sickly smell that the woman thought she would die of
it. She went to her window and listened to matins rather calmly.

When matins was over, she went back to bed. Right away someone
extinguished her light, and she heard a little bell ring from afar, approaching
her room, just as when a priest carries communion to someone. Then two
demons arrived dressed in white albs and carrying two lighted torches. Then
came two little demons in the shape of angels, who with their censers spread
incense in the room. Then came two demons dressed in white albs, carrying
two vials and a golden chalice. They proceeded to decorate the table in her
room with beautiful and rich golden cloths. They also decorated the woman's
bed with a rich cover and then put their vials and the golden chalice on the
table. Finally a priest arrived dressed in a cape of beautiful golden fabric held
together on his chest with a beautiful golden clasp. This priest was carrying
a beautiful vessel with a cover, similar to those used for carrying communion
to people, but there was no cross on the cover as there usually is. The priest
deposited his vessel on the table next to the other objects and then
approached the woman's bed and said: "At this moment, Ermine, beautiful
young woman, consider the honor God does you by sending us to you with
such a beautiful company. I am Saint Augustine who was one of the great
doctors of the Church, and God sends me to you in order to teach you the
truth. You actually believe the subprior who, by his pernicious teachings,
destroys himself as well as you and numerous other people. I want you to
know with great certainty that the priest who gave you communion today
gave you only bread. And this morning at the great mass, when you heard
the voice, all you saw at Elevation was just a bit of bread. But now I have
brought you your creator, Jesus Christ, whom you will see with your own
eyes, and at that moment God will judge your faith. You have seen the
demons and still see them; you have seen the saints; and for this reason God
has accorded you more grace than any living woman, and now He will see
the goodness that is in you."

Then he sat down next to her on the bed and said, "You now have to
confess a little, then I will give you communion and show you your creator
in his true shape." The woman replied, "One hears confession of and brings

communion in bed to people who are ill. I'm not ill, thank God. I have someone who hears my confessions and gives me communion whenever I desire it, God be praised. When I want to confess and take communion, I go to church or, if I'm ill, I ask someone to fetch my parish priest. I don't want to have anything to do with you or your company." Then he said, "You're not thinking straight." They began to sing with such elegance that no singer in the whole world could sing as melodiously. When they finished singing, the priest said, "Ermine, dear girl, you believe that you are not seeing anything; pay attention now for you will see your creator in his true form and you will also see only bread."

At this moment those who had brought the vials, the chalice, and the ornaments knelt down and someone put a white sheet before them just as one does in church when people take communion. Then they folded their hands, and the priest took from his chalice a round and white Host and put it in the mouth of one of them. Then the priest said, "Watch carefully; now we come to the tricky part." Then he again took from his vessel a round and white Host, elevated it a bit, and right away the Host took the form of a small and very beautiful child; and from this child burst forth such a bright light that the woman, dazzled by its éclat, thought she had gone blind. And the priest put the child in the mouth of the other one, and the little child cried a little, thus showing that it was alive. Then the priest gave them to drink, one after the other, from the golden vessel. Then he went back to the woman's bed and said, "Right now you have seen with your own eyes the true form of your creator, and you have also seen a bit of bread. You therefore must believe firmly that the one who received the bread only got bread, but the one who received the child received his Savior." "I believe firmly," said the woman, "that he received a devil from hell." The priest answered, "You believe wrongly, and I can state that the subprior is not as slow as you to believe for if he had seen what you just saw, he would have believed a lot faster than you."

Then the two little angels who were holding the censers approached the woman's bed and said to her, "Ermine, dearest friend, if you believe us, you will have confidence in this valorous doctor, lord Saint Augustine, for he is the flower of doctors of the Christian faith, and God sent him to you in order to inform you of the truth. And now we come to the heart of the matter: your damnation or your salvation. For if you believe what he says, you will be saved, and if you don't, you will be damned. This is your only chance; we will not be back." And the woman said, "I certainly hope you won't be back, if it please my sweet Savior Jesus Christ. You are all demons, and I believe you less than ever. I am firmer in my faith and love of Jesus Christ than I ever was, for you bring me nothing but deception and perfidy. You tire yourselves out for nothing by coming to see me so often, for I'm certainly not grateful to you nor will I do anything you advise me to do." The woman then turned away her eyes and began to pray. And a moment later when she looked at the place where the demons had been, she saw nothing.

On Easter Monday she came to our chapter house and told me, "What a strange thing; if I heard someone tell of such a strange occurrence without having seen it myself, I would not believe it. But I pray to God that I may be carried away into hell if I did not tell you the truth as much as I am able to."

[June 11–17, 1396: This passage is part of a long series of Ermine's eucharistic visions. It comes right after the moment when Jean le Graveur sought the counsel of his learned friends, analyzed in Chapter 3.]

And it seems that God wanted these things to be written down because several times it happened that the priest elevated something that related to the Passion, and this was so distressing that the woman could not remain upright but fell face down to the ground, and therefore she could no longer contemplate what she had seen and could not tell it to me with accuracy. And it happened sometimes that I asked her what she had seen and she answered simply, "This was such a distressing thing that I could not look at it long enough for me to tell you exactly what I saw." And I told her, "When you hear mass, look closely at what the priest elevates so that you can tell me the truth about it." And sure enough, at the next mass she heard, the priest elevated something very similar to what he had elevated earlier, and she looked more closely, in response to what I had said to her, and told me all about it. But when the priest elevated the Host in the shape of a child, she was filled with such joy that her whole body trembled.

[June 12, 1396:] On the following Monday, when she heard two masses, she saw that at the first one the priest elevated a beautiful and shining child, whose light reached all the way to the woman who was kneeling down; and the child moved his little wrists and his little hands and it had blonde curls and a pudgy body, and one could see the folds of flesh on his wrists. The priest was holding him by the two sides. And at the other mass she saw that the priest at Elevation lifted a crucified man, all covered with wounds and blood, and it seemed that he had just been nailed to the cross because blood sprang forth abundantly in five places: the two hands, the two feet, and the side. And the woman emitted a cry, right where she stood, and she fell to the ground when she saw such a pitiful thing, and she remained on the ground for quite a while, very distressed and sobbing desperately.

And you should know that at that time there were two friars in our house who had been ordained as priests by bishops who had received their bishoprics from Pope Clement VII. At their masses the woman also saw the child and things related to the Passion just as she saw them at masses said by friars who had been ordained by bishops who had received their bishoprics from popes before Clement VII. Later, the woman heard several masses in churches that were not ours; some of them were said by priests rumored to live together with women, but even at their masses she saw the child and things related to the Passion, just as she saw them with the priests of our house who lead honest lives.[26]

[June 13, 1396:] The following Tuesday the woman heard five masses where she saw at the moment of Elevation once a very beautiful child; at two masses she saw the Host as bread; and at the other two she saw the Host in the priest's hands red as blood, round and of normal size.

[June 14, 1396:] On the following Wednesday she saw at Elevation during mass the Host in the priest's hands, and it was red and round and was about a foot across.

[June 16, 1396:] On the following Friday at mass the woman saw the priest elevate a red hand that could signify God's power. And at the other mass she saw that the priest elevated a crucified man who had a crown of thorns on his head; he was all covered with blood, which ran down from the thorns of his crown. His feet were cruelly nailed together, and he seemed drained of blood, for he was so opened on the side that it seemed that one could look into his body; but it seemed as if he was not yet dead.

[June 17, 1396:] On the following Saturday she saw the priest elevate at mass a crucified man even more pitiful than at the two previous masses. He was crowned with a very cruel crown of thorns all covered with blood. And this time she saw him as he was at the moment of his death, that is, with closed eyes, head hanging down and his mouth open as if he was giving up the ghost. And at the two other masses she saw at one a dove being elevated and at the other a child. On that same Saturday, at night, it happened that the woman was in bed, and as soon as she was asleep, it seemed to her that matins was being sung, and she got up and went to her window. She heard that the chanting was very loud, or so it seemed to her, and she knelt down and said a psalm and an Ave Maria and several other things. Afterward the first ring of matins was sounded in our house, and the singing immediately stopped; thus the woman knew that demons had deceived her.

[June 23, 1396: Although this passage does not mark the end of Ermine's eucharistic visions, they become much less frequent after June 22—or rather Jean decides not to chronicle all of them anymore, unless they have some new imagery. A certain fatigue on Jean's part is visible here.]

I have not written down all the accounts of days between the octave of the feast of the Holy Sacrament and today. I have left them aside for the sake of brevity and will now also omit the things that the woman has seen or heard at mass and also the things that she will see, unless they are some new things that she has not previously seen. But you should know that there was not a day (except two) between the octave of the Holy Sacrament and the feast of Saint John that the woman did not see the Host in some form other than the normal one.[27] And on the two days that she saw the Host in the normal form, she was overjoyed, for she was afraid to see it differently from other people because she feared being deceived, for she felt that she was not worthy of seeing anything that was good.

[July 3, 1396: This is an example of how Ermine hates and mortifies her body in order to ward off temptation.]

It happened on the evening of the third of July that the woman began to pray in her room. And immediately she experienced such horrible and strong bodily temptations that she could not think of anything to say in her prayers. And so she said in her heart, "Oh, you dirty, stinking carrion, no demon in hell is more hostile and opposed to your salvation than you are yourself; do you want to lead me into hell? You are too content to enrage your Creator; I will treat you soon enough in such a way that you will no longer want to amuse yourself." Then she stripped herself naked, took two thin cords made from horse hair and fashioned from them a scourge, and she beat herself in front and back until the blood spurted forth and she had several wounds. And she sobbed while beating herself hard because she felt terrible pain. And then she put on her hair shirt over the wounds. She suffered intensely, and the pain she felt made her forget her bodily temptations; she did not sleep at all that night.

[Ermine's death on August 25, 1396; Jean's epilogue and Ermine's return as an apparition in January 1397.]

It happened that on the Sunday of the octaves of mid-August[28] when the woman got up to hear Monday matins, a mortal illness befell her and she went to bed extremely sick. And although she had already taken communion and confessed herself that Sunday, she said on Tuesday that she wanted to confess again and receive the extreme unction, and thus it was done. And because one believes more what a person says at the hour of her death than what she says when in good health, I decided to ask her at that time if the adventures she had told me were true, not so much for myself, for I completely believed her, but for those who had heard about them and did not know as much about them as I did. And it happened that before her bed there stood three religious, well-known men of good reputation and honesty and three honest women of good morals. I said to her, "Ermine, dear friend, you are very ill; I beg you to tell me the truth. Are these things that you told me true or not for they are very hard to believe." She answered me before the six people I mentioned: "By the judgment that awaits my soul I never lied with a single word, and if I did not always say the exact words I always told you the substance of everything as much as I could and I will affirm this before anyone you want me to." And again I asked her in the presence of the priest who had given her extreme unction and of all the people who were there if the things she had told me were true, and she affirmed and confessed that what she had said was the entire truth.

I have said earlier, in the prologue to this book, that this woman about whom I spoke was a simple woman, and I certainly never lied because she was of a good simplicity and a working woman who went into the fields in summer to cut straw and into the marshes to cut grass in order to provide for herself before the adventures happened to her. And you have seen how wisely she responded to the demons and how well she told me about her adventures and that her mind and her body were preserved throughout these cruel adventures; it seems to me that this is a true miracle of God. And she always had God's help with her who showed His power through her. But He cleansed her from her sins through the attacks that the demons leveled at her, before showing her the things He wanted to show her. Her good master, sweet Jesus, comforted her as did the voice that said it had come from God to comfort her and which promised her when it departed, "I will not speak to you again but will comfort you from inside." And she found this to be true several times, for when the demons spoke to her, all she had to do was open her mouth and the words came out, without her having to think about them, or so it seemed to her.

[August 21, 1396:] You should know that she was lying in bed sick from the Monday after the middle of August until she passed away the following Friday, the feast day of Saint Louis, around noon.[29] And she was so sick on that Monday and also the following night that she could hardly speak. And when I told her, "Ermine, think of God, and of His Passion, and of your sins," she answered me simply: "Sir, I have placed Him so firmly in my heart that I will not be able to forget Him, God be praised. And I hope that you will not be displeased if I am silent for speaking causes me great pain, blessed be God." A monk from Saint-Denis came to see her who was a friend of hers, and when she saw that he was without a hat she said, "Ah, sir, I am so happy to see your hair." And a number of people who were present were astonished because they did not know why she said this, but I myself was not astonished for she had told me that this monk had hair exactly like that of God that she had seen in the hand of the priest at mass.[30] And later, on Tuesday night, she spoke more easily than on Monday. [Ermine praises God and states that there are no more demons to vex her. When secular people come to see her she seems to sleep but when devout people visit she prays with them.] And she was always holding a crucifix in her hand even when she was eating; if it happened that someone took it away from her, it had to be returned to her immediately to keep her happy, and she kissed it so often and ardently that it seemed that she was going to eat it; and when someone took it from her one hand, she grabbed it with the other.

And when someone said to her, "Ermine, think about Our Lord's Passion, about the column and the cross," it seemed that she was about to cry, and she said, "Oh, the great pity." And when we, who stood near her bed, lifted our hands toward heaven and said, "Praise God, Ermine," it seemed that her entire body trembled with joy. And she lifted her head and her body as much as she could and began to smile, saying (quite inaudibly and with great difficulty, but we could understand her well), "I have seen the child." [Her joy is such that she forgets the anguish of death.] And her end arrived as follows: she passed away on Friday around noon, holding her crucifix in one hand and a holy candle in the other. And she had asked me for the absolution of her sins, and I had given it to her in the hour of her death. And three priests and other good people were present at her death and the crucifix was lifted up. And you should know that when she died, her bodily members were unharmed, but she was weakened from all the torments she had experienced. And she died at the time when there was an epidemic in Reims for she had two buboes[31] which she acquired, people said, when she helped bury a woman who was contaminated.

During her illness Ermine had requested that for the love of God she be buried in our house; this is what she said: "When you see my grave, you will pray for me, for the love of God." And she was buried in our house, in our church, between the portal and the holy water font, about four feet from it. May God take her soul, *amen.*

[Epilogue]

You who have read or listened to this book, I beg you, for the love of God and His sweet mother, do not think that I used bad judgment in this matter but truly, all I have sought is God's honor and the welfare of my fellow men, without trying to do any harm to any living being by writing the truth of my conscience as much as I could according to what she told me, or in any case the gist of it, and I would not have written anything at all if I had believed it to be a sin. But several good people told me that these were the deeds of God and that I would do a bad thing if I hid them, and also my conscience judged me. And I wrote these things in my name, may it not displease you, for truly I am not happy about it. But I could not do otherwise because I knew the facts better than anyone and what happened involved me as well. For you can see that all this was truly a struggle, for from the beginning the demons appeared in the shape of male and female saints and wanted her to move out and leave me and trust only in them. By contrast, the good voice of the hermit who said that he had been sent by God to help her and also all the spirits who came to her and in whom she could trust said to her back then, "Do not abandon your room or the subprior, and trust in Jesus Christ." But through God's help the demons have been vanquished, for she died in her room and she never left me; she always had strong faith in Jesus Christ and never believed in the demons. And for that reason, if anyone thinks badly of me, this makes me unhappy, and may sweet Jesus forgive them. May all the glory, praise and honor be God's without end and may we receive forgiveness for our sins, *amen.*

May it please you to know that when Ermine was sick in her last illness from which she died, the prior of Saint-Denis, who knew her well and knew about her adventures, wrote to me to say that it would be good if I told her to promise me that, if it pleased God, when she died she could let us know how things are after death. And when I told her in front of several people that I would really like to know and that she should promise (if it pleased God), she answered me, "Alas, for the love of God, why do you ask me something like this; I am a poor sinner worthy of the fire of hell. And if God did not grant me His grace I would go to hell directly after my death. Pray to God for me with these good people who are here, for the love of God." Then I said to her, "You truly should be afraid for your salvation, but you should also have hope for God's mercy. I am telling you this because if we knew that after your death you would be in a state of grace, we would praise God, and if you were in trouble, we would make every effort to pray for you." She answered, "Ah, sir, if it is a question of praying for me, I will gladly do it." And then I said to her, "You have seen the trickiness of the demons, so when you come back, make sure you do it with circumspection so that the demon won't deceive us in your name."

[January 25, 1397:] So it happened that she died on the feast day of Saint Louis, in the year I mentioned above. On the Thursday after the day of the Conversion of Saint Paul, after we had chanted the noon office, I walked toward the portal of our church in order to close the door, when I found a good old woman whom I knew well by sight, for she lived in our street, in a house where Ermine used to live, but I had not spoken with her in about eight years. And she sat by Ermine's grave and looked very unhappy. I said to her, "What are you doing here, good woman? You have to leave because I want to lock the church. It seems to me that you are very angry." "Indeed I am," she said. "You are telling the truth, for Ermine has taken away my companion." "What is that supposed to mean?" I said. "Do not lie to me."

She answered, "By my conscience, sir, I won't. I am a widow and all alone, and because I am sad when I am alone, I asked my son, who has several children, to lend me one of his children to keep me company. He gave me a little girl named Ysabelet who was just under five years old. She was a good and very sweet child who sometimes went to church with me. She swore only by Saint Nothing[32] and spoke very carefully, and I loved her very much for her goodness. And it happened that last Sunday she fell ill, and I put her in my bed. I came here to get some holy water, but I did not dare stay for mass because of my child whom I had left alone. So I went back to my little daughter—for she called me mother and I called her daughter. And when I arrived, she said, 'Mother, lady Ermine just left; she came to visit me.' And I said to her, 'Which lady Ermine? I think you've been dreaming. Lady Ermine is dead, you don't know what you are saying.' 'Lady

Ermine from the Val-des-Ecoliers, who sometimes came here, by Saint Nothing, she just left. But she did not have the cloak she used to wear for she was dressed all in white, and she spoke to me.' And I said to her, 'What did she tell you?' 'She said to me, 'How are you, beautiful girl?' And I answered, 'I am very sick, lady Ermine.' And she answered, 'You will be all right this night, God willing, and I will come back to see you. I commend you to God.' And then she left; she was here for only a moment, and she smiled at me and had a joyous face.' And when Vespers came, I ate my supper next to my little girl. She looked at me and said, 'Oh, mother, you do not believe what I told you about lady Ermine coming to be next to me. And I answered, 'I truly do not believe you.' Then she said, 'By Saint Nothing, mother, I am not lying. She was right here and she was not wearing her headdress.' A little later she said, 'Mother, prepare me for burial for I will die this night, and please leave me in this shirt that I am wearing, I don't want another.' I answered her, 'By God, my daughter, you will not die tonight, if it pleases God.' She answered, 'I will too, I tell you, mother.' And when night fell, I was so puzzled by what this child had told me that I did not go to sleep but lit a light and sat by her side.

"And when it was about ten o'clock that same Sunday night, she began to laugh and celebrate and said, 'Mother, do you see lady Ermine who has come back? And with her a great company of beautiful ladies, all white, and they are holding each other by the hand. And there is one who is more beautiful than all the others.' I said to her, 'Truly, child, I see no one.' And then the child with one hand took my arm and with the other showed me where she said they were, saying, 'There they are, mother, don't you see them? I am so astonished, see them right there, by Saint Nothing. And lady Ermine just told me that I will go with them to paradise.' [Isabelle exhorts her grandmother not to cry for her because she will be in paradise. While Isabelle continues to see and hear the ladies, her grandmother sees nothing.] Then her face began to turn pale and her breath became short, and it seemed to me that she was about to die. I went to fetch the holy candle and put it in her hand, and because I was afraid she would drop it. I helped her hold it with my right hand and made the sign of the cross with my left. And when I thought she could no longer speak, she said to me in a very low voice, 'Mother, you are not doing it right. Hold the candle in the left hand and make the sign of the cross with the good hand.' And I answered crying, 'You are right, my child, this is what I will do.' So I did it the way she had taught me. And then she turned her head away. After a little while she wanted to give up the ghost, she let the candle fall and joined her hands and smiled; at that moment she died."

It seems to me that what happened to this child, who was in a state of ignorance and only four-and-three-quarters years old, was supernatural. And because all this is difficult to believe, some people might say or think that she had become mad. But God in His mercy, in order to take away all doubt, allowed that the good woman made the sign of the cross with her left hand and that the child corrected her mistake in order to show that she had all her senses about her and did not lie, and had not lied in anything she had said.

[This is the end of the narrative about Ermine. The last part of the manuscript tells how Jean Morel took this book to Paris to submit it for approval to the chancellor of the University of Paris, Jean Gerson. Gerson's response is appended in several manuscripts.][33]

Gerson's Letter to Jean Morel:[34]

To the religious and good man, most beloved in fraternal charity in Christ, Lord Jean Morel, regular canon of the church of Saint Denis of Reims, Jean Gerson, unworthy chancellor of the church of Paris, wishes that he reaches the harbor of true religion.

Several times before now, sometimes by letter, sometimes in person, you have asked me to consider a book that has been edited in many manuscripts concerning the life, habits, and death of a certain plain and pious woman, called Ermine. This is especially because the book contains wondrous and unusual visions which that woman asserts were given her and shown while she was awake, recently from the vigil of the feast of All Souls of the year 1395 until the following feast of Saint Louis, on which day she left the world. Most recently you asked me with many pleas and supplications and begged me so much[35] that I could not delay any longer. In order to instruct the less learned and to close the mouths of those who want to undermine the faith of the simple and to harm the reputation of those who live well and piously, I decided to describe in brief what I judged should be thought about the contents of that little book.

I complied with your concern, which I have no doubt is from God. I reviewed that book and studied it as long and as much as I thought required. Without any rash attachment and in submitting the matter to the judgment of the Holy See and the resident Sovereign Pontiff, and to the discretion of all who know better, I can say as a triple conclusion what follows:

First conclusion: In the said book there is nothing that should be considered contrary to the Catholic faith or any of its articles of belief. The basis for this finding is that everything there set forth is possible in itself or in similar cases for divine omnipotence. Divine law also permits such things. For events of the same type or from which the same judgment can be made are read about in authentic stories in the *Lives of the Fathers*.[36] We find how they were attacked or deluded many times by demons and how similar things were done to them.

Second conclusion: Although it is not necessary for salvation to believe that each individual event happened as a fact and in the way in which it is told in the book, I think, nevertheless, that it is rash and crude[37] to insist on dissenting from such things or to attack them with stubborn ill will. The rationale of the first point is that very many such events are concerned with matters that are irrelevant for the faith; many occurrences are asserted to be miracles that can be naturally explained, even though similar events can take place miraculously. Still, not everything, as is asserted, can be excluded from the category of miracle.

The rationale of the second point is that a natural sense of equity insists that someone who wants to be believed in his assertions, especially if they are strengthened by an oath, at least should not be attacked in a stubborn manner for falsity or perjury. In this way all political discourse would perish if no faith were entrusted in anyone.[38] This is a principle of natural law confirmed by divine law, that what you hate to have done to you by someone else, you are careful not ever to do to another.[39] Thus no one who lives in a civilized manner should stubbornly refuse to believe what another person says when no falsity or clear breach of truth is apparent.

The contents of the book of which we speak have been put forward through serious and repeated attestation and in the face of death. It is especially important that they breech no truth of the faith. In fact, the faith is rather corroborated and honored. Also, a pious belief in the book's contents does not seem to give rise to any danger in morals. Thus what already has been said is clear. Add to this that the hand of God should not be shortened (Is. 59:1), for it formerly could do similar and greater things than in our times. Nor does it have to follow that if many such events can take place, that these can be denied to be miracles. For as the same death can be attributed to different causes, so the same effect can happen in various ways. When something doubtful happens with a miracle, it seems that divine omnipotence is more honored, as well as Christian religion, in attributing to a miracle that which happened, rather than in stubbornly denying the miraculous.

Here I always assume that true doctrine remains unharmed. For in the spreading of heresy even the raising of the dead would be wholly suspect for me and worthy of detestation. In this matter it is true what the wise man says: "He who believes too easily is shallow in his heart" (Sir. 19:4). And certainly this one fact does not prevent one's admiration or the possibility of a miracle, namely that it was an uneducated countrywoman who knew how to express all that is described in this book.[40]

Third conclusion: Both because of the limited learning of many people in scripture and sacred history and because of the obstinate incredulity of some people, whose minds are hardened, it is not appropriate now to make this book available to the general public without restriction, but only to make it known to those who will likely be edified by it.

The reason for the first statement is so that what is holy not be cast to the dogs, as pearls are thrown before swine (Mt. 7:6). All the thoughts of such people are of drinking and carousing. For such persons, all talk of religion, of angels and demons, is a fable. They reject and trample on these as if they were unworthy of their assent, for their minds are puffed up and gross.

The reason for the second assertion is that great profit can be gathered through the matters that there are narrated for those who are stable in their way of life and concerned with their own salvation. First, because that woman is a model for penance,[41] austerity, and tears. It is the gospel truth that the kingdom of heaven is given to those who do penance (cf. Mt. 3:2). Therefore this woman, being poor, old, uneducated, seems to be given to us to provide a powerful example of the apostolic truth that God has chosen what is weak in the world to overcome what is powerful (1 Cor. 1:27). Are not the demons strong, of whose prince the Bible says that there is no power on earth that can be compared to his?[42] But what greater confusion could be made for the strong, or what finer trick could be played on the dragon who was made for deception than that he be conquered so often and so basely by an insignificant woman, and such a woman? Clearly it seems to me that I see them, being outraged, frothing at the mouth and gnashing their teeth and being consumed with envy when she overcame the desire to sin.

In such a matter there is nothing surprising if similar things do not happen with even stronger persons. For graces are divided in such a way that one and the same spirit operates, giving out individual graces to individual persons as it desires (1 Cor. 12:11), It has done so with the humble and the great.

But as for those who have conquered the world (here I refer to lesser enemies), the flesh and the blood, God spares them so that he does not let them be overwhelmed by the weight of spiritual temptations and to be opposed beyond what they can bear (cf. 1 Cor. 10:13). God chose that woman, poor in spirit, rich in faith, so that no flesh be glorified in her sight (1 Cor. 1:29). But from the deeds of this type one can consider how shrewd is the iniquity of demons, how base and extreme their desire to harm, how full of fury and cleverness they are in seducing people, at one time with terror, at another with allurements, and again with a thousand kinds of false miracles.

In the face of all these devices, it is necessary and sufficient to have the triple assistance of the virtue that we read abounded in this woman. The first is a profound and true humility by which she judged herself to be unworthy of all good and deserving all evil. This she expressed not only with her mouth, as many do, but interiorly, with all her heart. This conviction came of a most passionate and conscientious awareness of her own weakness and imperfection with respect to divine power and goodness. Such humility is that which avoids the snares that have been set out everywhere, according to the oracle given by God to Saint Anthony.[43]

The second source of assistance is a firm faith that is alive and trusts God, so that without his consent, will, and providence, no adverse power can harm a person. Thus when the madness of enemies is boldly provoked to harm us, we will have an unshakable faith that they can do nothing, except insofar as the Most High should allow it. In this manner I think is fulfilled the saying about hell's lion: Resist him, they say, you who are strong in faith (1 Pt. 5:9).

The third source of help is prudent simplicity and, as I might say, an untaught wisdom that does not depend on its own prudence but does all things with counsel (Prv. 13:10). This is dove-like and at the same time serpent-like discretion (cf. Mt. 10:16), the director and the helmsman of the virtues, without which virtue lapses into vice. For as soon as someone is wise in his own eyes and spurns advice, virtue is driven from him and he is exposed to all the contempt of demons. Indeed, according to one of the sayings of a holy father, he now is made a demon unto himself.[44]

It appears at the end of the said book[45] how terrible will be the sufferings of hell and how great the joys of heaven. I am not unaware, most beloved

brother in Christ, that many more things could be said in a useful manner
about the admirable life of this devout and pious woman, but I think what I
have said is enough to satisfy your request. The time will come perhaps when
I will have more leisure, so that I can respond at great length. There is no
doubt that objections can be made in almost all matters, even those that are
most true.

I have signed this letter in my own hand in testimony of both my agree-
ment and consent. This is the hand which you know, which cannot be imi-
tated and has no desire to deceive, and which I think could not lie with
impunity. Farewell.

NOTES

PROLOGUE

1. Jean le Graveur, *Entre Dieu et Satan: Les visions d'Ermine de Reims (†1396)*, ed. Claude Arnaud-Gillet (Florence, 1997). André Vauchez's study *The Laity in the Middle Ages*, first published in French in 1987, has served as an inspiration for much of my work over the last fifteen years or so.

2. Renate Blumenfeld-Kosinski, *Poets, Saints, and Visionaries of the Great Schism (1378–1417)* (University Park, PA, 2006), 89–93 and "The Strange Case of Ermine de Reims (c. 1347–1396)," *Speculum* 85:2 (2010): 321–56.

3. Paul Gerhard Schmidt, "Die Visionärin Ermine von Reims (†1396) und der Freiburger Universitätsrektor Johannes Sutter (†1559)," *Mittellateinisches Jahrbuch* 44:3 (2009): 471–83; at 479. Although, as we will see later in this book, the thirteenth-century Christina of Stommeln could have competed with Ermine when it came to demonic vexations.

4. Paula M. Kane, *Sister Thorn and Catholic Mysticism in Modern America* (Chapel Hill, NC, 2013).

5. Oliver Sacks, *Hallucinations* (New York, 2012), 60.

6. See Barbara Newman, "Possessed by the Spirit: Devout Women, Demoniacs, and the Apostolic Life in the Thirteenth Century," *Speculum* 73 (1998): 733–70. This question of discernment is one of the major topics of my book.

7. Jerome Kroll, "A Reappraisal of Psychiatry in the Middle Ages," *Archives of General Psychiatry,* 29:2 (1973): 281.

8. Andreas Mavromatis, *Hypnagogia: The Unique State of Consciousness Between Wakefulness and Sleep* (London, 1991). Sacks describes in which brain cortex such images could be produced (*Hallucinations*, 206). Sacks uses numerous quotes from Mavromatis on pp. 205–15 but without page numbers from *Hypnagogia*.

9. See Gábor Klaniczay, "The Process of Trance: Heavenly and Diabolic Apparitions in Johannes Nider's *Formicarius*," in *Procession, Performance, and Ritual: Essays in Honor of Bryan R. Gillingham,* ed. Nancy van Deusen (Ottawa, 2007), 203–58.

10. Sacks, *Hallucinations*, 215.

11. Ariel Glucklich, *Sacred Pain: Hurting the Body for the Sake of the Soul* (Oxford, 2001), 84.

12. Kroll, "A Reappraisal," 277–78.

13. Muriel Laharie, *La folie au moyen âge, XIe-XIIIe siècles* (Paris, 1991), 23.

14. Cristina Mazzoni, *Saint Hysteria: Neurosis, Mysticism, and Gender in European Culture* (Ithaca, NY, 1996), 27. Sigmund Freud also used the term *neurosis* in a 1923 article about a seventeenth-century case of a woman "possessed" by demons. See Laharie, *La folie*, 35.

15. Glucklich, *Sacred Pain*, 86. Laharie also warns against "retrospective diagnostics" in *La folie*, 8 and 17.

CHAPTER I. ERMINE AND HER WORLD

1. Sharon Farmer, *Surviving Poverty in Medieval Paris: Gender, Ideology, and the Daily Lives of the Poor* (Ithaca, NY, 2002), 23.

2. Michel Mollat, *The Poor in the Middle Ages: An Essay in Social History*, trans. Arthur Goldhammer (Chicago, 1986; French ed., 1978), 295.

3. Peter Biller, "The Common Woman in the Western Church in the Thirteenth and Early Fourteenth Centuries," in *Women in the Church*, ed. W. J. Sheils and Diana Wood (Oxford, 1990), 129.

4. This is the subtitle of Barbara W. Tuchman's *A Distant Mirror* (New York, 1978).

5. See Desmond Seward, *The Hundred Years War: The English in France, 1337–1453* (New York, 1978).

6. On late medieval Reims see Pierre Desportes, *Reims et les Rémois aux XIIIe et XIVe siècles* (Paris, 1979). Chapter 21 deals with difficulties in Reims during the early phase of the war and during the plague.

7. The first true *sacre* was that of Pipin the Short in 751, and the first French king to be anointed in Reims was Louis the Pious in 816. A later exception was King Henri IV, who was crowned in Chartres in 1593.

8. Pierre Desportes goes so far as to call the citizens' reactions to the news of the defeat a "psychosis of betrayal" (*Reims*, 550).

9. A concise account is in Robert Gottfried, "The Black Death," *Dictionary of the Middle Ages*, ed. Joseph Strayer (New York, 1983), 2: 257–67. For a classic account see Philip Ziegler, *The Black Death* (New York, 1969), and more recently the very entertaining book by John Kelly, *The Great Mortality: An Intimate History of the Black Death, the Most Devastating Plague of All Time* (New York, 2005).

10. Most of the following details come from Desportes, *Reims*, 544–49.

11. Guillaume de Machaut, *The Judgment of the King of Navarre*, ed. and trans. R. Barton Palmer (New York, 1988), vv. 1–458.

12. *Judgment*, vv. 215–22. Generally on the Jews in medieval France see William C. Jordan, *The French Monarchy and the Jews: From Philip Augustus to the Last Capetians* (Philadelphia, 1989). There is much literature on the accusation of poisoning wells. See Séraphine Guerchberg, "The Controversies over the Alleged Sowers of the Black Death

in Contemporary Treatises on the Plague," in *Change in Medieval Society*, ed. Sylvia L. Thrupp (New York, 1964), 208–24, and the analysis by Carlo Ginzburg in his chapter "Jews, Heretics, Witches," in *Ecstasies: Deciphering the Witches' Sabbath*, trans. Raymond Rosenthal (New York, 1991), esp. 63–68.

13. *Chronique de Jean le Bel*, ed. Jules Viard and Eugène Déprez (Paris, 1904), 2:225. On Jewish martyrdom see Susan Einbinder, *Beautiful Death: Jewish Poetry and Martyrdom in Medieval France* (Princeton, 2002).

14. For a concise summary of this crisis see Renate Blumenfeld-Kosinski, *Poets, Saints, and Visionaries of the Great Schism (1378-1417)* (University Park, PA, 2006), 2–11. Just before the introduction there are maps showing the division of Europe between the two and eventually three papacies, as well as a list of all the popes that reigned during the Great Schism. For more detail see Walter Ullmann, *The Origins of the Great Schism: A Study in Fourteenth-Century Ecclesiastical History* (Hamden, CT, 1948).

15. Jean Froissart, *Chroniques*, ed. Le Baron Kervyn de Lettenhove, 28 vols. (Brussels, 1867–1877), 9:46.

16. See André Vauchez, "Un réformateur religieux dans la France de Charles VI: Jean de Varennes (†1396?)," *Académie des Inscriptions et Belles-Lettres, Comptes rendus* (1998), 1111–30 ; and Blumenfeld-Kosinski, *Poets, Saints, and Visionaries*, 90–91.

17. For a map of Reims and of the cloth trade see Desportes, *Reims*, 68, 426.

18. Desportes, *Reims*, 575–76.

19. For these and the following details see Jean le Graveur, *Entre Dieu et Satan*, 14–15.

20. Desportes, *Reims*, 304.

21. On the Augustinian rule and friars see Frances Andrews, *The Other Friars: Carmelite, Augustinian, Sack and Pied Friars in the Middle Ages* (Woodbridge, UK, 2006), part 2. On the Val-des-Ecoliers in particular see Catherine Guyon, *Les Ecoliers du Christ: L'ordre canonial du Val des Ecoliers, 1201–1539* (Saint-Etienne, France, 1998), 351–57.

22. Jean le Graveur, *Entre Dieu et Satan*, 15.

23. Andrews, *Other Friars*, 94.

24. Christine de Pizan, *Selected Writings*, ed. Renate Blumenfeld-Kosinski, trans. R. Blumenfeld-Kosinski and Kevin Brownlee (New York, 1997), 169–70, 189–90. For widows' legal positions and activities see Harry A. Miskimin, "Widows Not So Merry: Women and the Courts in Late Medieval France," in *Upon My Husband's Death: Widows in the Literature and Histories of Medieval Europe*, ed. Louise Mirrer (Ann Arbor, MI, 1992), 207–19.

25. Margaret Wade Labarge, "Three Medieval Widows and a Second Career," in *Aging and the Aged in Medieval Europe*, ed. Michael M. Sheehan (Toronto, 1983), 159–72.

26. Blumenfeld-Kosinski, *Poets, Saints, and Visionaries*, 33–46.

27. On Yvette of Huy see Anneke B. Mulder-Bakker, *Lives of the Anchoresses: The Rise of the Urban Recluse in Medieval Europe*, trans. Myra Heerspink Scholz (Philadelphia, 2005), chap. 3. But at age thirty-three Yvette abandoned her newfound profession and had herself enclosed as an anchoress (69).

28. For Christine's biography and literary production see Charity Cannon Willard, *Christine de Pizan: Her Life and Works* (New York, 1984), and Nadia Margolis, *An Introduction to Christine de Pizan* (Gainesville, FL, 2011).

29. See Christine de Pizan, *The Treasure of the City of Ladies, or The Book of the Three Virtues*, trans. Sarah Lawson (Harmondsworth, UK, 1985), 1.5–7. On Christine de Pizan's views of sanctity see Renate Blumenfeld-Kosinski, "Saintly Scenarios in Christine de Pizan's *Livre des trois vertus*," *Mediaeval Studies* 62 (2000): 255–92; for Gerson's opinion see 262 and note 22.

30. Lynn Botelho and Pat Thane, "Introduction," in *Women and Ageing in British Society Since 1500*, ed. Botelho and Thane (Harlow, UK, 2001), 1–12.

31. Desportes, *Reims*, 331.

32. See Chantal Amman Doubliez, "Vieillir en Valais à la fin du Moyen Âge d'après les actes privés et les auditions des témoins," in *Le poids des ans: Une histoire de la vieillesse en Suisse Romande*, ed. Geneviève Heller (Lausanne, Switzerland, 1994), 13–35.

33. Gabriela Signori, "Alter und Armut im späten Mittelalter. Überlegungen zu den lebenszyklischen Dimensionen von sozialem Abstieg und den formellen und informellen 'Strategien' der Überwindung" [Old age and poverty in the late Middle Ages: Reflections on the life-cyclical dimensions of social descent and the formal and informal strategies to overcome it], in *Armut im Mittelalter*, ed. Otto Gerhard Oexle (Ostfildern, Germany, 2004), 213–58.

34. Margaret Pelling, "Old Age, Poverty, and Disability in Early Modern Norwich: Work, Remarriage, and Other Expedients," in *Life, Death, and the Elderly*, ed. Margaret Pelling and Richard M. Smith (London, 1991), 82.

35. Sona Rosa Burstein, "Care of the Aged in England from Medieval Times to the End of the 16th Century," *Bulletin of the History of Medicine* 22 (1948): 738–46. Burstein points out that in mid-fourteenth-century Europe rural migration to cities increased the problem of the unemployed and the unemployable (740).

36. Isabelle Chabot, "Widowhood and Poverty in Late Medieval Florence," *Continuity and Change* 3 (1988): 301, 303.

37. On the various charitable institutions see Mollat, *The Poor*, chap. 8.

38. Farmer, *Surviving Poverty*, 149.

39. Jean le Graveur, *Entre Dieu et Satan*, 51. I will give page numbers in parentheses for all quotes from Ermine's *Visions*. All translations are my own.

40. Giulia Barone, "Society and Women's Religiosity, 750–1450," in *Women and Faith: Catholic Religious Life in Italy from Late Antiquity to the Present*, ed. Lucetta Scaraffia and Gabriella Zarri, trans. Keith Botsford (Cambridge, MA, 1999), 51.

41. See chap. 3, 00 and *Translations*, 175.

42. For details on Lateran IV and confession see chap. 3.

43. For a history of urban beguines in France, see Tanya Stabler Miller, *The Beguines of Medieval Paris: Gender, Patronage, and Spiritual Authority* (Philadelphia, 2014).

44. On the beguines see Walter Simons, *Cities of Ladies: Beguine Communities in the Medieval Low Countries, 1200–1565* (Philadelphia, 2001). On different modes of life of lay

religious women see Bernard McGinn, *The Flowering of Mysticism: Men and Women in the New Mysticism (1200–1350)*, vol. 3 of *The Presence of God: A History of Western Christian Mysticism* (New York, 1998), esp. chap. 4; and Barbara Newman's excellent introduction to Thomas of Cantimpré's *The Collected Saints' Lives* (Turnhout, 2008): 15.

45. See the detailed study by Elizabeth Makowski, *"A Pernicious Sort of Woman": Quasi-Religious Women and Canon Lawyers in the Middle Ages* (Washington, DC, 2005). The decree is cited on 22–23.

46. Makowski, *Pernicious*, xxiv and 104.

47. Michael D. Bailey, *Fearful Spirits, Reasoned Follies: The Boundaries of Superstition in Late Medieval Europe* (Ithaca, NY, 2013), 36. Chapters 2 to 4 are particularly relevant since they deal with Ermine's time and several of the Churchmen involved in her case. The fundamental study is that of Werner Tschacher, "Der Flug durch die Luft zwischen Illusionstheorie und Realitätsbeweis: Studien zum sog. Kanon Episcopi und zum Hexenflug," *Zeitschrift der Savigny-Stiftung für Rechtsgeschichte* 85 (1999): 225–76.

48. See Martine Ostorero, *Le diable au sabbat: Littérature démonologique et sorcellerie (1440–1460)* (Florence, 2011), 580–617.

49. Makowski, *Pernicious*, 45. An amusing example of how this fear could come true is my illustration at the opening of Chapter 2 (fig. 3) that shows the beguine of the *Roman de la rose* as a Dominican nun.

50. Makowski, *Pernicious*, 41.

51. Makowski, *Pernicious*, xxx.

52. For biographies of all of these French holy women as well as an up-to-date bibliography and a list of primary sources, see Renate Blumenfeld-Kosinski, "Holy Women in France: A Survey," in *Medieval Women in the Christian Tradition, c. 1100–c. 1500*, ed. Alastair Minnis and Rosalynn Voaden (Turnhout, 2010), 241–66.

53. See Sean Field, *Isabelle of France: Capetian Sanctity and Franciscan Identity in the Thirteenth Century* (Notre Dame, IN, 2006).

54. See Blumenfeld-Kosinski, *Poets, Saints, and Visionaries*, chap. 3.

55. See ibid., 61–75. For an English translation see Renate Blumenfeld-Kosinski and Bruce L. Venarde, *Two Women of the Great Schism: The Revelations of Constance de Rabastens by Raimond de Sabanac and the Life of Ursulina of Parma by Simone Zanacchi* (The Other Voice in Early Modern Europe) (Toronto, 2010).

56. Two manuscripts of the French text survive: Paris, Bibliothèque nationale de France fr. 25213 and fr. 25552. Jean de Balay, a subprior at Saint Denis in Reims, translated the *Visions* into Latin around 1402, and three manuscripts of this translation survive. See the Epilogue for what we can learn from these manuscripts about Ermine's afterlife.

57. For the *rapiaria* see John van Engen, *Sisters and Brothers of the Common Life: The Devotio Moderna and the World of the Later Middle Ages* (Philadelphia, 2008), 278–81. For diaries see also Mulder-Bakker, *Lives of the Anchoresses*, 139.

58. See the translation by Ulrike Wiethaus of Agnes Blannbekin, *Life and Revelations* (Woodbridge, UK, 2002).

59. See Katharine Tucher, *Die "Offenbarungen" der Katharina Tucher*, ed. Ulla Williams and Werner Williams-Krapp (Tübingen, 1998).

CHAPTER 2. ERMINE AND HER CONFESSOR, JEAN LE GRAVEUR

1. Jean le Graveur, *Entre Dieu et Satan: Les Visions d'Ermine de Reims (†1396)* (Florence, 1997), 50–51. I will again indicate all page numbers for this edition in parentheses.

2. For the variety of female orders and their development see Bruce L. Venarde, *Women's Monasticism and Medieval Society: Nunneries in France and England, 890–1215* (Ithaca, NY, 1997).

3. Based on documented events, this black-and-white film (1993) was directed by Chris Newby and starred Natalie Morse as Christine Carpenter, a simple young woman who persuaded the Church authorities in Surrey, England, in 1329 to permit her to be immured in a rural anchorhold. On the connections between the documented story and the film see Miri Rubin, "An English Anchoress: The Making, Unmaking, and Re-making of Christine Carpenter," in *Pragmatic Utopias: Ideals and Communities, 1200–1630*, ed. Sarah Rees-Jones and Rosemary Horrox (Cambridge, UK, 2001), 204–23.

4. Mulder-Bakker, *Lives of the Anchoresses*, 46.

5. Johannes of Marienwerder, *The Life of Dorothea von Montau, a Fourteenth-Century Recluse*, trans. Ute Stargardt, Studies in Women and Religion, vol. 39 (Lewiston, NY, 1997), 150.

6. We will return to the question of the frequency of the Eucharist in Chap. 3.

7. C. H. Talbot, ed. and trans., *The Life of Christine of Markyate, a Twelfth Century Recluse* (Oxford, 1959), 173, 175.

8. Katherine Kong, *Lettering the Self in Medieval and Early Modern France* (Cambridge, UK, 2010), chap. 1.

9. Jacques Dalarun, *Robert of Arbrissel: Sex, Sin, and Salvation in the Middle Ages*, trans. with an introduction and notes by Bruce L. Venarde (Washington, DC, 2006).

10. Ibid., 49.

11. Ibid., xii.

12. Fiona J. Griffiths and Julie Hotchin, eds., "Introduction,"*Partners in Spirit: Women, Men, and Religious Life in Germany, 1100–1500*, Medieval Women: Texts and Contexts 24 (Turnhout, 2014), 22.

13. An exception was baptism. Midwives were not only allowed but even urged to perform baptism in emergency situations. On the Church councils and medical texts that dealt with this issue, see Renate Blumenfeld-Kosinski, *Not of Woman Born: Representations of Caesarean Birth in Medieval and Renaissance Culture* (Ithaca, NY, 1990), esp. 26–27, 118.

14. For medieval Germany this problem in all its complexity is explored in Griffiths and Hotchin, *Partners in Spirit*.

15. See Brenda Bolton, "*Mulieres sanctae*," in *Women in Medieval Society*, ed. Susan Mosher Stuard (Philadelphia, 1976), 141–58.

16. Venarde, *Women's Monasticism*, 11–12 and fig. 3.

17. Jody Bilinkoff, *Related Lives: Confessors and Their Female Penitents, 1450–1750* (Ithaca, NY, 2005), 31, 117. For the holy couples of this section see John W. Coakley,

Women, Men, and Spiritual Power: Female Saints and Their Male Collaborators (New York, 2006); and Catherine Mooney, ed., *Gendered Voices: Medieval Saints and Their Interpreters* (Philadelphia, 1999). For "couples" who wrote together see Kimberley M. Benedict, *Empowering Collaborations: Writing Partnerships Between Religious Women and Scribes in the Middle Ages* (New York, 2004).

18. A striking visual representation of this kind of relationship can be found in an illumination of the *Life of Lutgard of Aywières* by Willem van Affligem, dating from around 1300. Lutgard (1182–1246), a Cistercian nun, appearing in a vision to the Benedictine Willem, reaches down from a kind of heavenly tabernacle and places a crown on Willem's head. Jeffrey Hamburger describes this image as one of "paradisical harmony" between the holy woman and the male witness to her deeds but not as representative of the relationships most nuns had with their confessors. ("Texts Versus Images: Female Spirituality from an Art Historian's Perspective," in *The Visual and the Visionary: Art and Female Spirituality in Late Medieval Germany* (New York, 1998), 13–34; at 19 and fig. 1.1. For more on Lutgard see Chapter 3.

19. Anneke Mulder-Bakker, "Introduction," *Mary of Oignies, Mother of Salvation* (Turnhout, 2006), 7; and Dyan Elliott, "Authorizing a Life: The Collaboration of Dorothea of Montau and Johannes of Marienwerder," in Mooney, ed., *Gendered Voices*, 173.

20. Brian McGuire, "Holy Women and Monks in the Thirteenth Century: Friendship or Exploitation?" *Vox Benedictina* 6 (1989), 360. On their relationship see also Coakley, *Women*, chap. 4.

21. See Chapter 1 for some of these issues.

22. See Coakley, *Women*, chap. 5; Mooney, ed., *Gendered Voices*, chap. 6; and especially the exhaustive and fascinating study by Christine Ruhrberg, *Der literarische Körper der Heiligen: Leben und Viten der Christina von Stommeln (1242–1312)* (Tübingen, 1995). Christine will make another appearance in our chapter on demons.

23. Ruhrberg, *Der literarische Körper*, 255. Vita 107 cited by Ruhrberg.

24. Very little is actually known about Angela's life, and many details mentioned by scholars are pure invention. For a sober assessment about what we can know about Angela, see Tiziana Arcangeli, "Re-Reading a Mis-Known and Mis-Read Mystic: Angela da Foligno," *Annali d'Italianistica: Women Mystic Writers* 13 (1995): 41–78; and Cristina Mazzoni, "Angela of Foligno," in *Medieval Holy Women in the Christian Tradition, 1100–1500*, ed. Alastair Minnis and Rosalynn Voaden (Turnhout, 2010), 581–600. Some scholars refer to Brother A. as Arnaldo, but this name is also only conjecture.

25. Angela of Foligno, *Complete Works*, trans. Paul Lachance, O.F.M. (New York, 1993), 136, 142.

26. Ibid., 138.

27. Ulrich Köpf, "Angela of Foligno: Ein Beitrag zur franziskanischen Frauenbewegung um 1300," in *Religiöse Frauenbewegungen und mystische Frömmigkeit im Mittelalter*, ed. Peter Dinzelbacher and Dieter Bauer (Cologne, 1988), 225–50. See also Coakley, *Women*, chap. 6.

28. For an in-depth analysis of their relationship see Dyan Elliott, *The Bride of Christ Goes to Hell: Metaphor and Embodiment in the Lives of Pious Women, 200–1500* (Philadelphia, 2012), 191–202.

29. Thomas of Cantimpré, *The Life of Margaret of Ypres*, in *Collected Saints' Lives*,, 174, 186–87, 192, n. 116. Dallas G. Denery II explores these kinds of vision problems in *Seeing and Being Seen in the Later Medieval World: Optics, Theology and Religious Life* (Cambridge, UK,2005), esp. chap. 4.

30. Johannes von Marienwerder, *Life of Dorothea von Montau*, book 2, chap. 27.

31. Ibid., 126.

32. Janette Dillon, "Holy Women and Their Confessors," in *Prophets Abroad: The Reception of Continental Holy Women in Late-Medieval England*, ed. Rosalynn Voaden (Woodbridge, UK, 1996), 128.

33. See Ute Stargardt, "Male Clerical Authority in the Spiritual (Auto)biographies of Medieval Holy Women," in *Women as Protagonists and Poets in the German Middle Ages: An Anthology of Feminist Approaches to Middle High German Literature*, ed. Albrecht Classen (Göppingen, Germany, 1991), 209–38.

34. The literature about Hildegard is enormous. See esp. Barbara Newman, *Sister of Wisdom: St. Hildegard's Theology of the Feminine* (Berkeley, 1987); *Voice of the Living Light: Hildegard of Bingen and Her World*, ed. Barbara Newman (Berkeley, 1998); Sabina Flanagan, *Hildegard of Bingen, 1098–1179: A Visionary Life* (London, 1990); and the large volume from the conference for Hildegard's 900th birthday held in Bingen in September 1998: Alfred Haverkamp, ed., *Hildegard von Bingen in ihrem historischen Umfeld* (Mainz, 2000).

35. Coakley, *Women*, 47.

36. Benedict, *Empowering Collaborations*, 32 (my emphasis).

37. This image, copied from the lost manuscript from the Rupertsberg, is often reproduced, for example, on the cover of Mooney, *Gendered Voices*.

38. Benedict studies modern uses of this image on book covers and shows how cropping and rearranging the image can reconfigure our perception of the working relationship between Hildegard and Volmar (*Empowering Collaborations*, 99–111).

39. See Guibert of Gembloux, *The Life of Holy Hildegard*, in *Jutta and Hildegard: The Biographical Sources*, trans. Anna Silvas (University Park, PA, 1998), 141.

40. Barbara Newman, "'Sibyl of the Rhine': Hildegard's Life and Times," in *Voice of the Living Light*, 21. For a wider perspective see Beverly Maine Kienzle and Pamela J. Walker, eds., *Women Preachers and Prophets Through Two Millennia of Christianity* (Berkeley, 1998).

41. Angela of Foligno, *Complete Works*, 136. Angela's work is usually referred to as the *Memorial* based on this passage.

42. See David Wallace, *Strong Women: Life, Text, and Territory, 1347–1645* (Oxford, 2011), 33, n. 71.

43. Angela of Foligno, *Complete Works*, 138.

44. Today we still have twenty-seven complete and incomplete manuscripts of her work. After 1497 about fifty Latin printed editions of her work appeared, along with

translations into Italian, Spanish, French, German, Flemish, and English. Köpf, "Angela of Foligno," 226.

45. Angela of Foligno, *Complete Works*, 137–38.

46. See Blumenfeld-Kosinski and Venarde, ed. and trans., *Two Women of the Great Schism*. For details on the Great Schism and Constance's complicated and sometimes contradictory view of it, see pp. 8–13.

47. Sue Niebrzydowski aligns Margery's age with the distances she traveled: in her thirties and forties Margery visited the most far-flung places like the Holy Land and Rome, while later in life she stayed closer to home ("The Middle-Aged Meanderings of Margery Kempe: Medieval Women and Pilgrimage," in *Medieval Life Cycles: Continuity and Change*, ed. Isabelle Cochelin and Karen Smyth, International Medieval Research 18 [Turnhout, 2013], 265–86).

48. Finke, *Feminist Theory*. My remarks here are based on pages 100–104. All quotes in this section come from these pages.

49. That, in any case, is the position of Felicity Riddy in her debate with Nicholas Watson, who has a different take on Margery's authorship. See Felicity Riddy, "Text and Self in the *Book of Margery* Kempe" and Nicholas Watson, "The Making of the Book of Margery Kempe," and the "Afterwords" by Riddy and Watson in *Voices in Dialogue: Reading Medieval Women*, ed. Linda Olson and Kathryn Kerby-Fulton (Notre Dame, IN, 2005), 435–453, 395–434, and 454–458, respectively. Riddy's quote is on 448.

50. See translation in the Appendix.

51. Generally, simplicity is a positive trait for visionary women, as we will see in Chapter 5.

52. On all the fake or counterfeit saints see Chapter 5.

53. See Doreen Fischer, *Witwe als weiblicher Lebensentwurf in deutschen Texten des 13. bis 16. Jahrhunderts* (Frankfurt, 2002), 41.

54. For examples see Fischer, *Witwe*, and Renate Blumenfeld-Kosinski, "The Compensations of Aging: Sexuality and Writing in Christine de Pizan, with an Epilogue on Colette," in *The Prime of Their Lives: Wise Old Women in Pre-industrial Society*, Groningen Studies in Cultural Change, ed. Anneke B. Mulder-Bakker and Renée Nip (Leuven, 2004), 1–16.

55. See Chapter 5 for other women tormented by sexual demons.

56. Thomas of Cantimpré, *The Life of Lutgard of Aywières*, in *Collected Saints' Lives*, 241.

57. Vauchez, "Un réformateur religieux"; Brian McGuire, *Jean Gerson and the Last Medieval Reformation* (University Park, PA, 2005), 76–78; and Blumenfeld-Kosinski, *Poets, Saints, and Visionaries*, 90–91.

58. McGuire, *Jean Gerson*, 77.

59. McGuire cites from de Varennes's document (*Jean Gerson*, 77).

60. Gerson also wrote extensively in French and his works in French occupy two hefty volumes of the Glorieux edition. Many of his sermons in which he addressed the court and advocated understanding and help for the poor were in French.

61. Vauchez, "Un réformateur religieux," 1112.

CHAPTER 3. ERMINE'S PIETY AND DEVOTIONAL PRACTICES

1. Ariel Glucklich, using the example of the late sixteenth-century Italian holy woman Maria Maddalena de' Pazzi, distinguishes between three kinds of pain: "voluntary self-inflicted pain," "pain inflicted by devils," and "natural pain" (*Sacred Pain*, 83). Ermine is subject to all three.

2. All references to the Arnaud-Gillet edition of Ermine's *Visions* are again given parenthetically.

3. "Et quant elle fu en oroison, a la nuit, en sa chambre, elle estoit si empechee de sa lecon, qu'elle ne povoit penser a ses oroisons, ne dire si devotement qu'elle souloit."

4. Jean Gerson, *Oeuvres complètes*, ed. P. Glorieux (Paris, 1960), 2:186. On this point see Katherine Zieman, *Singing the New Song: Literacy and Liturgy in Late Medieval England*, The Middle Ages Series (Philadelphia, 2008), 125.

5. Paul Saenger, "Books of Hours and the Reading Habits of the Later Middle Ages," in *The Culture of Print: Power and the Uses of Print in Early Modern Europe*, ed. Roger Chartier (Cambridge, UK, 1989), 141–73.

6. Zieman, *Singing the New Song*, 128.

7. The best study on women's education in the Middle Ages is still Charles Jourdain, "Mémoire sur l'éducation des femmes au moyen âge," *Mémoires de l'Institut National de France: Académie des Inscription et Belles-Lettres* 28 (1874): 79-133. See also James W. Thompson, *The Literacy of the Laity in the Middle Ages* (rep. New York, 1960); Nicolas Orme, *Medieval Schools: From Roman Britain to Renaissance England* (New Haven, 2006); and Elke Kleinau and Claudia Opitz, eds., *Geschichte der Mädchen—und Frauenbildung*, vol. 1 (Frankfurt, 1996).

8. While much research on the Latin/vernacular issue in religious literature and practice has been done for late medieval England, this is not the case for France. Zieman's *Singing the New Song* carefully investigates, for example, how much English nuns could understand of the Latin liturgy and demonstrates that there is a wide variety of "extra-grammatical literacies." For France such studies are lacking. In any case, since French as a Romance language is much closer to Latin, the linguistic problems are not the same.

9. Jourdain, "Mémoire," 102. On Isabelle see Sean Field, *Isabelle of France: Capetian Sanctity and Franciscan Identity in the Thirteenth Century* (Notre Dame, IN, 2006).

10. Jourdain, "Mémoire," 128 (*licentiam docendi puellis in litteris grammaticalibus*). For Liège see Mulder-Bakker, *Lives of the Anchoresses*, 237n.31. Note that the few schools for which at least some records survive are located in urban milieus.

11. See Zieman, *Singing the New Song*, chap. 4.

12. Ruhrberg, *Der literarische Körper*, 105.

13. Thomas of Cantimpré, *Collected Saints' Lives*, 226–27. The terms Thomas uses in the original Latin are *idiotae et rustice et laicae moniali*.

14. On this phenomenon see Christine Cooper-Rompato, *The Gift of Tongues: Women's Xenoglossia in the Later Middle Ages* (University Park, PA, 2010). For Lutgard see Thomas of Cantimpré, *Collected Saints' Lives*, 239.

15. Barbara Newman, introduction to *Collected Saints' Lives*, 46–48.

16. Thomas of Cantimpré, *Collected Saints' Lives,* 148. Barbara Newman speculates that this last sentence "was probably added by Thomas to give Christina respectability in the eyes of the hierarchy" (n. 50).

17. Cooper-Rompato, *Gift of Tongues,* 70.

18. On this issue see again Zieman, *Singing the New Song,* chap. 4.

19. Jane Tylus, *Reclaiming Catherine of Siena: Literacy, Literature, and the Signs of Others* (Chicago, 2009), esp. 54–57, 87–89; quote on 62.

20. Petrarch and Boccaccio, for example, wrote in both Latin and Italian.

21. It is possible that the rather frightening fiery-red seraphims reminded Ermine of stereoyped depictions of Muslims that she may have seen in paintings or even in a play like the *Jeu de Saint Nicolas,* which was at that time peformed in easily accessible outdoor venues. Saracens were usually shown as dark or even red-skinned and often monstrous. See Debra Higgs Strickland, *Saracens, Demons, and Jews: Making Monsters in Medieval Art* (Princeton, 2003), chaps. 2 and 4.

22. Among the vast literature on this topic see especially Peter Biller and Alastair Minnis, eds., *Handling Sin: Confession in the Middle Ages* (Woodbridge, UK, 1998). For a concise presentation of the normative and psychological aspects of confession see Dallas Denery, "The Devil in Human Form: Confession, Deception and Self-Knowledge," chap. 2 in his *Seeing and Being Seen in the Middle Ages.* On confession and gender see Dyan Elliott, "Women and Confession: From Empowerment to Pathology," in *Gendering the Master Narrative: Women and Power in the Middle Ages,* ed. Mary C. Erler and Mary-anne Kowaleski (Ithaca, NY, 2003), 31–51.

23. See Norman P. Tanner, ed. and trans., *Decrees of the Ecumenical Councils* (Washington, DC, 1990), 1:245. See also *Dictionnaire de spiritualité* (Paris, 1953), 2:cols. 1253–54.

24. A comprehensive study of Gerson's attitude toward teaching laypeople is D. Catherine Brown's *Pastor and Laity in the Theology of Jean Gerson* (Cambridge, UK, 1987). See also Daniel B. Hobbins, "Gerson on Lay Devotion," in *A Companion to Jean Gerson,* Brill's Companions to the Christian Tradition 3, ed. Brian Patrick McGuire (Leiden, 2006), 41–78.

25. Gerson, *Le doctrinal aux simples gens,* in *Oeuvres complètes,* 10:295–321.

26. Other articles of the Creed, not listed here, are the Holy Spirit, Holy Catholic Church, and baptism.

27. Gerson, *Doctrinal,* 315.

28. Miri Rubin has shown how "the Man of Sorrows converges with Eucharistic themes in the late medieval visual representation" of that mass (*Corpus Christi: The Eucharist in Late Medieval Culture* [Cambridge, UK, 1991], 308–10).

29. Reproduced for example in Hamburger, *The Visual and the Visionary,* 208, fig. 4.3; and in Elisabeth Vavra, "Bildmotiv und Frauenmystik—Funktion und Rezeption," in *Frauenmystik im Mittelalter,* ed. Peter Dinzelbacher and Dieter Bauer (Ostfildern, Germany, 1985), 201–30, at 226.

30. For an exhaustive study of this military imagery as it can be applied to women, see Gia Toussaint, *Das Passional der Herzogin Kunigunde von Böhmen: Bildrhetorik und Spiritualität* (Paderborn, Germany, 2003), chap. 4 (with many illustrations).

31. See Bella Millet and Jocelyn Wogan-Browne, eds., *Medieval English Prose for Women: Selections from the Katherine Group and* Ancrene Wisse (Oxford, 1990), 115–16.

32. This was the relatively simple conclusion to a complicated argument. See Rubin, *Corpus Christi*, 32.

33. Richard Kieckhefer, *Unquiet Souls: Fourteenth-Century Saints and Their Religious Milieu* (Chicago, 1984), 171. For the feminization of eucharistic visions see Caroline Walker Bynum, "Women Mystics and Eucharistic Devotion in the Thirteenth Century," in *Fragmentation and Redemption: Essays on Gender and the Human Body in Medieval Religion* (New York, 1991), 119–50.

34. Bynum, "Women Mystics," 126.

35. On the issue of doubt see Steven Justice, "Eucharistic Miracles and Eucharistic Doubt," *Journal of Medieval and Early Modern Studies* 42 (2012): 307–32.

36. Rubin, *Corpus Christi*, 118.

37. Caroline Walker Bynum, *Holy Feast and Holy Fast: The Religious Significance of Food to Medieval Women* (Berkeley, 1987).

38. Kieckhefer, *Unquiet Souls,* 171 n.43.

39. Bynum, *Holy Feast,* 67. Accounts of experiences like these led Protestant reformers to charge that taking the Host as "literally" Christ's flesh, that is, to believe in transubstantiation, was akin to cannibalism. See Maggie Kilgour, *From Communion to Cannibalism: An Anatomy of Metaphors of Incorporation* (Princeton, 1990), 83.

40. For background on and a thorough study of the idea of the Christ child as sacrifice visible in the Host, see Leah Sinanoglou, "The Christ Child as Sacrifice: A Medieval Tradition and the Corpus Christi Plays," *Speculum* 48:3 (1973): 491–509.

41. For more details see the introduction to Margaret of Oingt, *The Writings of Margaret of Oingt, Medieval Prioress and Mystic,* trans. Renate Blumenfeld-Kosinski (Newburyport, MA, 1990), 17–18.

42. *The Life of the Virgin Saint Beatrice of Ornacieux* in *The Writings of Margaret of Oingt,* 55.

43. Ibid., 55–56.

44. Cited by Sinanoglou, "Christ Child," from the *Summa Theologiae* Pt. III, ques. 76, art. 8. She also points out that it was this miracle in particular that "was a target of early Protestant reformers" (493).

45. Bynum, "Women Mystics," 119.

46. Angela of Foligno, *Complete Works,* 147.

47. Cited by Jeffrey Hamburger, *Nuns as Artists: The Visual Culture of a Medieval Convent* (Berkeley, 1997), 144.

48. Elina Gertsman, *The Dance of Death in the Middle Ages: Image, Text, Performance* (Turnhout, 2010), 152.

49. For more on this mass see Chapter 5.

50. See Kilgour, *From Communion to Cannibalism,* and Stuart Clark, *Vanities of the Eye: Vision in Early Modern European Culture* (Oxford, 2007), 187–91, on the Protestant critique of the mass and transubstantiation, focused in part on the imagery of the mass of

Saint Gregory, that was "a blunt reassertion of the value of sensory experience against a doctrine that seems radically to undermine it" (187).

51. For a translation of the next passages see the Appendix, 178.

52. See Rubin, *Corpus Christi*, and Mulder-Bakker, *Lives of the Anchoresses*, chaps. 4 and 5.

53. Sinanoglou, "Christ Child," 498.

54. For a full translation of this passage see the Appendix, 175.

55. André Vauchez believes that Jean de Varennes expressed the same ideas here as the "Patarins" of eleventh-century Italy who believed that immoral and unchaste priests could not offer valid sacraments. See "Un réformateur religieux," 1119.

56. See McGuire, *Jean Gerson*, 270. Gerson likened the myths of Narcissus and Pygmalion to visions of the child in the Host by showing how fantasies or deceptions by images—be they a reflection in water, an image made from stone, or the Christ child—can lead to depression and madness.

57. Bynum, "Women Mystics," 145.

58. See Rubin, *Mother of God*, chap. 16.

59. Goswin of Bossut, *Send Me God: The Lives of Ida the Compassionate of Nivelles, nun of la Ramée, Arnulf, Lay Brother of Villers, and Abundus, Monk of Villers*, trans. Martinus Cawley, O.C.S.O., with a preface by Barbara Newman (University Park, PA, 2006), 232. Abundus's confusion on this subject is not surprising given the lack of scriptural authority on Mary's bodily assumption. If Mary was assumed in body, how could there be relics? On the anxiety surrounding this problem as well as solutions proposed in cult and liturgy, see Rachel Fulton, "'Quae est ista quae ascendit sicut aurora consurgens?': The Song of Songs as the *Historia* for the Office of the Assumption," *Mediaeval Studies* 60 (1998): 55–122.

60. See Vavra, "Bildmotiv," and Hamburger, *The Visual and the Visionary*.

61. Kathleen Garay and Madeleine Jeay, trans., *The "Life" of Saint Douceline, Beguine of Provence*, Library of Medieval Women (Woodbridge, UK, 2001), 118. Extreme mortifications have been interpreted by some scholars as "sainte folie." Muriel Laharie in her study of medieval madness, for example, suggests that the "masochistic and self-destructive, even suicidal, character of these practices, when pushed to extremes, seems contrary to human nature" and akin to madness (*La folie*, 102).

62. Kieckhefer, *Unquiet Souls*, 147.

63. Giles Constable, *Attitudes Toward Self-Inflicted Suffering in the Middle Ages* (Brookline, MA, 1982), 10.

64. Katrien Heene, "Deliberate Self-Harm and Gender in Medieval Saints' Lives," *Hagiographica* 6 (1999): 213–33; at 226.

65. Laurie Finke, *Feminist Theory, Women's Writing* (Ithaca, NY, 1992), 94–95.

66. Goswin of Bossut, *Send Me God*, 139. While dreadful, Arnulf's idea was not wholly original. Margaret of Hungary (1242–1270), for example, owned a whole arsenal of "instruments of self-torture," which included a hedgehog vest. See Gábor Klaniczay, *Holy Rulers and Blessed Princesses: Dynastic Cults in Medieval Central Europe*, trans. Eva Pálmai (Cambridge, UK, 2002), 266.

67. Kieckhefer, *Unquiet Souls*, 148.

68. Werner Williams-Krapp, "Henry Suso's *Vita* Between Mystagogy and Hagiography," in *Seeing and Knowing: Women and Learning in Medieval Europe 1200–1550*, ed. Anneke B. Mulder-Bakker (Turnhout, 2004), 35–47; at 40. See also David E. Tinsley, "Dying with Christ in the Revelations of Elsbeth von Oye," chap. 2 in his *The Scourge and the Cross: Ascetic Mentalities of the Later Middle Ages* (Leuven, 2010).

69. Williams-Krapp, "Henry Suso's *Vita*," 40.

70. Elliott, *Bride of Christ*, 220 and 222. See also *Life of Dorothea von Montau*, 47–48.

71. For this story see Chapter 1.

72. See the translation in the Appendix, 160–61.

73. For a handy list of examples see Garay and Jeay, *"Life" of Saint Douceline*, 122 n.20.

74. Mulder-Bakker, *Mary of Oignies*, 54.

75. Hobbins, "Gerson on Lay Devotion,"at 55, 62.

76. Goswin of Bossut, *Send Me God*, 169.

77. Aviad Kleinberg, *Prophets in Their Own Country: Living Saints and the Making of Sainthood in the Later Middle Ages* (Chicago, 1992), 90.

78. Johannes of Marienwerder, *Life of Dorothea von Montau*, 54.

79. Margery Kempe, *The Book of Margery Kempe*, trans. B. A. Windeatt (Harmondsworth, U.K., 1985), 42. See Denery, "Devil in Human Form," for an interpretation of this scene in the context of medieval confession (in *Seeing and Being Seen*, 51–52).

80. In the fifteenth century Johannes Nider tells about the Dominican Katharinenkloster in Nürnberg where a few sisters were terrified by demons trying to induce them to resist reform of their convent, thus showing the involvement of demons in Church politics and dogmatic issues. The demons actually "contribut[ed] inadvertently to the progress of reform" by sending the terrified sisters to Nider for comfort. See Michael D. Bailey, *Battling Demons: Witchcraft, Heresy, and Reform in the Late Middle Ages* (University Park, PA, 2003), 116.

81. Ruhrberg, *Der literarische Körper*, 391. Demons are "eine Art kulturell und soziales Kürzel für grundsätzlich alles, womit die religiöse Norm fertig werden will, was sie ablegen und ausgrenzen will." See also Joachim Ehlers, "Gut und Böse in der hochmittelalterlichen Historiographie" in *Die Mächte des Guten und Bösen: Vorstellungen im XII. und XIII. Jahrhundert über ihr Wirken in der Heilsgeschichte*, ed. Albert Zimmermann (New York, 1977), 27–71; at 51–52.

82. The latter two are the subjects of Chapters 4 and 5.

83. "Mais on le dit mie publiquement pour ce que les gens ne vouroyent nul bien faire" (75).

84. The verb *corner* and the noun *corneur* are used hundreds of times in *Visions*; they designate the demons and their actions: deceivers who deceive.

85. "Qu'elle allast par le pays querant les pardons pour l'amour de Dieu, et qu'elle estoit cy trop aise."

86. "Car tu puez bien aler voir les bonnes gens et aler querre les pardons par les eglises aval la ville sans pechié et si en seras plus haitee."

87. See Anke Passenier, "'Women on the Loose': Stereotypes of Women in the Stories of the Medieval Beguines," in *Female Stereotypes in Religious Traditions,* ed. Ria Kloppenborg and Wouter J. Hanegraaff, Studies in the History of Religions 66 (Leiden, 1995), 61–88, at 63. See also the *Life* of Ida of Nivelles (Goswin of Bossut, *Send Me God*), 33, n.10, on "public asking of pardons" (Eccl. Office 70.54 "chapter of faults"). On attempts to rein in these begging women and their relation to accusations of heresy and witchcraft, see Bailey, *Battling Demons*, chap. 3.

88. Passenier, "'Women on the Loose,'" 63.

89. Thomas of Cantimpré, *Collected Saints' Lives*, 37; for the scene of her wanting to go begging see chap. 22, 184.

90. Begging was strictly controlled after the Fourth Lateran Council of 1215. See Simons, *Cities of Ladies*, 66–67.

91. Tanya Stabler Miller explores beguines' involvement with various labor practices, especially the silk trade. See her *Beguines of Medieval Paris*.

92. As we will see in Chapter 4, Francesca Romana's biographer also made a strict division between Francesca's holy visionary experiences and the awful torments demons subjected her to.

93. For this vision see Goswin of Bossut, *Send Me God*, 164–66.

94. Goswin of Bossut, *Send Me God*, 166 n.103.

95. See Chapter 5 for the many manifestations of Paul the Simple.

CHAPTER 4. ERMINE AND HER DEMONS

1. Jean le Graveur, *Entre Dieu et Satan*, 80. Page numbers are in parentheses.

2. See Clark, *Vanities of the Eye*, 151–52.

3. As Peter Dinzelbacher shows, it is the nature of apparitions as opposed to visions that the surroundings of the person seeing the apparitions remain in their ordinary daily form (*Vision und Visionsliteratur im Mittelalter* [Stuttgart, 1981], 33). We saw in Chapter 3 that her divine visions take a different form.

4. The term *sorcière* dates from the twelfth century. In Middle French it could mean "ugly and malicious woman," but it also had magical connotations (especially related to the throwing of lots, *sorts* in Middle French).

5. See Claude Gauvard, "Renommées d'être sorcières: Quatre femmes devant le prévôt de Paris en 1390–1391," in *Milieux naturels, espaces sociaux: Etudes offertes à Robert Delort*, ed. Elisabeth Mornet and Franco Morenzoni (Paris, 1997), 711.

6. See Bailey, *Fearful Spirits, 143*. See also Françoise Bonney, "Autour de Jean Gerson: Opinions des théologiens sur les superstitions et la sorcellerie au début du XVe siècle,"*Le Moyen Age* 78 (1971): 85–98.

7. The text of the condemnation can be found in Alan C. Kors and Edward Peters, *Witchcraft in Europe 400–1700: A Documentary History*, 2nd ed. (Philadelphia, 2001), 129–32. For a study see Jean-Patrice Boudet, "Les condamnations de la magie à Paris en 1398,"

Revue Mabillon n.s. 12 (2001): 121–57; and Jan Veenstra, *Magic and Divination at the Courts of Burgundy and France: Text and Context of Laurent Pignon's Contre les devineurs (1411)* (Leiden, 1998). Veenstra studied and edited Jean de Bar's confession on pp. 343–55. See the Epilogue to this book for more details on this manuscript.

8. For background on different conceptions of demonology in this period see Fabian Alejandro Campagne, "Demonology at the Crossroads: The Visions of Ermine de Reims and the Image of the Devil on the Eve of the Great Witch-Hunt," *Church History* 80 (2011): 467–97.

9. See Richard Kieckhefer, *European Witch Trials: Their Foundations in Popular and Learned Culture, 1300–1500* (Berkeley, CA, 1976); Kieckhefer, *Magic in the Middle Ages* (Cambridge, UK, 1989); Michael D. Bailey, "From Sorcery to Witchcraft: Clerical Conceptions of Magic in the Later Middle Ages," *Speculum* 76 (2001): 960–90; and Bailey, "The Feminization of Magic and the Emerging Idea of the Female Witch in the Late Middle Ages," *Essays in Medieval Studies* 19 (2002): 120–34, esp. pp. 120–21.

10. Tamar Herzig, "Witches, Saints, and Heretics: Heinrich Kramer's Ties with Italian Women Mystics," *Magic, Ritual, and Witchcraft* 1:1 (2006): 51.

11. Caesarius of Heisterbach, *The Dialogue on Miracles*, trans. H. von E. Scott and C. C. Swinton Bland (London, 1929), book 3, chaps. 6 and 8.

12. For pictorial examples of both see Ivan Gerát, *Legendary Scenes: An Essay on Medieval Pictorial Hagiography* (Bratislava, Slovakia, 2013), chap. 5; and Strickland, *Saracens, Demons, and Jews*, chap. 2.

13. See Paul Gerhard Schmidt, "Von der Allgegenwart der Dämonen: Die Lebensängste des Zisterziensers Richalm von Schöntal," *Literaturwissenschaftliches Jahrbuch* 36 (1995): 339–46. See also Peter Dinzelbacher, *Angst im Mittelalter: Teufels-, Todes-, und Gotteserfahrung: Mentalitätsgeschichte und Ikonographie* (Paderborn, Germany, 1996), 96.

14. This is the opinion of Schmidt, "Allgegenwart," 344.

15. David Brakke, *Demons and the Making of the Monk: Spiritual Combat in Early Christianity* (Cambridge, MA, 2006), 175. In this passage Brakke speaks specifically of demons in the shape of black Ethiopians.

16. See Norman Cohn, *Europe's Inner Demons: The Demonization of Christians in Medieval Christendom*, rev. ed. (Chicago, 2000), 29.

17. Walter Stephens, *Demon Lovers: Witchcraft, Sex, and the Crisis of Belief* (Chicago, 2002), 57. For many stories showcasing these copulations see Lyndal Roper, *Witch Craze: Terror and Fantasy in Baroque Germany* (New Haven, 2004), chap. 4, "Sex with the Devil." For the erotic aspects of saints' lives—also often linked to demons—in the earlier centuries of the Christian era, see Virginia Burrus, *The Sex Lives of Saints: The Erotics of Ancient Hagiography* (Philadelphia, 2004).

18. Ruhrberg, *Der literarische Körper*, 360.

19. Stuart Clark, *Thinking with Demons: The Idea of Witchcraft in Early Modern Europe* (Oxford, 1997), 174.

20. That demons are large and black is a commonplace in Christian literature. For the many shapes the devil could take in the Middle Ages see Jeffrey Burton Russell,

Lucifer: The Devil in the Middle Ages (Ithaca, NY, 1984), chap. 4; and Gerát, *Legendary Scenes*, chap. 5.

21. Dyan Elliott, *Proving Woman: Female Spirituality and Inquisitional Culture in the Later Middle Ages* (Princeton, 2004), 251–52.

22. Goswin of Bossut, *Send Me God*, 169–70. Of course, echoes of Saint Anthony surface here. He was accosted by just such demonic temptresses, usually dressed in the most fashionable outfits in medieval art.

23. See P. N. Stearns, "Old Women: Some Historical Observations," *Journal of Family History* 5 (1980): 44–57.

24. I use the passive here in order to reproduce the French "*on fist*" (one did such and such), a construction that leaves the "doer" unnamed.

25. "Soudainement elle vit emmy sa chambre ung beau et jeune varlet et une belle jeune femme, si se commencerent a acoler et baisier l'un l'autre, et puis se coucherent a terre et firent ensemble pechié; et tout ce faisoit l'ennemy devant elle, pour ce que il vouloit qu'elle eust mauvaise plaisance a pechié de corps."

26. For an example of an annoyingly snoring demon bothering Richalm of of Schöntal, see Dinzelbacher, *Angst*, 96.

27. Late fourteenth-century fashions seem indeed to have been quite revealing at times. Philippe de Mézières (1327–1405), a politician and writer contemporary with Ermine, has one of his allegorical vices (*Luxure*, or Voluptuousness) complain that men wear such short garments that "the instruments of my forge" (i.e., their genitals) as well as their buttocks hang out for everyone to see (*Le Songe du Vieux Pèlerin*, trans. Joël Blanchard [Paris, 2008], 298.)

28. *Vita venerabilis Lukardis, Analecta Bollandiana* 18 (1899), 313. See Kane, *Sister Thorn*, 58, for a comparison between Lukardis and the twentieth-century Sister Thorn (Margaret Reilly) from the perspective of "sexual purity."

29. Jean specifies that their breasts were "troussez hault," which makes one think of a medieval push-up bra. Philippe de Mézières's Luxure character also complains about this kind of fashion.

30. We will explore the vast demonic zoo that haunts Ermine later in the chapter.

31. Kleinberg, *Prophets in Their Own Country*, 90, n.34. Kleinberg points to a similar scene depicted in the second *Life* of Saint Francis composed by Thomas of Celano. On this scene see also Elliott, *Bride of Christ*, 231.

32. See Gábor Klaniczay, "Miraculum and Maleficium: Reflections Concerning Late Medieval Female Sainthood," in *Problems in the Historical Anthropology of Early Medieval Europe*, ed. Ronnie Po-Chia Hsia and R. W. Scribner (Wiesbaden, 1997), 66.

33. See Rudolph M. Bell, *Holy Anorexia* (Chicago, 1985), 138–39.

34. Kempe, *Book of Margery Kempe*, 183–84.

35. Kramer and Sprenger, *Hammer of Witches*.

36. Stephens, *Demon Lovers*, 54: "Kramer had to argue for a momentous historical change just to defend the idea that modern women were voluntarily copulating with demons," and 13.

37. Brakke, *Demons*, 175.

38. Jerome Kroll and Bernard Bachrach, *The Mystic Mind: The Psychology of Medieval Mystics and Ascetics* (New York and London, 2005), 190. See also the Prologue to this book.

39. See Brakke, *Demons*. See also Louis Leloir who speaks not of a zoo but of Noah's ark when it comes to the variety of animals assaulting the desert fathers. He also sees these animals as an "extériorisation d'assauts intérieurs" ("Anges et démons chez les Pères du Désert," in *Anges et démons: Actes du colloque de Liège et de Louvain-la-Neuve, 25–26 novembre 1986* [Louvain-la-Neuve, Belgium, 1989], 320–35; at 322).

40. Jacobus de Voragine, *The Golden Legend. Readings on the Saints*, trans. William Granger Ryan, 2 vols. (Princeton, 1993), 1:93.

41. William J. Short, *Saints in the World of Nature: The Animal Story as Spiritual Parable in Medieval Hagiography (900–1200)* (Rome, 1983), 173.

42. Ruhrberg, *Der literarische Körper*, 360-61.

43. Kleinberg, *Prophets in Their Own Country*, 88–89.

44. Ibid., 90; and Elizabeth Avilda Petroff, *Body and Soul: Essays on Medieval Women and Mysticism* (Oxford, 1994), 103.

45. Kleinberg, *Prophets in Their Own Country*, p. 90.

46. Dyan Elliott, "The Physiology of Rapture and Female Spirituality," in *Medieval Theology and the Natural Body*, ed. Peter Biller and Alastair Minnis (Norfolk, Suffolk, UK, 1997), 155.

47. Short, *Saints in the World of Nature*, 190.

48. Petroff, *Body and Soul*, 123.

49. As Pierre Boglioni puts it, "l'angoisse s'est installée de façon permanente" (anxiety has taken up permanent residency). See his "Les animaux dans l'hagiographie monastique," in *L'animal exemplaire au moyen âge, Ve-XVe siècle*, ed. Jacques Berlioz and Marie Anne Polo de Beaulieu (Rennes, 1999), 72.

50. A somewhat less dramatic pig, in fact a piglet, haunted Christina of Val-Duc. As Thomas of Cantimpré recounts in his *De apibus*, one night she could not sleep because her bed straw was "disturbed as if by a piglet wriggling and rooting anxiously about." Cited by Newman in "Possessed by the Spirit," 743.

51. Ruhrberg, *Der literarische Körper*, 369.

52. Jacques Berlioz tells us that the great medieval historian Jacques Le Goff never failed to greet a toad that crossed his path! See Jacques Berlioz and Marie Anne Polo de Beaulieu, "Le saint, la femme et le crapaud," in *L'ogre historien: Autour de Jacques Le Goff* (Paris, 1998), ed. Jacques Revel and Jean-Claude Schmitt, 224–25. See also Berlioz, "Le crapaud, animal diabolique: une exemplaire construction médiévale," in *L'animal exemplaire au moyen âge, Ve-XVe siècle*, ed. Berlioz and Polo de Beaulieu (Rennes, France, 1999), 267–88; Ermine is briefly mentioned on 285.

53. For more examples see Paul Gerlach, "Kröte, Frosch," in *Lexikon der Christlichen Ikonographie*, ed. Engelbert Kirschbaum (Rome, 1970), vol. 2, cols. 676–77. For other negative associations see Mary E. Robbins, "The Truculent Toad in the Middle Ages," in *Animals in the Middle Ages: A Book of Essays*, ed. Nora C. Flores (New York, 1996), 25–47.

54. Berlioz and Polo de Beaulieu, "Le saint," 31–32.

55. See Peter Assion, "Das Krötenvotiv in Franken," *Bayerisches Jahrbuch für Volkskunde* (1968), 65–79; and Blumenfeld-Kosinski, *Not of Woman Born*, 120–21.

56. Berlioz and Polo de Beaulieu, "Le saint," 234.

57. Goswin of Bossut, *Send Me God*, trans. Cawley, 48–49 (italics in Cawley).

58. Ruhrberg, *Der literarische Körper*, 227.

59. Kleinberg, *Prophets in Their Own Country*, 88. Ruhrberg speaks of a "pattern of suffering and victory" (*Der literarische Körper*, 228).

60. Short, *Saints in the World of Nature*, 189.

61. Another association, but one that does not come to the fore in our text, is that between the toad and heresy and idolatry. See Bernd-Ulrich Hergemöller, *Krötenkuss und schwarzer Kater: Ketzerei, Götzendienst und Unzucht in der inquisitorischen Phantasie des 13. Jahrhunderts* (Warendorf, Germany, 1996).

62. In all my reading in bestiaries and medieval natural history I have not come across the feature of the beautiful eyes. For toads linked to the punishment of sinners after death, which seems to be what Ermine sees in her dream, see Robbins, "Truculent Toad," esp. 31-32.

63. Petroff, *Body and Soul*, 103. Her chapter 6, "Transforming the World: The Serpent-Dragon and the Virgin Saint," explores the multiple roles of serpents. See also the essays in *L'animal exemplaire*, edited by Berlioz and Polo de Beaulieu, where almost every essay touches on the serpent's many different functions, be it in bestiaries, encyclopedias, saints' lives, or moral allegories.

64. See Chapter 5 for analyses of these counterfeit saints.

65. The third part of Berlioz and Polo de Beaulieu's *L'animal exemplaire* explores these rich and important traditions.

66. See Tamar Herzig, "Flies, Heretics, and the Gendering of Witchcraft," *Magic, Ritual, and Witchcraft* 5 (2010): 51–80.

67. I will return to Gerson and his dramatic change of opinion about twenty years later in Chapter 5.

68. Wolfgang Behringer, "How Waldensians Became Witches: Heretics and Their Journey to the Other World," in *Communicating with the Spirits*, ed. Gábor Klaniczay and Eva Pócs (Budapest, 2005), 160.

69. Alexander Murray, "Demons as Psychological Abstractions," in *Angels in Medieval Philosophical Inquiry: Their Function and Significance*, ed. Isabel Iribarren and Martin Lenz (Aldershot, UK, 2008), 178.

70. Guibert of Nogent, *Self and Society in Medieval France: The Memoirs of Abbot Guibert of Nogent*, ed. and intro. John F. Benton (repr. Toronto, 1984), 85. On the dreams in Guibert's text see Jean-Claude Schmitt, "Rêver au XIIe siècle," in *I sogni nel medioevo*, ed. Tullio Gregory (Rome, 1985), 290–316; and Steven F. Kruger, *Dreaming in the Middle Ages* (Cambridge, 1992), chap. 7.

71. See Stephens, *Demon Lovers*, who states that "contrary to modern cliché, witches could not actually fly because they were defined as powerless in themselves" (126).

72. Roper, *Witch Craze*, 108.

73. See Michael D. Bailey, "The Medieval Concept of the Witches' Sabbath," *Exemplaria* 8 (1996), 419–39; and *L'imaginaire du Sabbat: Edition critique des textes les plus anciens (1430 c.–1440 c.)*, ed. Martine Ostorero et al. (Lausanne, Switzerland, 1999). On the broomstick see Ostorero and Jean-Claude Schmitt, "Le balai des sorcières. Note sur une illustration marginale du manuscrit Paris, BnF, fr. 12476, f. 105v," 501–508, in the same volume, studying the image of witches flying on broomsticks in the margins of Martin Le Franc's 1451 *Champion des dames* (BnF fr. 12476, fol. 105v). This image and other images of the Sabbath are reproduced in Behringer, "How Waldensians Became Witches," 161. For the development of this belief see Werner Tschacher, "Der Flug durch die Luft zwichen Illusionstheorie und Realitätsbeweis. Studien zum sog. Kanon Episcopi und zum Hexenflug," *Zeitschrift der Savigny-Stiftung für Rechtsgschichte* 85 (1999): 225–76.

74. For Jean de Varennes see Chapters 1 and 2 and the translations, in the Appendix, 170–71.

75. Nanteuil is about ten miles from Reims.

76. In later periods the idea of "demonic impersonation," that is, the devil's ability to create "human simulacra," provided both excuses and reasons for accusing people that were supposedly seen attending Witches' Sabbaths. Either they claimed they were at home and a simulacrum attended the Sabbath in their form or else their accusers asserted that a simulacrum remained at home while the real person attended the Sabbath. See Stuart, *Vanities of the Eye*, 144–52.

77. See Stuart, *Vanities of the Eye*, for early modern developments of this skepticism.

78. See Campagne, "Demonology at the Crossroads," for the history of these ideas.

CHAPTER 5. ERMINE AND THE DISCERNMENT OF SPIRITS

1. On the discernment of spirits see Rosalynn Voaden, *God's Words, Women's Voices: The Discernment of Spirits in the Writing of Late-Medieval Women Visionaries* (York, UK, 1999); Cornelius Roth, *Discretio spirituum: Kriterien geistlicher Unterscheidung bei Johannes Gerson* (Würzburg, Germany, 2001); Nancy Caciola, *Discerning Spirits: Divine and Demonic Possession in the Middle Ages* (Ithaca, NY, 2003); Elliott, *Proving Woman*; Clark, *Vanities of the Eye*, chap. 6; Gábor Klaniczay, "The Process of Trance,"; Moshe Sluhovsky, *Believe Not Every Spirit: Possession, Mysticism, and Discernment in Early Modern Catholicism* (Chicago, 2007); and Wendy Love Anderson, *The Discernement of Spirits: Assessing Visions and Visionaries in the Late Middle Ages* (Tübingen, 2011). For a concise definition and a discernment text see Renate Blumenfeld-Kosinski, "Raimond de Sabanac, Preface to Constance de Rabastens, *The Revelations*," in *Medieval Christianity in Practice*, ed. Miri Rubin (Princeton, 2009), 290–95. A complete translation of the *Revelations* is in Blumenfeld-Kosinski and Venarde, ed. and trans., *Two Women of the Great Schism*, 35–73.

2. Elliott goes so far as to state "The tumultuous spiritual life of Ermine de Reims consisted almost entirely of her correct identification of demonic impostors" (*Proving Woman*, 254).

3. Elliott, *Proving Woman*, 1.

4. Constance's visions were bound up with the Great Schism of the Western Church, which pitted two popes against each other. Her visions were very much in favor of the Roman pope Urban VI, a stance that put her in opposition to the authorities in her own region, which adhered to the Avignon pope Clement VII (whom Constance saw burning in hell!). For details see Blumenfeld-Kosinski, *Poets, Saints, and Visionaries*, 61–75.

5. Cited by Voaden, *God's Words*, 50.

6. See Jean Gerson, *Early Works*, trans. Brian Patrick McGuire (New York, 1998), 334–64.

7. Johannes of Marienwerder, *Life of Dorothea von Montau*, 193.

8. Voaden, "Women's Words, Men's Language: *Discretio spirituum* as Discourse in the Writing of Medieval Women Visionaries," in *The Medieval Translator*, ed. Roger Ellis and René Texier (Turnhout, 1996), 65.

9. Dyan Elliott, "*Dominae* or *Dominatae*? Female Mysticism and the Trauma of Textuality," in *Women, Marriage, and Family in Medieval Christendom: Essays in Memory of Michael M. Sheehan, C.S.B.*, ed. Constance M. Rousseau and Joel T. Rosenthal (Kalamazoo, MI, 1998) 47–77.

10. Ibid., 48. For a brief biography and more on Francesca Romana see below.

11. This story is popular with medievalists; it is told and analyzed not only by Peter Dinzelbacher in *Heilige oder Hexen? Schicksale auffälliger Frauen in Mittelalter und Frühneuzeit* (Zurich, 1995), 77–78; but also by Caciola, *Discerning Spirits*, 87–98, and by Elliott, *Proving Woman*, 194–97.

12. Anne Jacobson Schutte, for example, examines sixteen cases of "pretense of holiness" of both men and women in *Aspiring Saints: Pretense of Holiness, Inquisition, and the Republic of Venice, 1618–1750* (Baltimore, 2001). See also the account of a "pretend-saint" in 1424 at the end of this chapter.

13. Dinzelbacher, *Heilige oder Hexen?* 82–86, and Stuart, *Vanities of the Eye*, 176.

14. Caciola, *Discerning Spirits*, 125.

15. See Françoise Bonney, "Jugement de Gerson sur deux expériences de la vie mystique de son époque: les visions d'Ermine et Jeanne d'Arc," in *Actes du 95e congrès national des Sociétés Savantes, Reims 1970*, vol. 2, 187–95 (Paris, 1974); and Dyan Elliott, "Seeing Double: John Gerson, the Discernment of Spirits, and Joan of Arc," *American Historical Review* 107 (2002): 26–54.

16. André Vauchez, "Préface," 9: preface to the edition of Ermine's visions. See Jean le Graveur, *Entre Dieu et Satan*. Discernment is a charisma of long standing, linked to the gift of visions. See Sluhovsky, *Believe Not*, 169–70; see also Ernst Benz, *Die Vision: Erscheinungsformen und Bilderwelt* (Stuttgart, 1969), 186–207, for many examples spanning the centuries.

17. Voaden, "Women's Words," 66.

18. Murray, in "Demons as Psychological Abstractions", speculates that "horror-stories about demons make better copy than goody-goody claims of angelic visions and both of our writers had a nose for good copy" (172). See Elliott, *Proving Woman* (250) for the quote on the primer.

19. Jane Tylus, "Mystical Enunciations: Mary, the Devil, and Quattrocento Spirituality," *Annali d'Italianistica* 13 (1995), in *Women Mystic Writers*, ed. Dino S. Cervigni, 221, 227.

20. For a definition see Dinzelbacher, *Vision und Visionsliteratur*, 33–35.

21. See Barbara Newman, "What Did It Mean to Say 'I Saw'? The Clash Between Theory and Practice in Medieval Visionary Culture," *Speculum* 80 (2005): 1–43.

22. Gerson uses the example of Saint Martin and the counterfeit Christ at the beginning of his 1415 treatise *De probatione spirituum* (in *Oeuvres complètes*, 9:177–78), thus stressing its paradigmatic character.

23. Jacobus de Voragine, *Golden Legend* vol. 2, 298. Intriguingly, in a painting from the Saint Martin's altar from Cerín (now at the Hungarian National Gallery in Budapest), both Saint Martin and the demonic Christ are dressed in equally luxurious outfits. If viewers could not see the counterfeit Christ's hooves and pointy ears, they might mistake the figures for two holy fashionplates. See Gerát, *Legendary Scenes*, fig. V/18 in the section "The Demon as a False Christ."

24. "Et vous plaise savoir que, es aventures qui sont avenues a ceste femmelete lesquelles j'ay devisees cy devant ou deviseray ci après, car quant aucuns bons esperis venoient a elle, se elle avoit paour non mie telle come aux mauvais, car elle estoit mendre aux bons et si aloit tousjours en amenuisant, et aux mauvais elle estoit plus grande et se cressoit ades; et toutesvoies, pour chose que ilz lui deissent, elle ne povoit croire seurement qu'il l'en venist nulz bons pour paour d'estre deceue et pour sa grant humilité."

25. For a consideration of this "mass" in the context of Ermine's devotion to the Eucharist see Chapter 3. Amusingly, Catherine Guyon in her book on the order of the Val-des-Ecoliers does not seem to realize that this Saint Augustine is actually a demon when she writes that Ermine's vision of "Saint Augustine" as one of the patron saints of the order "reflects certain elements of the friars' spirituality" (*Les Ecoliers du Christ*, 357).

26. See Bell, *Holy Anorexia*, 135–40, for the story of her life and an analysis of her life of self-punishment and especially of her eating patterns.

27. The *Life*, Francesca's visions, and other relevant texts have been printed in the *Acta sanctorum*, March II (Paris, 1865), 89–219.

28. All of these scenes are reproduced in Giovanni Brizzi, *Iconografia dei santi Bernardo Tolomei e Francesca Romana (secoli XV-XX)* (Cesena, Italy, 2009), figs. 1–37, and in several of the articles in Alessandra Bartolomei Romagnoli's edited volume, *Francesca Romana: La santa, il monasterio e la Città alla fine del medioevo* (Florence, 2009).

29. See Chapter 4 for the scene where demons have sex in front of Ermine.

30. Francesca Romana, *Acta sanctorum*, 155.

31. Ibid., 151. A total of ninety-seven divinely sent visions are described in that part of the text (104–54).

32. The demon clearly thinks that Francesca knows that he is a hermit of the desert and therefore loves deserted places.

33. Francesca Romana, *Acta sanctorum*, 161 (my translation).

34. Alessandra Bartolomei Romagnoli makes this point in "Nel segno dell' oblazione: Francesca Romana e la regola di Tor de' Specchi," in *Francesca Romana*, ed. Bartolomei Romagnoli, 87–142; at 100.

35. Blumenfeld-Kosinski, "Raimond de Sabanac," 291.

36. For a wider contextualization of this fear of deception see Benz, *Die Vision*, chap. 4.section 4, "Die Angst vor der Illusion."

37. See Chaps. 2 and 4.

38. Ermine is thus granted a vision similar to that of Saint Anthony, who also saw his friend ascend to heaven.

39. See the Appendix for a translation of this letter. Arnaud-Gillet details the circumstances of Gerson's judgment in *Entre Dieu et Satan*, 21–27. For a translation of Gerson's 1401 treatise see McGuire's translation of Gerson's *Early Works*, 334–64.

40. Nancy Caciola even mistakenly attributes the *Visions* to Jean Morel. See her *Discerning Spirits*, 303.

41. Elliott, *Proving Woman*, 279.

42. Letter to Jean Morel in Jean le Graveur, *Entre Dieu et Satan*, 172; Gerson, *Early Works*, 247.

43. Jean le Graveur, *Entre Dieu et Satan*, 28. These manuscripts have dissappeared. For more on the manuscripts and the seventeenth-century interest in Ermine see the Epilogue.

44. See Elliott, *Proving Woman*, 280–81. It would go too far here to detail the possible reasons for Gerson's change of mind. They undoubtedly are related to the Great Schism and Gerson's conviction that visionaries like Catherine of Siena and Birgitta of Sweden had contributed to the Church's division through their insistence that Pope Gregory XI (1370–1378) return to Rome, points addressed in Gerson's treatise *De probatione spirituum*, written in August 1415 during the Council of Constance, which finally ended the Great Schism. See Blumenfeld-Kosinski, *Poets, Saints, and Visionaries*, 35–46.

45. See Moshe Sluhovsky, "Discerning Spirits in Early Modern Europe," in *Communicating with the Spirits,* Demons, Spirits, Witches, vol. 1, ed. Gábor Klaniczay and Éva Pocs (Budapest, 2005), 53–70.

46. Ibid., 55.

47. For Gerson moderation was bound up with discernment. In his 1401–1402 *On Distinguishing True from False Revelations* (in *Early Works*) he states that people who overdo their fasts, vigils, and weeping lack *discretio*, the very quality necessary for the discernment of spirits. See Sluhovsky, *Believe Not*, 176.

48. See Chapter 1 on Christine de Pizan.

49. See Claire Le Ninan, *Le Sage Roi et la clergesse: L'Ecriture du politique dans l'oeuvre de Christine de Pizan* (Paris, 2013), 166–72.

50. Jean Gerson, *Oeuvres complètes*, 7:2, 1137–85; at 1143 and 1163.

51. See the Appendix, 177–79.

52. See the Appendix, 177–78.

53. Schutte, *Aspiring Saints*, 44.

54. See Chapter 1.

55. On this period of Gerson's life see McGuire, *Jean Gerson*, chap. 10.

56. Gerson, *Oeuvres complètes*, 9: 458–75.

57. Gerson, *De examinatione doctrinarum*, in *Oeuvres complètes*, 9:474.

58. Ibid. See Elliott. *Proving Woman*, 278–81, for an anaysis of gender issues related to this case.

59. Du Pin inlcuded this story in his 1706 edition of Gerson's complete works (Gerson, *Opera omnia*, vol. 1, columns 19–20), but Glorieux in 1973 did not. The story appears only in German manuscripts of the later fifteenth century. I thank Daniel Hobbins for this information. See Elizabeth A. R. Brown, "Jean Gerson, Marguerite Porete and Romana Guarnieri: The Evidence Re-Examined," *Revue d'histoire ecclésiastique* 108:3–4 (2013): 693–734. Brown reedits the text and conjectures that a Carthusian brother was responsible for adding this story to Gerson's treatise. I thank Peggy Brown for the lively discussions of this subject and sharing this piece with me before publication. Schutte in *Aspiring Saints* attributes this story to Gerson (44–45).

60. "Unam vel duas sine difficultate, aliam seu alias cum poena majori ut dicebat" (Du Pin, *Opera*, vol. 1, col. 19).

EPILOGUE

1. Claude Arnaud-Gillet, the editor of the *Visions*, did a meticulous study of the text's afterlife and of the manuscripts (Jean le Graveur, *Entre Dieu et Satan*, 27–29, 35–43). She did not, however, examine the composition of the manuscripts.

2. Cited by Arnaud-Gillet in Jean le Graveur, *Entre Dieu et Satan*, 41.

3. See the excellent article by Raymond Clemens, "Medieval Women Visionaries in the Renaissance: Jacques Lefèvre d'Etaples' *Liber trium virorum et trium spiritualium virginum* (1513)," in *From Knowledge to Beatitude: St. Victor, Twelfth-Century Scholars, and Beyond, Essays in Honor of Grover A. Zinn, Jr.*, ed. E. Ann Matter and Lesley Smith (Notre Dame, IN, 2012), 358–83.

4. Paul Gerhard Schmidt, "Die Visionärin Ermine von Reims (†1396) und der Freiburger Universitäsrektor Johannes Sutter (†1559)," *Mittellateinisches Jahrbuch* 44:3 (2009): 471–83.

5. Arnaud-Gillet lists the manuscripts that were mentioned between the seventeenth and nineteenth centuries but which have now been lost (Jean le Graveur, *Entre Dieu et Satan*, 43). Several of them were the copies Gerson had made in Paris while he was deliberating how to answer Jean Morel's letter.

6. This section largely reproduces pages 326–28 in my article "The Strange Case of Ermine de Reims (c. 1347–1396): A Medieval Woman Between Demons and Saints," *Speculum* 85 (2010): 321–56.

7. For details on the manuscripts see Jean le Graveur, *Entre Dieu et Satan*, 35–43. For an edition of Gerson's approving letter see pages 271–74; for the translation the Appendix. One of the Latin manuscripts (BnF lat. 13782) features an epitaph and a black-and-white sketch of Ermine's tomb cover on the *page de garde*, probably made in the early seventeenth century. She is shown in what looks like a nun's habit, fingering a rosary. See Figure 10.

8. For a translation of this letter see the section "Gerson's Letter to Jean Morel" in the Appendix.

9. For a detailed description see Danièle Calvot and Gilbert Ouy, *L'Oeuvre de Gerson à Saint-Victor de Paris: Catalogue des manuscrits* (Paris, 1990), 62–69. It is no. 10 in the catalogue. Folios 1–151 of the manuscript were written by three different scribes. For the sections on Ermine, Calvot and Ouy identify two different hands: "*une minuscule semi-humanistique*" by Pierre Duduit and "*une petite cursive gothique livresque*" attributed to a Victorin, André Hausselet (68).

10. See Jean-Patrice Boudet, "Les condamnations de la magie à Paris en 1398," *Revue Mabillon* n.s. 12 (=73) (2001): 121–57; and Veenstra, *Magic and Divination*. Veenstra studied and edited Jean de Bar's confession on pages 343–55.

11. Veenstra, *Magic and Divination*, 346. On Gerson's involvement in and texts related to this condemnation see pages 347–50.

12. See above; and Elliott, *Proving Woman*, 280–81.

13. This transition has been studied in detail by Bailey in "From Sorcery to Witchcraft." On Nider see Klaniczay, "The Process of Trance," and Bailey, *Battling Demons*. On the much-studied *Hammer of Witches* see also Stephens, *Demon Lovers*.

APPENDIX. THE VISIONS OF ERMINE DE REIMS

1. The word *enemy* always refers to the devil in this text.

2. On the history of this order see Chapter 1.

3. Hugues de Nizy, see Chapter 1.

4. That is, the Eucharist.

5. Here Jean articulates the tenets of the discernment of spirits (see Chapter 5).

6. Matins is the early morning prayer.

7. *Mechief* is the word Jean always uses to describe the mischief, that is, the physical and psychic attacks against Ermine, wrought by demons.

8. There were many feast days of the Virgin Mary. The most popular were Mary's Nativity (September 8), the Annunciation (March 25), the Purification (February 2), and the Assumption (August 15). The fifth feast day varied by region and could include the Visitation (July 2).

9. The fact that Jean repeats this phrase here makes it into a kind of motto, not just for Ermine but for late medieval piety in general.

10. *Aventure* is the word Jean uses to describe Ermine's visions and demonic visitations.

11. Luke 7.47.

12. This tablet appears many times in Ermine's *Visions*. It shows the Instruments of the Passion (Fig. 5). These tablets were popular in late medieval lay devotion, as we saw in Chapter 3.

13. The term *deux enfers* appears several times in the text, always uttered by demons. They claim that since Ermine will go to hell after death anyway, she should not create another hell for herself on earth by practicing asceticism and torturing herself.

14. A stringed instrument similar to a violin.

15. See Chapter 3 (asceticism), Chapter 4 (demons),, and Chaptere 5 (discernment) for analyses of these passages.

16. See Figure 7 for the many different shapes devils could assume.

17. A pear-shaped instrument with two or three strings, played with a bow.

18. This reference is to January 8, 1396.

19. This rather convoluted explanation speaks to Jean's desire to tie Ermine's adventures to specific passages in the Gospels that were read on certain Sundays. But alas, her experiences do not correspond to the biblical passages as much as Jean would like.

20. The first Sunday of Lent. See Chapter 3.

21. About ten miles from Reims.

22. See Chapter 4 for an analysis of these passages.

23. It is hard to see how this story illustrates the Gospel passage, as Jean intended it to do. The woods of Nanteuil can, at a stretch, evoke the "desert" mentioned in the first Gospel passage.

24. This is the moment when the priest holds up the Host and transubstantiation takes place: the Host is changed into Christ's flesh.

25. These flies were also demonic.

26. On this passage see Chap. 3 where I discuss the Donatist controversy concerning the efficacy of the sacraments if administered by unworthy or compromised priests. The Champagne region, as did the rest of the French kingdom, adhered to Pope Clement VII, who, with Pope Urban VI, formed the first "couple" of popes during the Great Schism of the Western Church (see Chapter 1).

27. The feast of the Holy Sacrament is the same as Corpus Christi, celebrated sixty days after Easter. The feast of Saint John is June 24.

28. August 20. Mid-August refers to the feast of the Assumption of the Virgin on August 15.

29. Saint Louis IX, king of France, died on August 25, 1270, during a crusade to North Africa and was canonized in 1297. Noon is the hour of Christ's death.

30. A reference to Ermine's vision of a human Christ in the Host during mass.

31. These buboes are signs of the plague. See Figure 2 in Chapter 1 for a depiction.

32. *Saint néant* seems to be a French version of Saint Nemo or Saint Nobody, a character from a Latin parody, *Life of Saint Nemo*, which states among other things that

Nemo (=nobody) has seen God because the Bible says that no one can see God and continue to live. On the cult of this peculiar saint see Lucie Doležalová, "Absolute Alterity in the Cult of the Saints: Saint Nobody," in *Identity and Alterity in Hagiography and the Cult of the Saints,* ed. Ana Marinković and Tripmir Vedriš. Biblioteca Hagiotheca. Series Colloquia I (Zagreb, Croatia, 2010), 89–102.

33. See Chap. 5 for the details. I discuss the manuscripts in the Epilogue. Gerson's response dates from 1401–1402.

34. This section is reproduced (with some minor changes) from Jean Gerson's *Early Works,* translated and introduced by Brian Patrick McGuire, and printed in 1998. Reprinted by permission of Paulist Press, Inc., www.paulistpress.com. Gerson wrote this letter in Latin. The notes in square brackets below come from McGuire's translation. McGuire began with the date of 1408 that he indicates here (244) but revised it later to 1401–1402.

35. The Latin word is *vehementer,* which expresses an almost obsessive urgency.

36. [Gerson is referring to the immensely popular collection known as *Vitae Patrum,* published in vol. 73 of the *Patrologia latina* (= PL 73).]

37. Latin *incivilis.*

38. [The Latin word for "discourse" here is *conversation,* which until now in medieval Latin has meant one's way of life. It was used for the most part in a monastic context, and so here we find Gerson opening it into a larger context and moving toward the modern sense of communication by speech.]

39. [The statement is a variant of the golden rule, cf. Mt. 7:12, Lk. 6:3.]

40. [Gerson emphasized in his *Mystical Theology* that training in scholastic theology is by no means necessary for someone to whom God chooses to reveal his truth.] The Latin adjectives Gerson used to describe Ermine are *idiota* and *rusticana.*

41. The Latin term Gerson uses is *speculum poenitentiae.* The word *speculum* (or mirror) thus echoes Jean le Graveur's use of the term *miroir* in the prologue to *Visions.*

42. [Cf. Is.14:12–17. For the fall of Lucifer, Rv. 12:9.]

43. [See *Vitae Patrum* (PL 73:953B, Bk. 15.3): "Again Abbot Anthony said: I saw all the traps of the enemy set up on earth. I moaned: Who can imagine that he will be able to get past them? And I heard a voice saying: Humility."]

44. [I cannot find a precise equivalent among the many sayings under the headings humility and discretion (note 43 above). The closest equivalent is the assertion that "our own wills become demons" (PL 73:923A: *Verba Seniorum* 10:62).]

45. That is, Ermine's *Visions.*

BIBLIOGRAPHY

PRIMARY TEXTS

Angela of Foligno. *Complete Works.* Translated by Paul Lachance, O.F.M., with a preface by Romana Guarnieri. New York, 1993.

Blannbekin, Agnes. *Life and Revelations.* Translated by Ulrike Wiethaus. Cambridge, UK, 2002.

Caesarius of Heisterbach. *The Dialogue on Miracles.* Translated by H. von E. Scott and C. C. Swinton Bland. 2 vols. London, 1929.

Christine de Pizan. *The Treasure of the City of Ladies or The Book of the Three Virtues.* Translated by Sarah Lawson. Harmondsworth, UK, 1985.

———. *Selected Writings.* A Norton Critical Edition. Edited by Renate Blumenfeld-Kosinski. Translated by R. Blumenfeld-Kosinski and Kevin Brownlee. New York, 1997.

Francesca Romana. *Vita,* Visions, and Other Texts. *Acta Sanctorum,* 89–219. March II (Paris, 1865).

Froissart, Jean. *Chroniques.* Edited by Le Baron Kervyn de Lettenhove. 28 vols., vol. 9. Brussels, 1867–1877.

Garay, Kathleen, and Madeleine Jeay, trans. *The "Life" of Saint Douceline, a Beguine of Provence.* The Library of Medieval Women. Woodbridge, UK, 2001.

Gerson, Jean. *Oeuvres complètes.* 10 vols. Edited by Palemon Glorieux. Paris, 1961–1973.

———. *Opera omnia.* 5 vols. Edited by Louis Ellies Du Pin. Antwerp, 1706. Repr. New York, 1987.

———. *Early Works.* Translated by Brian McGuire. New York, 1998.

Goswin of Bossut. *Send Me God: The Lives of Ida the Compassionate of Nivelles, Nun of la Ramée, Arnulf, Lay Brother of Villers, and Abundus, Monk of Villers.* Translated by Martinus Cawley, O.C.S.O., with a preface by Barbara Newman. University Park, PA, 2006.

Guibert of Gembloux. *The Life of Holy Hildegard.* In *Jutta and Hildegard: The Biographical Sources,* 118–210. Translated by Anna Silvas. University Park, PA, 1998.

Guibert of Nogent. *Self and Society in Medieval France: The Memoirs of Abbot Guibert of Nogent.* Edited with an introduction by John F. Benton. Repr. Toronto, 1984.

Guillaume de Machaut. *The Judgment of the King of Navarre*. Edited and translated by R. Barton Palmer. New York, 1988.

Jacobus de Voragine. *The Golden Legend: Readings on the Saints*. Translated by William Granger Ryan. 2 vols. Princeton, 1993.

Jean le Bel. *Chronique de Jean le Bel*. Edited by Jules Viard and Eugène Déprez. 2 vols. Paris, 1904.

Jean le Graveur. *Entre Dieu et Satan: Les Visions d'Ermine de Reims (†1396)*, recueillies et transcrites par Jean le Graveur. Edited by Claude Arnaud-Gillet. Florence, 1997.

Johannes of Marienwerder. *The Life of Dorothea von Montau, a Fourteenth-Century Recluse*. Translated by Ute Stargardt. Studies in Women and Religion, vol. 39. Lewiston, NY, 1997.

Kempe, Margery. *The Book of Margery Kempe*. Translated by B. A. Windeatt. Harmondsworth, UK, 1985.

Kramer, Heinrich, and Jakob Sprenger. *The Hammer of Witches: A Complete Translation of the* Malleus Maleficarum. 2 vols. Edited and translated by Christopher S. Mackay. Cambridge, MA, 2006.

Margaret of Oingt. *The Writings of Margaret of Oingt, Medieval Prioress and Mystic*. Translated by Renate Blumenfeld-Kosinski. Newburyport, MA, 1990.

Mézières, Philippe de. *Le Songe du Vieux Pèlerin*. Translated by Joël Blanchard. Paris, 2008.

Mulder-Bakker, Anneke B., ed. *Mary of Oignies: Mother of Salvation*. Translated by Margot H. King and Hugh Feiss, with contributions by Brenda Bolton and Suzan Folkerts. Medieval Women: Texts and Contexts 7. Turnhout, Belgium, 2006.

Talbot, Charles H., ed and trans. *The Life of Christine of Markyate, A Twelfth Century Recluse*. Oxford, 1959.

Tanner, Norman P., ed. and trans. *Decrees of the Ecumenical Councils*. Washington, DC, 1990.

Thomas of Cantimpré. *The Collected Saints' Lives: Abbot John of Cantimpré, Christina the Astonishing, Margaret of Ypres, and Lutgard of Aywières*. Edited with an introduction by Barbara Newman. Translated by Margot H. King and Barbara Newman. Medieval Women: Texts and Contexts 19. Turnhout, Belgium, 2008.

Tucher, Katharina. *Die "Offenbarungen" der Katharina Tucher*. Edited by Ulla Williams and Werner Williams-Krapp. Tübingen, 1998.

Vita venerabilis Lukardis, Analecta Bollandiana 18 (1899): 305–67.

CRITICAL AND HISTORICAL WORKS

Anderson, Wendy Love. *The Discernement of Spirits: Assessing Visions and Visionaries in the Late Middle Ages*. Tübingen, 2011.

Andrews, Frances. *The Other Friars: Carmelite, Augustinian, Sack and Pied Friars in the Middle Ages*. Woodbridge, UK, 2006.

Arcangeli, Tiziana. "Re-Reading a Mis-Known and Mis-Read Mystic: Angela da Foligno." *Annali d'Italianistica* 13 (1995), 41–78. Women Mystic Writers. Edited by Dino S. Cervigni.

Assion, Peter. "Das Krötenvotiv in Franken." *Bayerisches Jahrbuch für Volkskunde* (1968): 65–79.

Bailey, Michael D. *Battling Demons: Witchcraft, Heresy, and Reform in the Late Middle Ages.* University Park, PA, 2003.

———. *Fearful Spirits, Reasoned Follies: The Boundaries of Superstition in Late Medieval Europe.* Ithaca, NY, 2013.

———. "The Feminization of Magic and the Emerging Idea of the Female Witch in the Late Middle Ages." *Essays in Medieval Studies* 19 (2002): 120–34.

———. "From Sorcery to Witchcraft: Clerical Conceptions of Magic in the Later Middle Ages." *Speculum* 76 (2001): 960–90.

———. "The Medieval Concept of the Witches' Sabbath." *Exemplaria* 8 (1996): 419–39.

Barone, Giulia. "Society and Women's Religiosity, 750–1450." In *Women and Faith: Catholic Religious Life in Italy from Late Antiquity to the Present.* Edited by Lucetta Scaraffia and Gabriella Zarri. Translated by Keith Botsford. Cambridge, MA, 1999.

Bartolomei Romagnoli, Alessandra. "Nel segno dell' oblazione: Francesca Romana e la regola di Tor de' Specchi." In *Francesca Romana: La santa, il monastero e la città alla fine del medioevo,* edited by Bartolomei, 87–142. Florence, 2009.

Behringer, Wolfgang. "How Waldensians Became Witches: Heretics and Their Journey to the Other World." In *Communicating with the Spirits* (Demons, Spirits, Witches vol. 1), edited by Gábor Klaniczay and Éva Pócs, 155–92. Budapest, 2005.

Bell, Rudolph M. *Holy Anorexia.* Chicago, 1985.

Benedict, Kimberley M. *Empowering Collaborations: Writing Partnerships Between Religious Women and Scribes in the Middle Ages.* New York, 2004.

Benz, Ernst. *Die Vision: Erscheinungsformen und Bilderwelt.* Stuttgart, 1969.

Berlioz, Jacques. "Le crapaud, animal diabolique: une exemplaire construction médiévale." In *L'animal exemplaire au moyen âge, Ve-XVe siècles,* edited by Jacques Berlioz and Marie Anne Polo de Beaulieu, 267–88. Rennes, France, 1999.

Berlioz, Jacques, and Marie Anne Polo de Beaulieu. "Le saint, la femme et le crapaud." In *L'ogre historien: Autour de Jacques Le Goff,* edited by Jacques Revel and Jean-Claude Schmitt, 223–42. Paris, 1998.

Bilinkoff, Jodi. *Related Lives: Confessors and Their Female Penitents, 1450–1750.* Ithaca, NY, 2005.

Biller, Peter. "The Common Woman in the Western Church in the Thirteenth and Early Fourteenth Centuries." In *Women in the Church,* edited by W. J. Sheils and Diana Wood, 127–57. Oxford, 1990.

Biller, Peter, and Alastair Minnis, eds. *Handling Sin: Confession in the Middle Ages.* Woodbridge, UK, 1998.

Blumenfeld-Kosinski, Renate. "The Compensations of Aging: Sexuality and Writing in Christine de Pizan, with an Epilogue on Colette." In *The Prime of Their Lives: Wise*

Old Women in Pre-industrial Society. Groningen Studies in Cultural Change, edited by Anneke B. Mulder-Bakker and Renée Nip, 1–16. Leuven, Belgium, 2004.

———. "Holy Women in France: A Survey." In *Medieval Women in the Christian Tradition, c. 1100-c. 1500.* Brepols Essays in European Culture 1, edited by Alastair Minnis and Rosalynn Voaden, 241–66. Turnhout, Belgium, 2010.

———. *Not of Woman Born: Representations of Caesarean Birth in Medieval and Renaissance Culture.* Ithaca, NY, 1990.

———. *Poets, Saints, and Visionaries of the Great Schism, 1378–1417.* University Park, PA, 2007.

———. "Raimond de Sabanac, Preface to Constance de Rabastens, *The Revelations.*" In *Medieval Christianity in Practice,* edited by Miri Rubin, 290–95. Princeton, 2009.

———. "Saintly Scenarios in Christine de Pizan's *Livre des trois vertus.*" *Mediaeval Studies* 62 (2000): 255–92.

———. "The Strange Case of Ermine de Reims (c. 1347–1396)." *Speculum* 85:2 (2010): 321–56.

Blumenfeld-Kosinski, Renate, and Bruce L. Venarde. *Two Women of the Great Schism: The Revelations of Constance de Rabastens by Raimond de Sabanac and the Life of Ursulina of Parma by Simone Zanacchi.* The Other Voice in Early Modern Europe. Toronto, 2010.

Boglioni, Pierre. "Les animaux dans l'hagiographie monastique." In *L'animal exemplaire au moyen âge, Ve–XVe siècles,* edited by Jacques Berlioz and Marie Anne Polo de Beaulieu, 51–80. Rennes, France, 1999.

Bolton, Brenda. "*Mulieres sanctae.*" In *Women in Medieval Society,* edited by Susan Mosher Stuard, 141–58. Philadelphia, 1976.

Bonney, Françoise. "Autour de Jean Gerson: Opinions des théologiens sur les superstitions et la sorcellerie au début du XVe siècle." *Le Moyen Age* 78 (1971): 85–98.

———. "Jugement de Gerson sur deux expériences de la vie mystique de son époque: les visions d'Ermine et Jeanne d'Arc." In *Actes du 95e congrès national des Sociétés Savantes, Reims 1970,* vol. 2, 187–95. Paris, 1974.

Botelho, Lynn, and Pat Thane. "Introduction." In *Women and Ageing in British Society Since 1500,* edited by Botelho and Thane, 1–12. Harlow, UK, 2001.

Boudet, Jean-Patrice. "Les condamnations de la magie à Paris en 1398." *Revue Mabillon* n.s. 12 (2001): 121–57.

Brakke, David. *Demons and the Making of the Monk: Spiritual Combat in Early Christianity.* Cambridge, MA, 2006.

Brizzi, Giovanni. *Iconografia dei santi Bernardo Tolomei e Francesca Romana (secoli XV-XX).* Cesena, Italy, 2009.

Brown, D. Catherine. *Pastor and Laity in the Theology of Jean Gerson.* Cambridge, UK, 1987.

Brown, Elizabeth A. R. "Jean Gerson, Marguerite Porete, and Romana Guarnieri: The Evidence Reconsidered." *Revue d'histoire ecclésiastique* 108:3–4 (2013): 693–734.

Burrus, Virginia. *The Sex Lives of Saints: An Erotics of Ancient Hagiography.* Philadelphia, 2004.

Burstein, Sona Rosa. "Care of the Aged in England from Medieval Times to the End of the 16th Century." *Bulletin of the History of Medicine* 22 (1948): 738–46.

Bynum, Caroline Walker. *Holy Feast and Holy Fast: The Religious Significance of Food to Medieval Women.* Berkeley, 1987.

———. "Women Mystics and Eucharistic Devotion in the Thirteenth Century." In *Fragmentation and Redemption: Essays on Gender and the Human Body in Medieval Religion*, 119–50. New York, 1991.

Caciola, Nancy. *Discerning Spirits: Divine and Demonic Possession in the Middle Ages.* Ithaca, NY, 2003.

Calvot, Danièle, and Gilbert Ouy. *L'oeuvre de Gerson à Saint-Victor de Paris: Catalogue des manuscrits.* Paris, 1990.

Campagne, Fabian Alejandro. "Demonology at the Crossroads : The Visions of Ermine de Reims and the Image of the Devil on the Eve of the Great Witch-Hunt." *Church History* 80 (2011): 467–97.

Chabot, Isabelle. "Widowhood and Poverty in Late Medieval Florence." *Continuity and Change* 3 (1988): 291–311.

Clark, Stuart. *Thinking with Demons: The Idea of Witchcraft in Early Modern Europe.* Oxford, 1997.

———. *Vanities of the Eye: Vision in Early Modern European Culture.* Oxford, 2007.

Clemens, Raymond. "Medieval Women Visionaries in the Renaissance: Jacques Lefèvre d'Etaples' *Liber trium virorum et trium spiritualium virginum* (1513)." In *From Knowledge to Beatitude: St. Victor, Twelfth-Century Scholars, and Beyond, Essays in Honor of Grover A. Zinn, Jr.*, edited by E. Ann Matter and Lesley Smith, 358–83. Notre Dame, IN, 2012.

Coakley, John W. *Women, Men and Spiritual Power: Female Saints and Their Male Collaborators.* New York, 2006.

Cohn, Norman. *Europe's Inner Demons: The Demonization of Christians in Medieval Christendom.* Revised edition. Chicago, 2000.

Constable, Giles. *Attitudes Toward Self-Inflicted Suffering in the Middle Ages.* Brookline, MA, 1982.

Cooper-Rompato, Christine. *The Gift of Tongues: Women's Xenoglossia in the Later Middle Ages.* University Park, PA, 2010.

Dalarun, Jacques. *Robert of Arbrissel: Sex, Sin, and Salvation in the Middle Ages.* Translated with an introduction and notes by Bruce L. Venarde. Washington DC, 2006.

Denery, Dallas G. II. *Seeing and Being Seen in the Middle Ages: Optics, Theology and Religious Life.* Cambridge, UK, 2005.

Desportes, Pierre. *Reims et les Rémois aux XIIIe et XIVe siècles.* Paris, 1979.

Dictionnaire de spiritualité. Vol. 2. Paris, 1953.

Dillon, Janette. "Holy Women and Their Confessors." In *Prophets Abroad: The Reception of Continental Holy Women in Late-Medieval England*, edited by Rosalynn Voaden, 115–40. Woodbridge, UK, 1996.

Dinzelbacher, Peter. *Angst im Mittelalter. Teufels-, Todes-, und Gotteserfahrung: Mentalitätsgeschichte und Ikonographie.* Paderborn, Germany, 1996.

————. *Heilige oder Hexen? Schicksale auffälliger Frauen in Mittelalter und Frühneuzeit.* Zurich, 1995.

————. *Mittelalterliche Frauenmystik.* Paderborn, Germany, 1993.

————. *Vision und Visionsliteratur im Mittelalter.* Monogaphien zur Geschichte des Mittelalters 23. Stuttgart, 1981.

Doležalová, Lucie. "Absolute Alterity in the Cult of the Saints: Saint Nobody." In *Identity and Alterity in Hagiography and the Cult of the Saints,* edited by Ana Marinković and Tripmir Vedriš, 89–102. Biblioteca Hagiotheca. Series Colloquia 1. Zagreb, Croatia, 2010.

Doubliez, Chantal Amman. "Vieillir en Valais à la fin du Moyen Âge d'après les actes privés et les auditions des témoins." In *Le poids des ans: Une histoire de la vieillesse en Suisse Romande,* edited by Geneviève Heller, 13–35. Lausanne, 1994.

Ehlers, Joachim. "Gut und Böse in der hochmittelalterlichen Historiographie." In *Die Mächte des Guten und Bösen. Vorstellungen im XII. und XIII. Jahrhundert über ihr Wirken in der Heilsgeschichte,* edited by Albert Zimmermann, 27–71. New York, 1977.

Einbinder, Susan. *Beautiful Death: Jewish Poetry and Martyrdom in Medieval France.* Princeton, 2002.

Elliott, Dyan. "Authorizing a Life: The Collaboration of Dorothea of Montau and John of Marienwerder." In *Gendered Voices: Medieval Saints and Their Interpreters,* edited by Catherine Mooney, 168–91. Philadelphia, 1999.

————. *The Bride of Christ Goes to Hell: Metaphor and Embodiment in the Lives of Pious Women, 200–1500.* Philadelphia, 2012.

————. "*Dominae* or *Dominatae?* Female Mysticism and the Trauma of Textuality." In *Women, Marriage, and Family in Medieval Christendom: Essays in Memory of Michael M. Sheehan, C.S.B.,* edited by Constance M. Rousseau and Joel T. Rosenthal, 47–77. Kalamazoo, MI, 1998.

————. "The Physiology of Rapture and Female Spirituality." In *Medieval Theology and the Natural Body,* edited by Peter Biller and Alastair Minnis, 141–73. Norfolk, UK, 1997.

————. *Proving Woman: Female Spirituality and Inquisitional Culture in the Later Middle Ages.* Princeton, 2004.

————. "Seeing Double: John Gerson, the Discernment of Spirits, and Joan of Arc." *American Historical Review* 107 (2002): 26–54.

————. "Women and Confession: From Empowerment to Pathology." In *Gendering the Master Narrative: Women and Power in the Middle Ages,* edited by Mary C. Erler and Maryanne Kowaleski, 31–51. Ithaca, NY, 2003.

Elm, Kaspar. "*Vita regularis sine regula:* Bedeutung, Rechtsstellung und Selbstverständnis des mittelalterlichen und frühneuzeitlichen Semireliogentums." In *Häresie und vorzeitige Reformation im Spätmittelalter,* edited by Frantisek Smahel, 239–73. Munich, 1998.

Farmer, Sharon. *Surviving Poverty in Medieval Paris: Gender, Ideology, and the Daily Lives of the Poor.* Ithaca, NY, 2002.

Field, Sean. *Isabelle of France: Capetian Sanctity and Franciscan Identity in the Thirteenth Century.* Notre Dame, IN, 2006.

Finke, Laurie. *Feminist Theory, Women's Writing.* Ithaca, NY, 1992.

Fischer, Doreen. *Witwe als weiblicher Lebensentwurf in deutschen Texten des 13. bis 16. Jahrhunderts.* Frankfurt, 2002.

Flanagan, Sabina. *Hildegard of Bingen, 1098–1179: A Visionary Life.* London, 1990.

Fulton, Rachel. "'Quae est ista quae ascendit sicut aurora consurgens?': The Song of Songs as the *Historia* for the Office of the Assumption." *Mediaeval Studies* 60 (1998): 55–122.

Gauvard, Claude. "Renommées d'être sorcières: Quatre femmes devant le prévôt de Paris en 1390–1391." In *Milieux naturels, espaces sociaux: Etudes offertes à Robert Delort,* edited by Elisabeth Mornet and Franco Morenzoni, 703–16. Paris, 1997.

Gerát, Ivan. *Legendary Scenes: An Essay on Medieval Pictorial Hagiography.* Bratislava, Slovakia, 2013.

Gerlach, Paul. "Kröte, Frosch." In *Lexikon der Christlichen Ikonographie,* edited by Engelbert Kirschbaum, vol. 2, cols. 676–77. Rome, 1970.

Gertsman, Elina. *The Dance of Death in the Middle Ages: Image, Text, Performance.* Turnhout, Belgium, 2010.

Ginzburg, Carlo. *Ecstasies: Deciphering the Witches' Sabbath.* Translated by Raymond Rosenthal. New York, 1991.

Glucklich, Ariel. *Sacred Pain: Hurting the Body for the Sake of the Soul.* Oxford, 2001.

Gottfried, Robert. "The Black Death." In *Dictionary of the Middle Ages,* edited by Joseph Strayer, vol. 2, 257–67. New York, 1983.

Griffiths, Fiona J., and Julie Hotchin, eds. *Partners in Spirit: Women, Men, and Religious Life in Germany, 1100–1500.* Medieval Women: Texts and Contexts 24. Turnhout, Belgium, 2014.

Guerchberg, Séraphine. "The Controversies over the Alleged Sowers of the Black Death in Contemporary Treatises on the Plague." In *Change in Medieval Society,* edited by Sylvia L. Thrupp, 208–24. New York, 1964.

Guyon, Catherine. *Les Ecoliers du Christ: L'ordre canonial du Val des Ecoliers, 1201–1539.* Saint-Etienne, France, 1998.

Hamburger, Jeffrey. *Nuns as Artists: The Visual Culture of a Medieval Convent.* Berkeley, 1997.

———. "Texts Versus Images: Female Spirituality from an Art Historian's Perspective." In *The Visual and the Visionary,* edited by Hamburger, 13–34. Cambridge, MA, 1998.

———. *The Visual and the Visionary: Art and Female Spirituality in Late Medieval Germany.* Cambridge, MA, 1998.

Hassig, Debra, *Medieval Bestiaries: Text, Image, Ideology.* Cambridge, UK, 1995.

Haverkamp, Alfred, ed. *Hildegard von Bingen in ihrem historischen Umfeld.* Mainz, 2000.

Heene, Katrien. "Deliberate Self-Harm and Gender in Medieval Saints' Lives." *Hagiographica* 6 (1999): 213–33.

Hergemöller, Bernd-Ulrich. *Krötenkuss und schwarzer Kater: Ketzerei, Götzendienst und Unzucht in der inquisitorischen Phantasie des 13. Jahrhunderts.* Warendorf, Germany, 1996.

Herzig, Tamar. "Flies, Heretics, and the Gendering of Witchcraft." *Magic, Ritual, and Witchcraft* 5 (2010): 51–80.

———. "Witches, Saints, and Heretics: Heinrich Kramer's Ties with Italian Women Mystics." *Magic, Ritual, and Witchcraft* 1 (2006): 24–55.

Hobbins, Daniel B. "Gerson on Lay Devotion." In *A Companion to Jean Gerson*, edited by Brian Patrick McGuire. Brill's Companions to the Christian Tradition 3, 41–78. Leiden, 2006.

Jordan, William C. *The French Monarchy and the Jews: From Philip Augustus to the Last Capetians.* Philadelphia, 1989.

Jourdain, Charles. "Mémoire sur l'éducation des femmes au moyen âge." *Mémoires de l'Institut National de France. Académie des Inscriptions et Belles-Lettres* 28 (1874): 79–133.

Justice, Steven. "Eucharistic Miracles and Eucharistic Doubt." *Journal of Medieval and Early Modern Studies* 42 (2012): 307–32.

Kane, Paula M. *Sister Thorn and Catholic Mysticism in Modern America.* Chapel Hill, NC, 2013.

Kelly, John. *The Great Mortality: An Intimate History of the Black Death, the Most Devastating Plague of All Time.* New York, 2005.

Kerby-Fulton, Kathryn, and Linda Olson, eds. *Voices in Dialogue: Reading Women in the Middle Ages.* Notre Dame, IN, 2005.

Kieckhefer, Richard. *European Witch Trials: Their Foundations in Popular and Learned Culture, 1300–1500.* Berkeley, 1976.

———. *Magic in the Middle Ages.* Cambridge, UK, 1989.

———. *Unquiet Souls: Fourteenth-Century Saints and Their Religious Milieu.* Chicago, 1984.

Kienzle, Beverly Maine, and Pamela J. Walker, eds. *Women Preachers and Prophets Through Two Millennia of Christianity.* Berkeley, 1998.

Kilgour, Maggie. *From Communion to Cannibalism: An Anatomy of Metaphors of Incorporation.* Princeton, 1990.

Klaniczay, Gábor. *Holy Rulers and Blessed Princesses: Dynastic Cults in Medieval Central Europe.* Translated by Eva Pálmai. Cambridge, 2002.

———. "Miraculum and Maleficium: Reflections Concerning Late Medieval Female Sainthood." In *Problems in the Historical Anthropology of Early Modern Europe*, edited by Ronnie Po-Chia Hsia and R. W. Scribner. Wolfenbütteler Forschungen 78, 49–74. Wiesbaden, Germany, 1997.

———. "The Process of Trance: Heavenly and Diabolic Apparitions in Johannes Nider's *Formicarius*." In *Procession, Performance, and Ritual: Essays in Honor of Bryan R. Gillingham*, edited by Nancy van Deusen, 203–58. Ottawa, 2007.

Kleinau, Elke, and Claudia Opitz, eds. *Geschichte der Mädchen- und Frauenbildung*. Vol. 1. Frankfurt, 1996.

Kleinberg, Aviad M. *Prophets in Their Own Country: Living Saints and the Making of Sainthood in the Later Middle Ages*. Chicago, 1992.

Kong, Katherine. *Lettering the Self in Medieval and Early Modern France*. Cambridge, 2010.

Köpf, Ulrich. "Angela of Foligno: Ein Beitrag zur franziskanischen Frauenbewegung um 1300." In *Religiöse Frauenbewegungen und mystische Frömmigkeit im Mittelalter*, edited by Peter Dinzelbacher and Dieter Bauer, 225–50. Cologne, 1988.

Kors, Alan C., and Edward Peters. *Witchcraft in Europe 400–1700: A Documentary History*, 2nd edition. Philadelphia, 2001.

Kroll, Jerome. "A Reappraisal of Psychiatry in the Middle Ages." *Archives of General Psychiatry* 29:2 (1973): 276–83.

Kroll, Jerome, and Bernard Bachrach. *The Mystic Mind: The Psychology of Medieval Mystics and Ascetics*. New York, 2005.

Kruger, Steven F. *Dreaming in the Middle Ages*. Cambridge, 1992.

Laharie, Muriel. *La folie au moyen âge, XIe-XIIIe siècles*. Paris, 1991.

Leloir, Louis. "Anges et démons chez les Pères du Désert." In *Anges et démons: Actes du colloque de Liège et de Louvain-la-Neuve, 25–26 novembre 1986*, 320–35. Louvain-la-Neuve, Belgium, 1989.

Le Ninan, Claire. *Le Sage Roi et la clergesse: L'Ecriture du politique dans l'oeuvre de Christine de Pizan*. Paris, 2013.

Makowski, Elizabeth. *"A Pernicious Sort of Woman": Quasi-Religious Women and Canon Lawyers in the Middle Ages*. Studies in Medieval and Early Modern Canon Law vol. 6. Washington, DC, 2005.

Margolis, Nadia. *An Introduction to Christine de Pizan*. Gainesville, FL, 2011.

Mavromatis, Andreas. *Hypnagogia: The Unique State of Consciousness Between Wakefulness and Sleep*. London, 1991.

Mazzoni, Cristina. "Angela of Foligno." In *Medieval Women in the Christian Tradition, c. 1100-c. 1500*, edited by Alastair Minnis and Rosalynn Voaden, 581–600. Turnhout, Belgium, 2010.

———. *Saint Hysteria: Neurosis, Mysticism, and Gender in European Culture*. Ithaca, NY, 1996.

McGinn, Bernard. *The Flowering of Mysticism: Men and Women in the New Mysticism (1200–1350)*. Vol. 3 of *The Presence of God: A History of Western Christian Mysticism*. New York, 1998.

McGuire, Brian Patrick. "Holy Women and Monks in the Thirteenth Century: Friendship or Exploitation?" *Vox Benedictina* 6 (1989): 343–73.

———. *Jean Gerson and the Last Medieval Reformation*. University Park, PA, 2005.

Miller, Tanya Stabler. *The Beguines of Medieval Paris: Gender, Patronage, and Spiritual Authority*. Philadelphia, 2014.

Millet, Bella, and Jocelyn Wogan-Browne, eds. *Medieval English Prose for Women: Selections from the Katherine Group and Ancrene Wisse*. Oxford, 1990.

Miskimin, Harry A. "Widows Not So Merry: Women and the Courts in Late Medieval France." In *Upon My Husband's Death: Widows in the Literature and Histories of Medieval Europe,* edited by Louise Mirrer, 207–19. Ann Arbor, MI, 1992.

Mollat, Michel. *The Poor in the Middle Ages: An Essay in Social History.* Translated by Arthur Goldhammer. Chicago, 1986.

Mooney, Catherine, ed. *Gendered Voices: Medieval Saints and Their Interpreters.* Philadelphia, 1999.

Mulder-Bakker, Anneke. *Lives of the Anchoresses: The Rise of the Urban Recluse in Medieval Europe.* Translated by Myra Heerspink Scholz. Philadelphia, 2005.

Murray, Alexander. "Demons as Psychological Abstractions." In *Angels in Medieval Philosophical Inquiry: Their Function and Significance,* edited by Isabel Iribarren and Martin Lenz, 171–84. Aldershot, UK, 2008.

Newman, Barbara. "Possessed by the Spirit: Devout Women, Demoniacs, and the Apostolic Life in the Thirteenth Century." *Speculum* 73 (1998): 733–70.

———. "'Sibyl of the Rhine': Hildegard's Life and Times." In *Voice of the Living Light: Hildegard of Bingen and her World,* edited by Newman, 1–29. Berkeley, 1998.

———. *Sister of Wisdom: St. Hildegard's Theology of the Feminine.* Berkeley, 1987.

———, ed. *Voice of the Living Light: Hildegard of Bingen and Her World.* Berkeley, 1998.

———. "What Did It Mean to Say 'I Saw'? The Clash Between Theory and Practice in Medieval Visionary Culture." *Speculum* 80:1 (2005): 1–43.

Niebrzydowski, Sue. "The Middle-Aged Meanderings of Margery Kempe: Medieval Women and Pilgrimage." In *Medieval Life Cycles: Continuity and Change,* edited by Isabelle Cochelin and Karen Smyth. International Medieval Research 18, 265–86. Turnhout, Belgium, 2013.

Orme, Nicolas. *Medieval Schools: From Roman Britain to Renaissance England.* New Haven, 2006.

Ostorero, Martine. *Le diable au sabbat: Littérature démonologique et sorcellerie (1440–1460).* Florence, 2011.

Ostorero, Martine et al., eds. *L'imaginaire du Sabbat: édition critique des textes les plus anciens (1430 c.-1440 c.).* Lausanne, 1999.

Ostorero, Martine, and Jean-Claude Schmitt. "Le balai des sorcières: Note sur une illustration marginale du manuscrit Paris, BnF, fr. 12476, f. 105v." In *L'imaginaire du Sabbat,* edited by Ostorero et al., 501–508. Lausanne, Switzerland, 1999.

Passenier, Anke. "'Women on the Loose': Stereotypes of Women in the Stories of the Medieval Beguines." In *Female Stereotypes in Religious Traditions,* Studies in the History of Religions 66, edited by. Ria Kloppenborg and Wouter J. Hanegraaff, 61–88. Leiden, 1995.

Pelling, Margaret. "Old Age, Poverty, and Disability in Early Modern Norwich: Work, Remarriage, and Other Expedients." In *Life, Death, and the Elderly,* edited by Margaret Pelling and Richard M. Smith, 74–101. London, 1991.

Petroff, Elizabeth Alvilda. *Body and Soul: Essays on Medieval Women and Mysticism.* New York, 1994.

Riddy, Felicity. "Text and Self in the *Book of Margery Kempe.*" In *Voices in Dialogue: Reading Women in the Middle Ages,* edited by Linda Olson and Kathryn Kerby-Fulton, 435–53. Notre Dame, IN, 2005.

Riddy, Felicity, and Nicholas Watson. "Afterwords." In *Voices in Dialogue: Reading Women in the Middle Ages,* edited by Linda Olson and Kathryn Kerby-Fulton, 454–58. Notre Dame, IN, 2005.

Robbins, Mary E. "The Truculent Toad in the Middle Ages." In *Animals in the Middle Ages: A Book of Essays,* edited by Nora C. Flores, 25–47. New York, 1996.

Roper, Lyndal. *Witch Craze: Terror and Fantasy in Baroque Germany.* New Haven, 2004.

Roth, Cornelius. *Discretio spirituum: Kriterien geistlicher Unterscheidung bei Johannes Gerson.* Würzburg, Germany, 2001.

Rubin, Miri. *Corpus Christi: The Eucharist in Late Medieval Culture.* Cambridge, UK, 1991.

———. "An English Anchoress: The Making, Unmaking, and Re-making of Christine Carpenter." In *Pragmatic Utopias: Ideals and Communities, 1200–1630,* edited by Sarah Rees-Jones and Rosemary Horrox, 204–23. Cambridge, 2001.

———. *Mother of God: A History of the Virgin Mary.* New Haven, 2009.

Ruhrberg, Christine. *Der literarische Körper der Heiligen: Leben und Viten der Christina von Stommeln (1242–1312).* Tübingen, Germany, and Basel, Switzerland, 1995.

Russell, Jeffrey Burton. *Lucifer: The Devil in the Middle Ages.* Ithaca, NY, 1984.

Sacks, Oliver. *Hallucinations.* New York, 2012.

Saenger, Paul. "Books of Hours and the Reading Habits of the Later Middle Ages." In *The Culture of Print: Power and the Uses of Print in Early Modern Europe,* edited by Roger Chartier, 141–73. Cambridge, UK, 1989.

Schmidt, Paul Gerhard. "Die Visionärin Ermine von Reims (†1396) und der Freiburger Universitätsrektor Johannes Sutter (†1559)." *Mittellateinisches Jahrbuch* 44:3 (2009): 471–83.

———. "Von der Allgegenwart der Dämonen: Die Lebensängste des Zisterziensers Richalm von Schöntal." *Literaturwissenschaftliches Jahrbuch* 36 (1995): 339–46.

Schmitt, Jean-Claude. "Rêver au XIIe siècle." In *I sogni nel medioevo,* edited by Tullio Gregory, 290–316. Rome, 1985.

Schutte, Anne Jacobson. *Aspiring Saints: Pretense of Holiness, Inquisition, and Gender in the Republic of Venice, 1618–1750.* Baltimore, 2001.

Seward, Desmond. *The Hundred Years War: The English in France, 1337–1453.* New York, 1978.

Short, William J. *Saints in the World of Nature: The Animal Story as Spiritual Parable in Medieval Hagiography (900–1200).* Rome, 1983.

Signori, Gabriela. "Alter und Armut im späten Mittelalter: Überlegungen zu den lebenszyklischen Dimensionen von sozialem Abstieg und den formellen und informellen 'Strategien' der Überwindung." In *Armut im Mittelalter,* edited by Otto Gerhard Oexle, 213–58. Ostfildern, Germany, 2004.

Simons, Walter. *Cities of Ladies: Beguine Communities in the Medieval Low Countries, 1200–1565.* Philadelphia, 2001.

Sinanoglou, Leah. "The Christ Child as Sacrifice: A Medieval Tradition and the Corpus Christi Plays." *Speculum* 48:3 (1973): 491–509.

Sluhovsky, Moshe. *Believe Not Every Spirit: Possession, Mysticism, and Discernment in Early Modern Catholicism.* Chicago, 2007.

———. "Discerning Spirits in Early Modern Europe." In *Communicating with the Spirits.* Demons, Spirits, Witches, vol. 1, edited by Gábor Klaniczay and Éva Pócs, 53–70. Budapest, 2005.

Stargardt, Ute. "Male Clerical Authority in the Spiritual (Auto)biographies of Medieval Holy Women." In *Women as Protagonists and Poets in the German Middle Ages: An Anthology of Feminist Approaches to Middle High German Literature,* edited by Albrecht Classen, 209–38. Göppingen, Germany, 1991.

Stearns, P. N. "Old Women: Some Historical Observations." *Journal of Family History* 5 (1980): 44–57.

Stephens, Walter. *Demon Lovers: Witchcraft, Sex, and the Crisis of Belief.* Chicago, 2002.

Strickland, Debra Higgs. *Saracens, Demons, and Jews: Making Monsters in Medieval Art.* Princeton, 2003.

Thompson, James W. *The Literacy of the Laity in the Middle Ages.* Repr. New York, 1960.

Tinsley, David E. *The Scourge and the Cross: Ascetic Mentalities of the Later Middle Ages.* Leuven, Belgium, 2010.

Toussaint, Gia. *Das Passional der Herzogin Kunigunde von Böhmen: Bildrhetorik und Spiritualität.* Paderborn, Germany, 2003.

Tschacher, Werner. "Der Flug durch die Luft zwichen Illusionstheorie und Realitätsbeweis: Studien zum sog. Kanon Episcopi und zum Hexenflug." *Zeitschrift der Savigny-Stiftung für Rechtsgeschichte* 85 (1999): 225–76.

Tuchman. Barbara W. *A Distant Mirror: The Calamitous Fourteenth Century.* New York, 1978.

Tylus, Jane. "Mystical Enunciations: Mary, the Devil, and Quattrocento Sprituality." In *Annali d'Italianistica* 13 (1995). Women Mystic Writers, edited by Dino S. Cervigni, 218–42.

———. *Reclaiming Catherine of Siena: Literacy, Literature, and the Signs of Others.* Chicago, 2009.

Ullmann, Walter. *The Origins of the Great Schism: A Study in Fourteenth-Century Ecclesiastical History.* Hamden, CT, 1948.

Van Engen, John. *Sisters and Brothers of the Common Life: The Devotio Moderna and the World of the Later Middle Ages.* Philadelphia, 2008.

Vauchez, André. *The Laity in the Middle Ages: Religious Beliefs and Devotional Practices.* Edited and introduction by Daniel Bornstein. Translated by Margery J. Schneider. Notre Dame, IN, 1993.

———. "Un réformateur religieux dans la France de Charles VI: Jean de Varennes (†1396?)." *Académie des Inscriptions et Belles-Lettres, Comptes rendus* (Paris, 1998): 1111–30.

Vavra, Elisabeth. "Bildmotiv und Frauenmystik—Funktion und Rezeption." In *Frauen-mystik im Mittelalter*, edited by Peter Dinzelbacher and Dieter Bauer, 201–30. Ost-fildern, Germany, 1985.

Veenstra, Jan. *Magic and Divination at the Courts of Burgundy and France: Text and Context of Laurent Pignon's* Contre les devineurs *(1411)*. Leiden, 1998.

Venarde, Bruce L. *Women's Monasticism and Medieval Society: Nunneries in France and England, 890–1215.* Ithaca, NY, 1997.

Voaden, Rosalynn. *God's Words, Women's Voices: The Discernment of Spirits in the Writing of Late-Medieval Women Visionaries.* York, 1999.

———. "Women's Words, Men's Language: *Discretio Spirituum* as Discourse in the Writing of Medieval Women Visionaries." In *The Medieval Translator*, edited by Roger Ellis and René Texier, 64–83. Turnhout, Belgium, 1996.

Wade Labarge, Margaret. "Three Medieval Widows and a Second Career." In *Aging and the Aged in Medieval Europe*, edited by Michael M. Sheehan, 159–72. Toronto, 1983.

Wallace, David. *Strong Women: Life, Text, and Territory 1347–1645.* Oxford, 2011.

Watson, Nicholas. "The Making of the Book of Margery Kempe." In *Voices in Dialogue: Reading Women in the Middle Ages,* edited by Linda Olson and Kathryn Kerby-Fulton, 395–434. Notre Dame, IN, 2005.

Willard, Charity Cannon. *Christine de Pizan: Her Life and Works.* New York, 1984.

Williams-Krapp, Werner. "Henry Suso's *Vita* Between Mystagogy and Hagiography." In *Seeing and Knowing: Women and Learning in Medieval Europe 1200–1550*, edited by Anneke B. Mulder-Bakker, 35–47. Turnhout, Belgium, 2004.

Ziegler, Philip. *The Black Death.* New York, 1969.

Zieman, Katherine. *Singing the New Song: Literacy and Liturgy in Late Medieval England.* Philadelphia, 2008.

INDEX

Abundus, monk of Villers, 75, 78; heavenly vision of, 92
Acts of the Apostles, 92
aerial journeys, 20, 121–25
Agincourt, battle of, 5
Agnes, saint, 25
Alberic of Metz, 20
Alfonso of Pecha: *Epistola solitarii ad reges*, 129–30
Alpais of Cudot, 21
Anchoress (film), 29
Ancrene Wisse (*Ancrene riwle*), 29–30, 69
Andrew, saint: as demon, 89
Andrews, Frances, 11
Angela of Foligno, 35–36, 40–42; *Memorial*, 36; Eucharistic vision of, 73
animals (see also demons as), ix
Anthony, saint, 51, 109, 113–14, 116, 125, 185
Aquinas, Thomas, 73
arma Christi, 47, 67–70, 105, 108, 162; fig. 5
Arnaud-Gillet, Claude, vii, 153
Arnulf, lay brother of Villers, 80–82, 85–86, 106, 109, 113; heavenly vision of, 92
asceticism, 50, 58, 79–85, 176
Augustine, saint, 52, 78; as demon, 73, 127, 136–37, 172–73

Bachrach, Bernard, 114
Bartholomeus Anglicus, viii; *De proprietatibus rerum*, fig. 6
Beatrice of Ornacieux, 71–72
Beelzebub, 121
begging, 90
beguines, beguinages, 3, 15, 19–20, 29, 89
Benedict XIII (1394–1423), pope, 9, 53, 56, 114
Benvenuta Bojani, 115
Benz, Ernst, 142
Biller, Peter, 3

Birgitta of Sweden, saint, 1, 129, 148
Black Death. *See* plague
Blannbekin, Agnes, 24
Boccaccio, Giovanni; *Decameron*, 6
Bocheta, Beatrice, 15
Boglioni, Pierre, 116
Boniface, IX (1389–1404), pope, 9
Brakke, David, 102, 108
Brother A., 35–36, 40–42, 73
Bynum, Caroline Walker, 70–71, 78

Caciola, Nancy, 132
Caesarius of Heisterbach, 101, 133
Caffarini, Tommaso, 63
canon Episcopi, 20
Catherine of Alexandria, saint, 21, 25
Catherine of Bologna, saint: *Setti armi spiri-tuali*, 134
Catherine of Siena, saint, 62, 148
Charcot, Jean-Martin, xi
Charles de Valois, 3
Charles V, king of France, 5
Charles VI, king of France, 5, 146, 153
Charles VII, king of France, 4
Charles the Bad of Navarre, 5
child in Host, 18, 23, 73, 77–79; in demonic mass, 74–75, 137, 173–74
Christina of Markyate, *Life*, 30
Christina of Stommeln, 35, 86, 102, 112, 115; and demonic toads, 117–18
Christina the Astonishing, 62
Cistercians, 32
civil war, French, 5
Clare of Assisi, saint, 32
Clare of Montefalco, 62
Clark, Stuart, 103
Clement VII (1378–1394), pope, 8–9, 22, 43, 53, 175

Valéry, Paul, 78
Vauchez, André, vii, 54
Verdiana of Castelfiorentino, 115
visions, ix, 14; eucharistic, 71–73, 79, 91, 147,
  174–76; heavenly, 92–95
Voaden, Rosalynn, 129, 133
Volmar, 33
Voragine, Jacobus de; *Golden Legend*, 67, 114,
  121, 135–36

widows, widowhood, xi, 12–18, 109; widows
  and sex, 52

Williams-Krapp, Werner, 81
Wimpfeling, Jakob, 152
witchcraft, witches, 3, 98–100, 102, 113, 122

xenoglossia, 62

Yvette of Huy, 14

Zeger of Lille (aka of Brabant), friar, 36–37,
  90
Zilboorg, Gregory, x

ACKNOWLEDGMENTS

Talking about Ermine de Reims with family, friends, and colleagues has been one of my great pleasures over the past few years. People have opinions—strong opinions—about her, whether they are medievalists, physicians, mathematicians, or primary school teachers, all represented in the group I would like to thank here for their interest and support. André Vauchez encouraged me early on to pursue a study of Ermine. In the Prologue to this book I briefly trace the scholarly trajectory that brought me to a book-length study of this peculiar woman. My most important interlocutors have been Barbara Newman, Gábor Klaniczay, and Paula M. Kane. Barbara, over many years, gave me brilliant advice, saved me from many errors, and shared my empathy for Ermine. Gábor listened tirelessly to my ideas, made great suggestions, and eventually read and commented on the entire manuscript. Paula helped me put Ermine into a wider perspective by sharing her work on the 1930s American stigmatic Sister Thorn with me over countless dinners, at the swimming pool, and even while watching *Downton Abbey*. Peggy Brown involved me in lively discussions on Jean Gerson and generously sent me her crucial 2013 article on Marguerite Porete and Gerson before publication. Ursula Sonn, my dear friend since fifth grade, helped me clarify my thoughts on this project in many wonderful get-togethers throughout the years. My stepdaughter Dr. Marta Kosinski supplied a physician's much-needed perspective. For help with various issues and good conversations I also thank Michael Bailey, Dyan Elliott, Daniel Hobbins, Brian McGuire (who generously let me reproduce his translation of Gerson's letter on Ermine's *Visions*), Bruce Venarde, and Lori Walters. Alessandra Bartolomei Romagnoli helped me get in touch with the Madre Presidente of the Tor de' Specchi in Rome, which allowed me to obtain the stunning image of Francesca Romana and the demonic Saint Onofrio. I had the privilege of presenting my work on Ermine at many institutions and conferences and am grateful to all the organizers and gracious hosts, notably Barbara Newman at Northwestern University and Ruth Mazo Karras at the University of Minnesota. My thanks also go, of course, to Jerry Singerman, who waited patiently and supportively after a major family crisis delayed the completion of the manuscript.

The title of this book reproduces the title of my article "The Strange Case of Ermine de Reims (c. 1347–1396)," *Speculum* 85:2 (2010): 321–56. Several pages in the Epilogue were drawn from this article. I reuse the title and the material from the article here with the kind permission of the editor of *Speculum* and of Cambridge University Press.

The Richard D. and Mary Jane Edwards Endowed Publication Fund at the University of Pittsburgh generously paid for the photographs and permission fees.

As has been the case for all my previous work, this book would not have seen the light of day without the constant intense interest and support of my husband, Antoni Kosinski. His wit and compassion helped me put Ermine in perspective.

CPSIA information can be obtained
at www.ICGtesting.com
Printed in the USA
BVOW03s1254281117
501067BV00005B/1/P

9 780812 224009